Cabell County's

[West] Virginia

EMPIRE FOR FREEDOM

The Manumission of Sampson Sander's Slaves

Carrie Eldridge

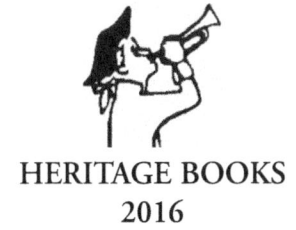

HERITAGE BOOKS
2016

HERITAGE BOOKS
AN IMPRINT OF HERITAGE BOOKS, INC.

Books, CDs, and more—Worldwide

For our listing of thousands of titles see our website
at
www.HeritageBooks.com

Published 2016 by
HERITAGE BOOKS, INC.
Publishing Division
5810 Ruatan Street
Berwyn Heights, Md. 20740

Copyright © 1999 Carrie Eldridge

Heritage Books by the author:

Cabell County's Empire for Freedom

Minute Books: Cabell County, [West] Virginia Minute Book 1, 1809–1815

*Miscellaneous Cabell County, West Virginia Records: Order Book Overseers of the Poor, 1814–1861;
Fee Book, 1826–1839; 1857–1859 (Rule Book); Cabell Land for Tax Purposes, 1861–1865*

Nicholas County, Kentucky Property Tax Lists, 1800–1811 with Indexes to Deed Books A & B (2), and C

*Nicholas County, Kentucky Records: Stray Book 1, 1805–1811; Stray Book 2, 1813–1819;
Stray Book 3, 1820–1870; and Execution Book A, 1801–1878*

Torn Apart: How Cabell Countians Fought the Civil War

Cover art from: *Routes and Resorts of the Chesapeake and Ohio Railway*, published in 1878

All rights reserved. No part of this book may be reproduced or transmitted in any form or by any means, electronic or mechanical, including photocopying, recording or by any information storage and retrieval system without written permission from the author, except for the inclusion of brief quotations in a review.

International Standard Book Numbers
Paperbound: 978-1-58549-884-0
Clothbound: 978-0-7884-6477-5

DEDICATION

This book is for Edith Alicia Allison Woodard. The lady who taught me the joy of reading, the understanding of knowledge and the importance of family history.

ACKNOWLEDGMENTS

Every project requires a multitude of people to bring it to culmination. I thank everyone who has assisted me and survived my intrusion into their lives, beginning with the descendants of Sampson Sanders both in Cabell County, West Virginia and Cass County, Michigan. Family notes compiled by Maurice Sanders were both helpful and appreciated.

Special gratitude is due the John Deaver Drinko Academy for Political and Civic Culture at Marshall University, and especially, its executive director, *Dr. Alan B. Gould*. Dr. Gould has been unfailing in his encouragement and insistence that this material should be published. He also arranged the commissioning and financial assistance necessary for the project. Financial assistance from the *John Deaver Drinko Academy for Political and Civic Culture*, the *Marshall University Foundation*, the *West Virginia Humanities Council*, and the *Cabell County Historical Landmark Commission* accents the desire these groups have to present viable local history information to the community.

I also wish to thank the following Marshall University staff. *Professor Lisle Brown*, Curator of the James E. Morrow Library, provided excellent editorial assistance. *Cora Teel*, research librarian, researched many odd requests. *Dr. Delores Johnson*, Writers Program, and *Dr. Ancella Bickley* deserve thanks for suggestions and directions. *Dr. Mack Gillenwater* and *Dr. Sam Clagg*, Professor Emeritus, both of the Geography Department are thanked for beginning a quest and supplying much needed support. *Amy Druskovich*, librarian at Cassopolis Public Library, provided numerous requested, both in person and through the mails. Finally, I would like to thank *Stella Lawson*, *Ruth Crawley* and the entire membership of the Chain Lake Baptist Church for their warm and friendly reception at their annual homecoming.

Table of Contents

	Foreword	xi
	Introduction	xiii
	Prologue	1
I.	Virginia Frontier, 1780-1801	5
II.	Kanawha County, Virginia, 1802-1809	19
III.	Cabell County, Virginia, 1810-1850	25
IV.	Sampson Sanders' Private Life, 1810-1850	27
V.	Sanders' Other "Family"	33
VI	Life as a Sanders Slave	41
VII.	1849-Sanders' Death and the Manumission	45
VIII.	Interlude - Traveling to Michigan with the Sanders	51
IX.	1850 - The New Citizens of Cass County	59
X.	The End of the Original Settlers	65
XI.	Sanders of Today	71
XII.	Tracing Lost Sanders	73
	Appendices	79
	Selected Bibliography	155
	Index	159

Illustrations

Figure		page
1	Following the Sanders	xv
2	Manumissions in 1850 and 1860	xvi
3	A Comparison of Slaves per Slaveholder	xvi
4	Sanders in Loudoun County	6
5	Virginia and West Virginia County Formation	8
6	Kanawha County, Virginia, 1800	17
7	Settlers Along the James River Turnpike	20
8	Cabell County Tax and Census Listings	24
9	The Community at the Mill	26
10	Sampson Sanders' Property	30
11	Kanawha and Cabell Personal Property Tax Lists	33
12	Determining the Slaves Freed	35
13	Sanders' Assets	38
14	Sanders' Obligations - The Relatives	38
15	Sanders' Obligations - The Slaves	39
16	Midwest Railroad Routes, 1860	47
17	Cass County, Michigan	49
18	Calvin and Porter Townships, 1860	57
19	Historic Chain Lake Baptist Church	63
20	Solomon Sanders' Tombstone Receipt	67
21	Dorcas Sanders' Settlement	68
22	Genealogy for Sanders of Cass County	71
23	Stella Sanders Lawson, 1997	76
24	Sanders' Graves in Cabell County	77
25	Sanders' in Chain Lake Cemetery	78
26	Sanders' Cabell Survey	110
27	Calvin and Porter Townships Maps	137-140

All maps drawn by Carrie Eldridge unless otherwise noted.
Pen and Ink illustrations are from *Routes and Resorts of the Chespeake/Ohio Railway*, Richwood: Baughman Brothers, 1878.

Foreword

This project had its origins several years ago when I was doing research on the evolution of slavery in Cabell County. It was then I stumbled upon the name of Sampson Sanders. About ten years ago, I introduced the story to Ms. Carrie Eldridge who took the material and ran with it! Ms. Eldridge, a noted local cartographer and historical geographer, has travel extensively in Virginia, West Virginia, Ohio and Michigan in compiling this wonderful historical account.

Sampson Sanders was an exceptional individual. Not only was he the wealthiest landowner in Cabell County, Virginia during the Ante-bellum Period, but also the master of fifty-one slaves. This placed him within the top 2.7% of slaveholders in the South. What is interesting about Sanders is that upon his death he manumitted all the slaves in his possession and provided them with the means and the land required to start a new life as free men and women in Cass County, Michigan. From the records it is evident that Sampson Sanders never purchased a slave, those he had came through inheritance, and he never sold a slave. Moreover, he never hired an overseer, but relied instead on teaching his slaves to run his holdings for him. It is also evident that some of his slaves could read, write and cipher.

Sampson Sanders' decision to manumit his slaves is made all the more remarkable because it ran counter to the prevailing trends. In fact, attitudes against manumission, as reflected in the action of state legislatures, are revealed in the move to restrict slaves access to freedom. For example, as early as 1806, legislation enacted in Virginia required newly freed blacks to leave the state or face re-enslavement. Indeed, this trend included the overturning of the manumission of slaves directed by the slave holders' will. Additionally, while restrictive legislation was haphazard, inconsistent and sporadically enforced, Virginia was one of only four states which had laws on the books throughout the last thirty years of slavery totally prohibiting teaching slaves to read and write. In the main, the plantation owner's concern for order, property rights and their own economic security exceeded interests in the rights of their slaves among all but the most exceptional slaveowners. Sampson Sanders was one of those exceptions.

Perhaps, however, the most unique and significant aspect of the story of Sampson Sanders is the nearly complete record and history of his slaves. Tracing their origins back to Hannah, the family matriarch, Ms. Eldridge has reconstructed a continuous history of an African-American family from 1780 to the present! One of the major assets of this book and a real value to historians and the interested lay public is found in the extensive appendices and impressive bibliography. The resource materials cited herein give the reader real insight into the "underside" of history.

In conclusion, this work provides a unique perspective of not only life on a Mid-Ohio Valley Ante-Bellum plantation; but thanks to the patience and persistence of Ms. Eldridge, an even rarer view of the history and evolution of an African-America family.

Dr. Alan Gould
John Deaver Drinko Academy
Marshall University

Introduction

For a student of local history, an unique event or a note worthy person is always a subject of interest and calls for further study. Cabell County, West Virginia, has had several such events and people, including the Sanders family. At a time when women just did not become involved in public affairs, the earliest county land deeds seem to have the name Martha Sanders on every page. Investigating Martha Sanders' life leads to her entrepreneur son, Sampson. Finally, the trail leads to one of the most unusual events in Cabell County history, Sampson Sanders' manumission of all his fifty slaves. A most remarkable event, not just in Cabell County, but in all of early Virginia in a period when very few slave masters freed even one slave.

Virginia, in the early Nineteenth Century, was represented by a landed gentry which displayed its wealth by possession of land and slaves. Although the plantation owners were few, the land, property and political influence they controlled far outweighed their numbers. These gentlemen were the entrepreneurs, the risk takers, the adventurers, and above all else, those people most respected by the rest of the community. They either appeared as justices and officers of the militia and controlled the fords and mills; or they owned the most profitable businesses in the small communities. Early court records, in any section of the state, abound with their various names and numerous deeds.

Most of the large Virginia plantations were located east of the mountains, but a few were found in the valleys along the Ohio and Kanawha rivers. Regardless of public opinion, most plantations in Virginia were peopled by less than twenty slaves; only ten percent of the plantations supported more than fifty slaves.[1] Of that ten percent, only three plantations were found west of the Allegheny Mountains.

Cabell County, in western most Virginia along the Ohio River, was created from Kanawha County in 1809. It was the site of two of those large plantations. Greenbottom with 4,444 acres, was one of the largest plantations in the state of Virginia. Throughout most of its history, Greenbottom supported about fifty slaves who were transferred with the plantation each time it was sold.[2] The other Cabell County plantation was owned by Sampson Sanders. Over time as he acquired land, the number of Sanders slaves increased until they numbered about fifty by 1849.

In 1850 Virginia had 472,528 slaves. Laws had been passed to continue the institution of slavery in the state. The 1850 census record reveals that only 218 slaves were manumitted.[3] In 1849 when a western Virginia plantation owner from Cabell County freed fifty-one slaves, that number was one fourth of the 218 slaves manumitted. Virginia law, at that time, required an owner to provide for any freed slave for the rest of the slave's natural life. Any former slave who remained in the state could be returned to servitude for failure to pay his taxes, failing to show

---

[1] Compiled from United States census statistics collected between 1830 and 1860.
[2] Cabell Co., Huntington, WV, County Clerk, Deeds, Bks. 1-10. Hereafter cited Cabell Records.
[3] Freed by legal means as opposed to self freedom through escape or purchase.

an acceptable means of support, forgetting to present himself before the county justices each year, or simply by someone claiming him an escaped slave.[4]

When Sampson Sanders decided to manumit his slaves, he not only provided his slaves with $15,000 cash, but encouraged them to select needed materials from his estate. Sanders also selected lawyers to go with the group to protect them in their travels, making sure everyone purchased good property, and ensuring they were fairly treated in all the legal dealings.[5] Studying county records, federal census reports and personal records has allowed for the reconstruction of the life and times of Sampson Sanders and his slaves. By piecing together various records, it has been possible to identify his slaves and to follow them into freedom. This story may begin as a story of empire building, but that empire was used to provide for the future freedom of the Negroes that Sanders manumitted.

---

[4] William W. Henning, *Statues at Large Being a Collection of the Laws of Virginia.* 15 Vols. (New York: R & W & G Burrow. 1823), Vol. 12, Chap. 37, pp. 531-532. Hereafter cited as Henning, *Statues at Large.*
[5] Cabell Records, Wills, Bk. 1, p. 391. Sampson Sanders' will.

Figure 1. Following the Sanders.

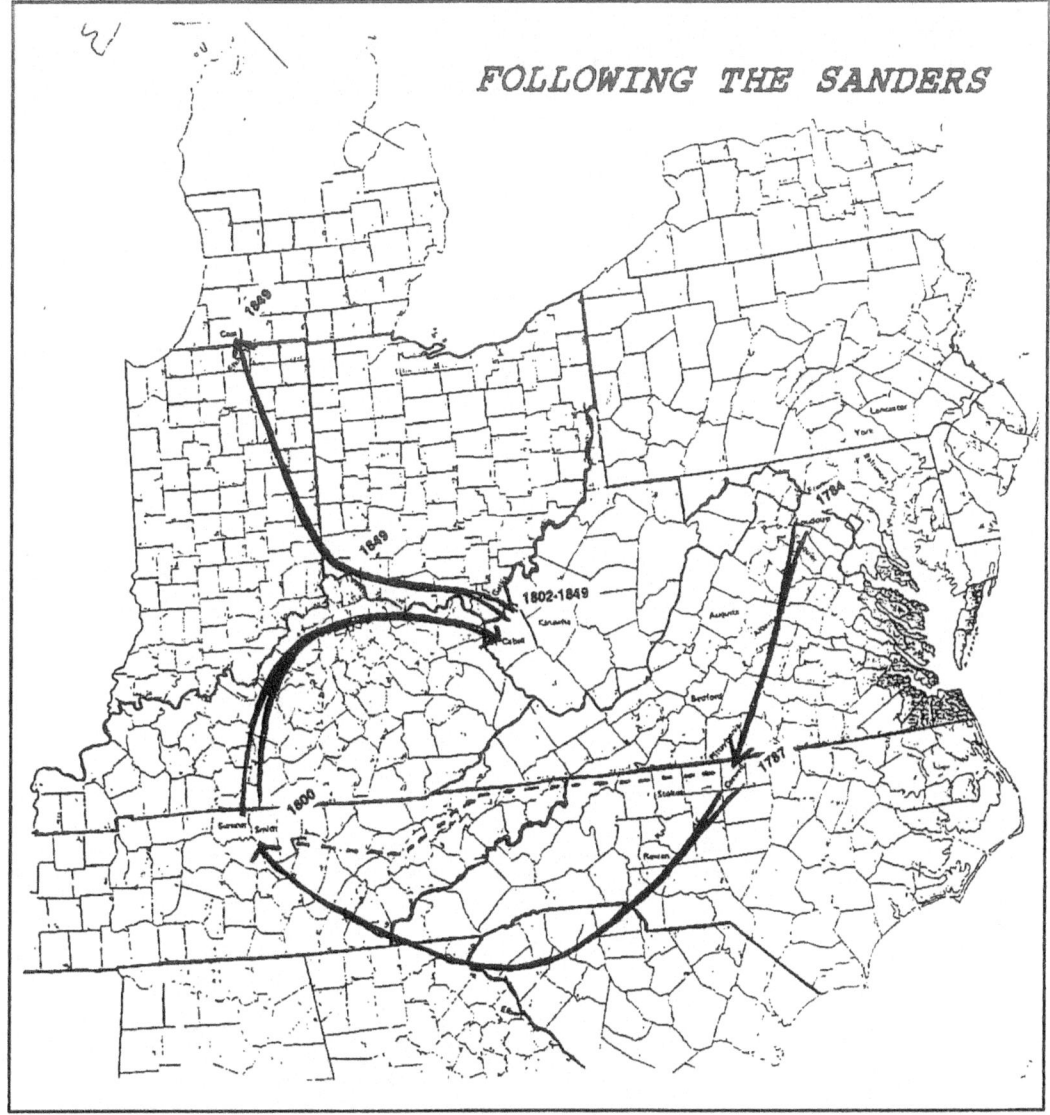

Figure 1. About 1784, William Sanders left Loudoun County, Virginia, and followed the Carolina Road south to either Pittsylvania County, VA, or Caswell County, NC. He and his family resided there several years before moving into northcentral Tennessee. (Sanders' friends from the same area are known to have been in Elbert County, GA.) From Smith County, TN, Sanders rushed to Kanawha County, VA, to claim property and settled in the area later to be Cabell County. In 1849, Sampson Sanders' manumitted slaves left Cabell County, floated on the Ohio to Cincinnati then took a train to Elkhart, IN, completing their trip to Cass County, MI by wagon.

Figure 2. Slave manumission in 1850 and 1860.

Manumitted slaves, according to the Seventh Census (1850) and the Eight Census (1860) respectively.

STATES	Seventh Census				Eighth Census			
	Slaves	Manumitted	One out of	Percent	Slaves	Manumitted	One out of	Percent
Alabama	342,844	16	21,427	.0046	435,080	101	4,310	.0231
Arkansas	47,100	1	47,100	.0021	111,115	41	2,711	.0369
Delaware	2,290	277	8	12.0960	1,798	12	149	.6674
Florida	39,310	22	1,786	.0559	61,745	17	3,632	.0275
Georgia	381,689	19	20,088	.0049	462,198	160	4,360	.0229
Kentucky	210,981	152	1,388	.0720	225,483	176	1,281	.0780
Indiana	244,809	159	1,539	.0649	331,726	517	641	.1558
Maryland	90,368	493	183	.5455	87,189	1,017	85	1.1664
Mississippi	300,878	6	51,646	.0019	436,631	182	2,399	.0416
Missouri	87,422	50	1,748	.0571	114,931	89	1,291	.0774
North Carolina	288,548	2	144,274	.0006	331,059	258	1,283	.0779
South Carolina	384,984	2	152,492	.0005	402,406	12	33,533	.0029
Tennessee	239,450	45	5,321	.0187	275,719	174	1,584	.0630
Texas	58,161	5	11,632	.0085	182,566	37	5,889	.0169
Virginia	472,528	218	2,167	.0461	490,865	277	1,771	.0564
TOTALS	3,200,364	1,467	2,181	.0458	3,953,696	3,018	1,309	.0763

Source: United States Eight Census of Agriculture

Figure 3. A comparison of slaves per slave holders.

SLAVEHOLDERS and SLAVES in VIRGINIA - 1860

number of slaves	1 only	2-9	10-19	20-49	over 50	total holders	total slaves	Average
Virginia holders	11,085	26,492	8,774	4,917	860	52,128	472,528	9
Cabell County holders	25	56	2	1	0	84	305	3+

DISTRIBUTION OF SLAVES

Virginian holders owning less than 10 slaves 37,577 = 72%
Virginian holders owning 10-49 slaves 13,691 = 26%
Virginian holders owning more than 50 slaves 860 = 2%

Cabell 1849 Sampson Sanders - 51 slaves
Cabell 1850 William Jenkins - 53 slaves

Author's Notes:

The time frame of this material predates the creation of the state of West Virginia, created in 1863. For that reason, all references to Cabell County, West Virginia, will be recorded as Cabell County, Virginia.

Sanders/Saunders was used interchangeably in records and will be used as Sanders in this record.

Webster's Deluxe Unabridged Dictionary:
Manumission- "to let go, a freeing from slavery; liberation, emancipation, to liberate from personal bondage." A legal term for freeing slaves through a Court Order such as a will opposed to a person freeing himself by self purchase or escape.

Prologue

Loudoun County, Virginia, 1780

Old James Green had worked hard to marry off his daughter, but he had succeeded and made a fine match at that. The announcement said Miss Martha Green was to marry the handsome William Sanders sometime next spring and had been made just as the blackberries bloomed. Hannah would have to wait almost a year, but she was thrilled for herself as well as Miss Martha. Hannah would soon be moving into a new home with her young mistress, and Miss Martha had promised to keep Hannah always. Hannah knew she would never have to worry about being sold because Miss Martha was one young lady who always kept her word.

Loudoun County, Virginia, 1784-1785

Martha Sanders was alarmed. Her husband had just informed her, he was going west. She did not understand much of what he said, but she had often heard him rave about the increasing taxes and land prices. He planned to sell the plantation. With that cash, he could buy at least three times as much of the cheap frontier land. They would follow the Carolina Trail and perhaps join some of his family near the Dan River. The trip would take several months and the trail was rough. He assured her, he could shoot well enough to get plenty of game. They would use pack horses, taking some cooking pots, a sack or two of flour and meal, a few tools and what clothes needed. Everything else must be left behind.

She could just hear her father, "You're leaving this fine plantation to go gallivanting over the country. I told you that man was a wanderer. He's too restless for his own good." In spite of her doubts and fears, Martha Sanders began to plan. Her china and silverware could be left with her father, even if he did not approve. Maybe, one of her sisters would like to have her furniture. She could remember her uncle's stories about the wild frontier and did not look forward to the hard life. Would she ever have a fine house again or a chance to wear her new gown? At least Hannah would be around to help her with the baby.

South Central Virginia, 1786

Aunt Hannah returned from the main house to her lively cabin and spread the word: the Colonel and Mrs. Sanders had a healthy new baby boy to share the nursery with his little sister Hetty. It was so very hot, everyone feared childbed fever would claim Miss Martha. Aunt Hannah was glad she had birthed Zeb a few weeks ago so she could wet nurse the new baby Sampson, if Miss Martha lost her milk again. Aunt Hannah would never forget just how close to death little Miss Hetty had been, before Hannah's milk came in when her Ada was born. She had happily nursed both babies. Hannah was saddened though, because Miss Martha would probably never have another child. The hard travel of the last year across Virginia had made Miss Martha quite ill on several occasions. Often the trail had been so narrow Miss Martha had to walk even through mud and snow, but the jolting horse was little improvement. Everyone was relieved to have a healthy baby and a living mother. The days ahead were worrisome. Colonel William planned to ride out in a day or so to look over more new land, and there was no way to know if Miss Martha would recover her strength before he was ready to leave.

Caswell County, North Carolina, 1787

Once more the Sanders family was settling into a new home, although this time Colonel William had simply borrowed a cabin. All of them were sure their stay would be short. The Colonel was anxiously talking to a neighbor, Tilman Dixon, about moving to the Cumberland Valley to settle and to reap a profit selling the Revolutionary claims he had been buying. Surveyors had already been sent to the new Sumner County to locate the best land, and Colonel William had sent his nephew to stake a claim before the best land was taken. As soon as North Carolina allowed, settlers would push into the virgin area. He had not decided how they would travel. Most of the local people talked about going to the Long Island of the Holston and then to follow the Cumberland River. His friend, Dixon, thought the best way was south to the head of the Savannah River. That route would go around the Indians. Then they could follow the Tennessee River and cut across country to locate their surveys along the Cumberland River.

Smith County, Tennessee, August 1801

Life was little changed at any one place along the frontier; all of it was hard. Where the Sanders family lived on the Cumberland River had become part of the new state of Tennessee, but that meant little to anyone but Colonel William Sanders and his political friends. Aunt Hannah was outside making soap as she saw Briscoe striding toward her cabin, and she laid the ladle aside. "Hannah, you best get up to the house to help Miss Martha. The Colonel just rode in and said we're leaving for the Ohio River as soon as possible. I'm to get Master Sampson and the boys to help round up the stock." Before the week was out, both cabins were emptied, all the possessions packed, logs cut and lashed together; and everyone, master and servant alike, loaded onto flat boats to start down the Cumberland River. Colonel William and Master Sampson Sanders rode their fine geldings along the bank, while Uncle Briscoe and Uncle Charley rode the mares and helped the boys herd along the stock of cattle, hogs and geese.

Floating down the broad Cumberland River in late summer was fair traveling, except the water was quite low and several times everyone had to get off the rafts and push them through the shallows. Once the families reached the Ohio River, there was more water to float the rafts; but they had to go up river against the current. The Colonel hired some extra men to help pole the rafts up the Ohio and finally up the Kanawha River to Charleston, the county seat of Kanawha County, Virginia.

The Colonel left the rafts at the mouth of the Guyandotte River and traveled overland on the James River Turnpike to conduct his business, but he met the travelers at the Charleston water front.[6] After weeks of work and toil everyone, white and black, was happy to climb up the muddy bank and enter the little frontier town.[7] Miss Martha was quite upset when the Colonel told her they must travel overland all the next day. The site he had chosen to live was a beautiful place on a pretty stream with the unlikely name of Mud River.[8]

---

[6] Rafts traveled by the indicated route, but a man on horse back could travel from the Ohio River to Charleston by the much quicker James River Turnpike which short cut a large section of river. The Turnpike had been established as an official road by Virginia in 1788. Colonel William Sanders may have selected his home site along the turnpike on this trip to Charleston.

[7] Kanawha Co., Charleston, WV, County Clerk, Deeds, Bk. B, p. 104. Hereafter cited Kanawha Records. William Sanders' Bill of Sale, 14 Oct. 1801, lists "Ader and her children and Hannah and her children." (See Appendix 2.) Cabell Co. Huntington, WV, County Clerk, Wills, Bk 1 p. 101, Martha Sanders' Inventory 1831, excludes the slaves Briscoe and Charles. (See Appendix 4B.) The events depicted above represent a probable life for Sanders family members prior to their settlement in the Cabell/Kanawha area.

[8] Colonel William Sanders apparently settled his family in Teays Valley just below Mud Bridge (now the site of Milton). It is possible that the land was situated near old neighbors. (See Addendices 1A &1B.)

PROLOGUE

Cabell County, Virginia, 1860

Aunt Hannah knew her time had almost run out. Hers had been a good life, serving the people she loved. Everyone told Hannah she was over one hundred years old.[9] She did not really know, all she remembered now were the many children for whom she had cared. Little Miss Martha Green had taken her as a personal servant when both of them were teenagers. Hannah had been Miss Martha's personal maid for almost twenty years until Martha's daughter, Hetty, had gotten married. Then she had moved into a new home to care for Miss Hetty's children, and there was really a group of them. When Miss Hetty's poor little girl, Miss Polly, died soon after her husband William Simmons, Hannah moved again. Although already ninety, she moved into the Simmons home because someone had to take care of all those poor orphaned children.

Lately, her many years had really begun to tell. Hannah could not see very well any more, and her hands and knees were in constant pain; but she had raised three generations of Miss Martha's family as well as her own. Hannah just had one regret. She would like to see all of young Master Sampson's people one more time because many of them were nieces and nephews. Since they had been freed and left home, she knew she would never see them again. Everyone in the group had come to her before they left, and she had cried long after the rafts were out of sight. Hannah had never been able to understand why all Master Sampson's people had to leave, if they were free.

---

[9] Fred B. Lambert Collection, 76B-9-9, Special Collections Department, James E. Morrow Library, Marshall University, Huntington, WV. Hereafter cited as Lambert Collection. Nephew Sampson Simmons stated, "Hannah was Shed's mother and belonged to Grandmother Kilgore. Brother Conwelsie inherited them. She (Hannah) lived to be 104 years old." Simmons was six when Sampson Sanders died, Grandmother Kilgore died when he was nine (1852). There is no other information about Hannah's age as she is never listed by name on any census. The census enumerator also missed the related families: Sanders, Simmons, Kilgore and Gallaher in various years.

Chapter One
Virginia Frontier 1780-1801

The story of Sampson Sanders and his slaves spans five states and a period of two hundred years. Records which should record the events of his life were never made or have been misplaced through the years. To understand the limited amount of information known about Sampson Sanders, one must look beyond him and compile circumstantial evidence for his early family. This story starts with his father, William, in Loudoun County, Virginia, and subsequently follows William and a Negro slave, Hannah, across the frontier into North Carolina, across Tennessee and back into Virginia.

William Sanders was one of the semi-silent frontiersmen. Only two years of his life are successfully documented. The rest must be inferred from records and events that involved the whole western frontier. Sanders should have fought in the Revolutionary War, but he died before that service was recorded.[10] About 1784, he joined the mass of settlers moving westward at the war's end. Subsequent events led the researcher to believe William Sanders had money when he began his travels, and he certainly was a rich man at his death. The life William Sanders led had a profound affect on the members of his family who traveled across the frontier. It especially touched the life of his heir, Sampson.

Loudoun County, Virginia, 1780's

The Loudoun County, Virginia, tithable records from 1772 through 1784 show at least one William Sanders, as well as a connection to the James Green family.[11] Sometime before 1783, a William Sanders married Martha Green while living next door to the family of James Green. Martha's brother, Gerrad Green, was shown living in both the William Sanders and the James Green households in different years. A wealthy landowner, James Green left a will naming his son Gerrard Green, his daughter Polly Sanders, his wife Frances and several other children.[12] Another sister was listed "Mary," making it quite probable that Martha Green Sanders was known as Polly at home. Just prior to the time Gerrard Green appeared in William Sanders' household, a Negro slave Hannah appeared on Sanders' tithable record. Hannah may have been a bride price from Martha to her new husband, or a gift to Martha from William.[13]

William Sanders was also listed with other males in his household prior to the appearance of Gerrard Green and Hannah. The information raises the possibility Martha may have been a second wife.[14] (See Figure 4.) There were far too many Sanders and Greens in Loudoun County to sort the various sons and cousins without extensive study, but it is interesting to note that William and Martha's first child was named Hetty Frances Sanders, probably for Martha's mother Frances Green. The tithable lists also name several Loudoun County neighbors, such as George Summers, Samuel Love, George Kilgore, Henry Peyton, and James Turley who appear as neighbors later in Cabell County.[15] Figure 7 describes the Cabell County neighborhood

---

[10] William died in 1801 before general pension laws were enacted. No war records have been verified, but a land bounty could be one reason for his movement.

[11] Tithable Records are the records of people paying taxes. The records referred to here listed adult males (over 21) and slaves (not always by name). (See: Marty Hiatt and Craig Roberts Scott, *Loudoun County, Virginia Tithables, 1758-1774, 1775-1786 and 1786-1790*; 3 Vols.[Athens, GA: Iberian Press, 1995].)

[12] The James Green will is significant because it places the families together and connects his wife to Martha's daughter Hetty Frances. (See: Loudoun Co., Leesburg, VA, County Clerk, Wills, Bk. E, pp. 237-238.)

[13] The Green family had several slaves, but none named Hannah.

[14] Hiatt and Scott, *Loudoun County, Virginia Tithables 1758-1786*. Vol.1, 165; Vol.2, pp. 165,610,669,809. (See appendix 1A for more complete list.)

[15] *Ibid*. Vol.3, pp. 1082-1085,1104,1156,1190,1326,1359. All (or similar names) lived within a few miles of the Sanders family in Cabell County, and a George Summers accompanied the freed slaves to Cass County, Michigan. Additional Loudoun County surnames which appear later in Cabell County include: Donoho, Roberts, Shelton, Morrison, Bryant, Yates, Pettit, Jenkins, Hampton, Lane, Lewis and Davis.

in which the families settled. (See page 20.)

Of those names associated with the Sanders family, the most interesting surname was Kilgore. That surname was listed in every area the Sanders' lived; and Thomas Kilgore aged 40, married Sampson's sister Hetty in Kanawha County in 1802. Thomas' birth place was listed "Pennsylvania" in the 1850 census, but perhaps the two families traveled together across the frontier.

Below is an abstract of the Loudoun County tithable lists showing a William Sanders over twenty-one in 1772 with a Sampson Sanders also over twenty-one. In 1775 another male over twenty-one is added to the list indicating possibly a father and two sons, making William about forty. If this supposition is true, William would have been about fifty when he married Martha and that age is given some credence by William's death in 1802, thirty years before his wife. The tithable list also shows the proximity of the Green family and the general location of the families.

Figure 4. Sanders in Loudoun County.

LOUDOUN COUNTY, VIRGINIA TITHABLES - LISTING THE FAMILIES OF SANDERS AND GREEN HEAD OF HOUSEHOLD - MALES OVER 16 - NEGROES

Year	Entry	Parish
1767	Near neighbors to William Sanders (Who later appeared in Cabell County) Francis George Summers, Thomas Lewis, George Kilgore, Sampson Turley (Both Summers & Turley with a negro Hannah)	
1772	William Sanders, Samson	Shelburn Parrish
1773	William, Samson Sanders	Cameron Parrish
1774	James Green	Cameron Parrish
1775	William Sanders Benjamin, Sampson	Shelburn Parrish
1774	James Green	Cameron Parrish
1777	James Green	Cameron Parrish
1778	James Green, Gerrard ,3n	Cameron Parrish
1780	William Sanders, Benja., Jas, & Negro Hannah	
1780	James Green, Gerrard, 5 Negroes	
1781	William Sanders, Benj. & n-Hanna	
1782	William Sanders, Benja., Jas. & n-Hannah	
1782	James Green, Gerrard, 5 Negroes	
1783	William Sanders 5w 1n	
1784	William Sanders, Jarrett Green, n-Hannah	
1784	next house James Green, Thos. & 4n	
1785	William Sanders, Garret Green, John Vincent, n-Hannah	
1785	next house James Green, Thos. 4n	

Compiled from Hiatt & Scott, Loudoun County Tithables.

Following any family along the frontier is quite a challenge. Often a researcher must follow travel patterns, neighbors or even communities instead of the main family. Several surnames listed in the Loudoun County Tithables also appeared in North Carolina, Tennessee and finally Cabell County, Virginia. Those families may have traveled as a group for protection or simply followed the frontier as it advanced. Many families felt they would find a better life in the new western lands.

People sold their possessions or just left what they could not pack on a couple of horses. They followed the trails westward long before wagon roads were improved. Such pioneers often arrived in the wilderness with just a skillet, an ax, a plow, some seeds and their gun, powder horn and bullet mold. Various records indicate William Sanders and his family were better situated than the average frontier family, but in many ways the Sanders were typical of the Virginians who traveled west. Moving south on the Carolina Road on the east side of the Blue Ridge, with hopes of making a fortune or just a new beginning on the frontier; they left everything behind.

Frontier records can be very confusing while adding a glimmer of hope. In 1787, a William Sanders appeared in Pittsylvania County, Virginia, near a Jeremiah Ward who had married a Sanders.[16] Fifteen years later, Ward was living in Cabell County, Virginia, and the owner of the mill which passed first to his son-in-law and then to Sampson Sanders.[17] The Ward and Sanders families were located in the same frontier areas and seemed to have had far reaching connections. A family connection might explain why William Sanders settled his family thirty miles from his business at the Kanawha County Court in 1801. Figure 5 shows the route followed by the Sanders family across Virginia.

Placing William Sanders in Pittsylvania County in 1787 causes a problem; for also in 1787 a William Sanders was taxed in Caswell County, across the disputed Virginia/North Carolina line. That Sanders lived near Tilman Dixon, with whom "Colonel" William Sanders moved into Tennessee. Dixon later signed the affidavits which Sanders took to Kanawha County. Possibly the same William was taxed in both states at the site of his property, or in that particular area, the tax collector may have been unsure of his territory.[18] Undoubtedly, the border dispute caused many settlers to move to other areas where the land titles would be secure.[19]

---

[16] Norris Wayne Jackson, *Our Ward Family*, (Salt Lake City: Artistic Printing Company, 1995), p. 10.

[17] Deeds in both Kanawha and Cabell counties, reference a mill site on the Guyandotte River. Joel Estis was a son-in-law to Ward, Sampson Sanders may have been a nephew.

[18] "Personal and Property Tax Lists", Pittsylvania Co. VA. Microfilm Roll 54, Library of Virginia, Richmond; and Alvaretta Kenan Register, *State Census of North Carolina 1784-1787* (Baltimore: Genealogical Printing Co., 1983), 42. Hereafter cited as: Register, *State Census of North Carolina 1784-1787*. A comparison of tax lists from Pittsylvania County, Virginia, and Caswell County, North Carolina, shows many of the same surnames. This was an area of early boundary dispute, not settled until the 1820's.

[19] One reason people moved south was the boundary disputes between Pennsylvania and Maryland resulting in unclear land titles.

Figure 5.
Virginia and West Virginia Formation

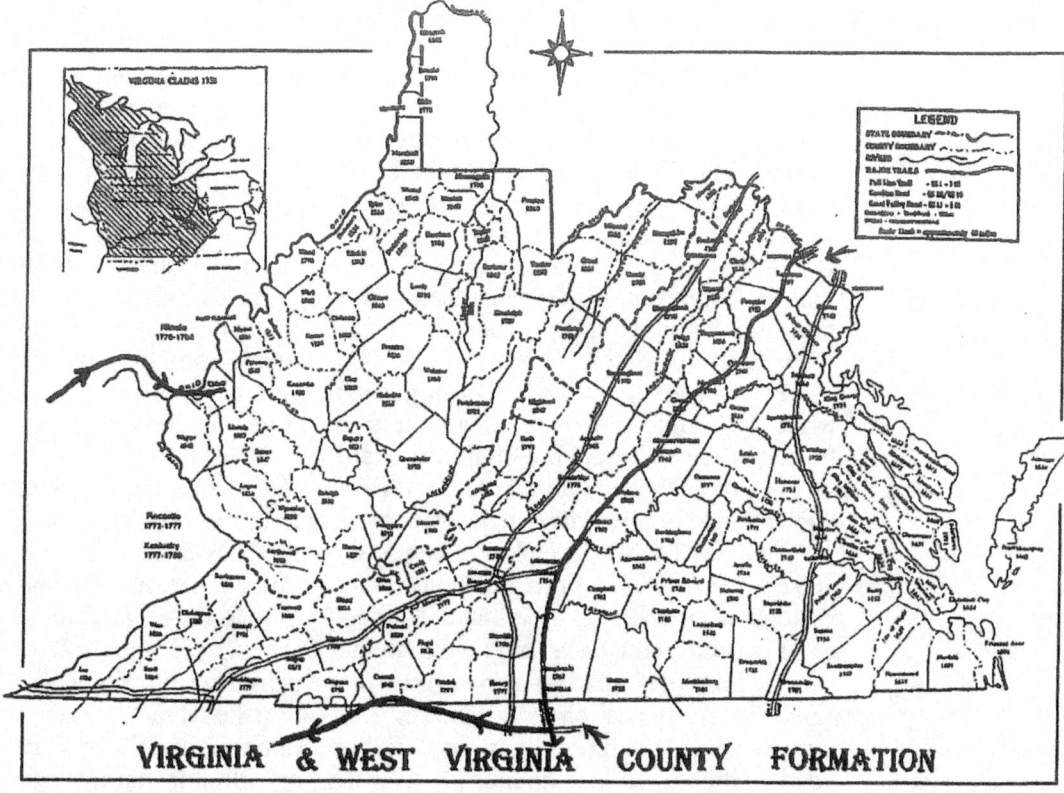

The Carolina Road, also known as the Piedmont Trail or the Rogues Road, entered northern Virginia through Loudoun County. It crossed Virginia on the east side of the Blue Ridge and entered Caswell County, North Carolina, along the Dan River from Pittsylvania County, Virginia.

Loudoun County to Pittsylvania County 1782-1787

William Sanders wed Martha Green of Loudoun County, Virginia, in late 1781 or early 1782, possibly after becoming good friends with her brother Gerrard.[20] The neighboring Green family had extensive land holdings in Loudoun County and James Green could see no future in moving west.[21] William Sanders, however, was probably upset with prices or unable to afford more land. As the Revolutionary War drew to a close, taxes throughout Virginia were steadily rising while inflation made currency practically worthless.[22] He may have resented his rich father-in-law, or made plans to become rich on the frontier by trading and through land speculation. Probably, a combination of reasons caused William to decided to sell everything and head west.

Several of his neighbors had already made the move southwest, and the letters they wrote home praised the good soil along the Dan River. Even more important to William Sanders was the price of land on the frontier, which could be purchased for pennies an acre or acquired by presenting

---

[20] Loudoun Co., Leesburg, VA, County Clerk, Bk. E, 237-238. The Will indicates they were married, but no date is available. See Figure 4 for relationships.
[21] Julia Hope Audrey, *Kentucky Records* (Baltimore: Genealogical Printing Co., 1997), p. 124. Gerrard Green may have soldiered with Sanders. Green claimed a pension and died in Harrison County, KY, and possibly went west with Sanders.
[22] Ray Allen Billington, *Westward Expansion* (New York: Macmillan Publishing Co., 1974), p. 190. Hereafter cited as Billington, *Westward Expansion*.

war certificates. When the war ended, soldiers received payment for their war services in bounty land. Land which the soldier could only claim by moving west. Most soldiers could ill afford to move and gladly sold their seemingly worthless bounty land for a few cents on the dollar.[23]

Pittsylvania County, Virginia, was one of the sites where bounty land could be located. It had been settled almost twenty years when the Sanders family arrived about 1787.[24] It offered a likely place of settlement because Loudoun County friends were nearby. William and his family traveled more than three hundred miles to reach Pittsylvania County. Although the trip took several months, they probably stayed in Pittsylvania County just long enough for Martha to deliver their son Sampson, and then recover her strength. Sanders thought there was greater opportunity further south.[25]

Sanders was interested in bounty land. The western land beckoned him because it was virtually free and local government nonexistent.[26] An aggressive man could make a fortune. He had already made money trading horses and seemed to be quite a good trader, but not all his profits were made from horse trading.[27] William Sanders traded anything that would make him a profit and bought bounty certificates every place he went. North Carolina records show William Sanders received over two hundred bounty warrants in 1786, representing at least three hundred acres each.[28] Land speculation was quite lucrative if you could locate your lands.[29]

Caswell County, North Carolina, just across the state line from Pittsylvania County, Virginia, was at the southern end of Virginia's Carolina Road. The land was good and farming was necessary to feed a family, but William preferred trading and speculating in land. By 1787 William Sanders had acquired nine slaves in addition to Martha's girl Hannah.[30] Dealing in slaves was as lucrative as buying and selling land and horses, but the costs and risks were much higher. Records of his partnership with Rogers show at least some of his trading was done in slaves.[31]

While in Caswell County, William Sanders met Tilman Dixon, a young man like himself with plans for the future. Together, these men may have talked about going west and starting their own community where the land was cheaper. It did not take much discussion to send Sanders into new territory and there were other settlers in the Caswell, area (mostly Revolutionary veterans) with the same idea. As soon as North Carolina opened her western land, many of them began moving westward.[32]

Sumner County and Smith County, Tennessee, 1790-1800

It had taken several years, but Tilman Dixon and William Sanders had finally been able to start their own communities in Tennessee.[33] Sandersville was just a family station on the Nashville Road about eight miles from Gallantin, but Dixon Springs was rapidly becoming a place of importance.[34]

---

[23] Edmund N. Leete and Ann J. Sheedy, "The Ohio Trail," *The Tallow Light*, (Marietta, OH: Summer, 1995): 25.
[24] Register, *State Census of North Carolina, 1784-1787*, p. 42.
[25] The exact location of Sampson's birth has not been identified, but it must have been either Pittsylvania County, Virginia, or Caswell County, North Carolina, as those were tax record locations for the family at the time of his birth. Relative surnames indicate Pittsylvania County.
[26] Billington, *Westward Expansion*, p. 200. North Carolina set aside a military reserve along the Cumberland River(later to become Tennessee) and opened the rest of its western territory for settlement at $5 per hundred acres. Land speculators bought four million acres in seven months of 1783.
[27] The subsequent trading venture with Bennett Rogers was well documented, probably from past experience.
[28] North Carolina Daughters of the American Revolution, *Roster of Soldiers from North Carolina in the American Revolution* (Baltimore: Genealogical Publishing Co., 1988), pp.505-558.(See Appendix 1C.)
[29] Register, *State Census of North Carolina 1784-1787*, p. 23. Caswell Co., NC, tax lists show William Sanders owned several Negroes and his ability to purchase various Revolutionary land warrants indicates ready cash.
[30] Ibid., p. 23.
[31] Kanawha Records, Deeds, Bk. B, pp. 101-110.
[32] *Caswell County, North Carolina Bonds*, (bound originals)located at the Carthage Library, Carthage, TN, has a listing for William Sanders and his surveyor, James Sanders:locating Revolutionary claims along the Cumberland River in Sumner County, Tennessee.
[33] Goodspeed's *History Of Tennessee* (Nashville, TN: Goodspeed Printing Co., 1887), p. 799.
[34] *Rural Sun*, Nashville, TN, June 19, 1873, Vol.1, No.37.

The Cumberland River area had gained so many people that a new county was soon to be formed. Tilman Dixon and William Saunders were two of the main reasons for Smith County's creation. It was only natural for the men to become leaders of the community for years of trading and acquiring property had made both men rich and influential.[35]

Whether he took part in the Revolution or was simply honored by his neighbors, William Sanders acquired the title of Colonel during his stay in Tennessee. He was not listed among Revolutionary officers so it may be assumed the title was acquired from the vast amount of land he located in the Cumberland area. "Colonel" William Sanders had many business dealings with such locally important persons as Tilman Dixon, Thomas Banks and Bennett Rogers, all gentlemen of central Tennessee.[36] William Sanders recognized quite early that a man with a little money and a lot of adventure could turn a handsome profit by supplying the right merchandise along the wilderness trails. The Colonel especially appreciated fine horses. Wherever he had settled, his neighbors soon knew that Colonel William Sanders had some of the best horses they had ever seen.[37]

1800 found the William Sanders family living among several Sanders families in Smith County, Tennessee, just created from a section of Sumner County. Events began to unfold in Smith County which would change many lives. Sometime in 1800, Bennett Rogers came to live with the Sanders family. Rogers had lived in the same neighborhood with a relative, Thomas Banks, for two years before joining the Sanders household.[39] By February 1801, Rogers and Sanders had arranged a partnership, with Sanders supplying the money and Rogers taking the risk. The deal would send Rogers with a group of horses and at least one slave down the Natchez Trail to New Orleans.[40] Once in New Orleans, Rogers intended to sell the merchandise and purchase cotton to sell in Baltimore. All went as expected, excellent trades were made; and the trip was relatively uneventful until it neared its end.

Rogers lead a string of horses from Nashville to Natchez where they were sold. He was able to buy cotton cheaply at Natchez, transport it to New Orleans and load his cargo aboard a ship bound for New York. After selling the cotton in New York, Rogers took the profit and journeyed to Baltimore where he set about buying slaves. He planned to take them back south, where the partners could realize a greater profit.[41] Rogers was diligent in his duties, and the following letters from Rogers to Sanders aptly describe his merchandise and trip.

---

[35] Worth S. Ray, *Tennessee Cousins* (Baltimore: Genealogical Publishing Co., 1994), p. 646.
[36] Kanawha Records, Deed Bk. B, p. 101-110. Among the Sanders/Rogers papers filed at the Court House in 1801, is a letter from Thomas Banks who stated, although a relative of Bennett Rogers, "he makes no claim to his property."
[37] *Ibid.*, p. 105. Bennett Rogers' letter shows the main merchandise in the partnership was horses. Later, Sampson Sanders bill of sale names the horses, but not the slaves.
[38] Ray, *Tennessee Cousins*, p. 646. Several records of Smith County show two William Sanders living in the county near Dixon Springs in 1800. The "other" William died in 1803 and left a young widow who remarried "Rowan Bill" Alexander, a county justice. Dixon Springs was near land called "the Revolutionary Grant".
[39] Kanawha Records, Deed Bk. B, pp. 104-111.
[40] *Ibid.*
[41] *Ibid.* Bennett Rogers letters to William Sanders, produced as evidence of partnership, detail his trip and intentions, including the difficulty in removing slaves from Maryland.

Mississippi Territory Natchez
March 31th 1801

Dear Sir
I take opportunity to Inform you that we got safe to this Country with much fertuge [fatigue], It has been a very hard mater to sell off our plunder for the cash, Yesterday I sold off the last horse we are safe so far in our trade the whole amount is 2252p Dollars 40 doll creadit while [Tall] I have just bought 2,000 Dollars worth of Bale Cotton & shall start down the River at the last of the week or the first of next. Cotton is now selling at 39 Dollars at New York. I think it is well to make a trial on Cotton as to take the money so, Capt. Ballow has sold off his horses and is much put to it to get his money he expects to stay till the first of May for his money. Mr.Terrell will start to that Country next Sunday on McConnel who will deliver you this and inform you every perticular. Ballow has it in Contemplation to go back by land and meet me at Baltimore. Should it be the case I want you to send a horse to me which will be much less than buying being so long on expenses makes it come very high, I think it is in my power to make a handsome speck, The price of Horses if much fell negros is selling verry well at this place If I can get here by the first of September next it will much in our favour, Cotton is selling at 22 Dollars p cwt I have some thought of taking water at Fort Pit and [{coming}] when I come to this place by reason geting here so much sooner. If I should you shall know I shall rite as soon as I get round You will please to excuse one for not riting no sooner my reasons will satisfy you when I see you, With respect to this Country I think it is the best that has ever been found yet Money seems tolerable plenty here you may make as much here as you please I should rite you more perticularly by Terrell can inform you everything you wish to know, Give my Compliment to Mrs.Saunders and the family & Nothing more but remains your Friend & c

Bennet Rogers

> New Orleans
> April 23rd 1801
>
> Dear Colo.
> I wrote you from Natchez by Mr. Terrell al the news particular concerning our affairs, there is nothin turned up since worth mentinoning. I have got safe to this place with my cotton, I am offered 25 dollars here but I see every body so anxious to buy Keeps me in good heart I got aboard Scooner & shall start for New York tomorrow, cotton selling from 36 to 39 dollars at New York, at this place Cumberland cotton is from 22 to 23 dollars p cwt. Natchez cotton is from to 25 dollars. Flower is 7 & 8 Dollars p Barrell Tobacco 3-p dollars Bacon 12p Dollars, Bacon hams 18 3/4-- I should be glad to hear from you, I have been very Onwell since I have been in this place but have got well nothing more but desires to be remembered to Mrs.Saunders & family & c
>
> Bennet Rogers

Kanawha County October Court 1801
Letters were presented in Court by Colo.William Saunders and the same is ordered to record teste John Reynolds (Kanawha Co., Charleston, WV, County Clerk, Deeds, Bk. B, 107.)

Obviously, the first part of Rogers' venture was a success. Not only was he able to sell the horses for a profit and purchase cotton, but he was also able to get prices on slaves and commodities, to look over the Mississippi territory, and to determine the availability of cash.[42] Rogers sent an itinerary of his proposed trip, even mentioning a fellow traveler would make the trip to Baltimore overland.[43] The reader will notice Rogers had some undisclosed concern, "my reasons will be good when I see you" and horses were so high priced, he requested one be sent to him. Rogers sent two more letters to Sanders in the next few months.

---

[42] Billington, *Westward Expansion*, p. 121. Cash money was in very short supply on the frontier. Most items were bartered.
[43] The Natchez Trail ran from the Mississippi north to Nashville where it connected other trails going east through Cumberland Gap and then north through the Virginia Valley and east again crossing the Potomac. It was the favored path in 1800 from New Orleans north.

New York,
May 29th 1801

Dear Colo.

I take up my pen once more to Inform you I have got safe to this place. I had a very disagreeable passage, I was sea sick the greater part of the voiage, we arrive here last Monday (this Tuesday) I saw nothing very particular on the passage, more than whales & porposes were as thick as the suierrels is on Dixon Creek, Cotton has taken a great fall here within a few weeks it has been selling as high as 40 cents, I have been offered only thirty yet I expect to get about 32, I am trying to sell as fast as possible as soon I can sell I shall start for [Menton] I expect to take water at Fort Pit or Whealing to go to Natchez my reasons will be good when I see you. You had better find me 2 horses to Natchez by the last of August it will be much better for us it save money if you have to hire some body to carry them to Natchez, You may rest continted without some accident I will pay every man we owe to you as soon as possible and some thing {clever} nothing more but remains. Yours with respect & c

Bennet Rogers

Baltimore
June 8th 1801

Dear Colo.

I am happy to Inform you I got so far on my Journey, I arrive here last evening I made sale of my Cotton at New york at 32p cents p lb (the profits were very small) the expense---------so high I am but little gainor Negros is selling tollarable high in this Country & it appears verry difficult in getting them from this state, there has been several people put in jail aboute trying to carry Negroes from this place & some has not got oute yet, I shall do the best I can, I am not much afraid of my self, I am going to see five or six tomorrow morning There appears to be a good maney for aboute here. It is uncertain which way I shall get oute from this place for the Ohio and go Down the River which I think much the best, I mentioned to you in my last letter from New York aboute sending me two horses to the Natchez which would be verry proper, Being in debt makes me so uneasy I am afraid it will make me do business too fast, I should be very glad to see a letter in the post office in Natchez when I get there from you concerning our affairs pray dont negelecting riting to me as soon as possible, You will hear from me every opertunity i want you to keep a sharp Eye upon that peace of land on Crick Creek I have nothing more perticular at the present but wish to be remembered to the family please give my complments to Jno C Henderson & his laidy & C

Bennet Rogers

These letters presented in Court by Colo. William Saunders (Kanawha Co., Charleston, WV, County Clerk, Deeds, Bk. B, pp. 108-109.)

Bennett Rogers was a good trader, and the partnership had already made money before he started his return; but Rogers acquired one slave too many. Apparently, Rogers was offered a good deal on a Negro blacksmith who had just been manumitted by his deceased owner. Although Rogers knew the man had been freed, getting a blacksmith slave was too good a deal to pass up.[44] Perhaps Rogers thought with his master dead no one would care about a former slave, and apparently he was right. No one protested or even seemed to notice as Rogers slipped out of Maryland and headed for Pittsburgh.

From the Baltimore letter and from subsequent events we learn that, Jack Neal, the blacksmith who thought himself a free man, was enslaved a second time, manacled to five other slaves, and headed west for the Natchez Trail. The trip began in Maryland going overland, perhaps along the proposed National Road route, to Pittsburgh where they continued down the Ohio River by canoe. Jack Neal reportedly told Rogers, "I am a free man and I will kill you if I have to."[45] Neal was a powerful blacksmith. True to his word, as the canoe floated past the mouth of the Kanawha River, Neal broke his chains, grabbed an ax, and killed Rogers while Rogers' assistant leaped overboard and swam ashore.

Neal quickly freed the other slaves, but the group was totally unprepared to live in the wilderness. Having noticed a settlement on the west river bank, the small group traveled back up the Ohio River and turned themselves over to officials at Gallipolis, where they also reported the crime.[46] Since the Ohio River where the crime occurred, belonged to Virginia, Gallipolis officials sent the group across the river to Point Pleasant where they were taken to the Kanawha County seat in Charleston.[47]

Once the legal system took over, many decisions were quickly made. The slaves were indicted for murder and Rogers' property was released for public auction. Somehow, William Sanders was notified of the murder, and he rushed to Kanawha County to claim his property, for the slaves alone were worth nearly $1800.00.[48] Sanders arrived in time for the October Court and presented his papers (gathered in Smith County, Tennessee) which claimed all of Rogers' property through partnership. Below is one of the letters which William Sanders produced to prove his partnership with Rogers.

---

[44] Henry & William Ruffner Papers, Kanawha County, (Montreat, NC, Historical Foundation of Presbyterian and Reformed Churches, unpaged [22 pages]). Hereafter cited as Ruffner Papers. Ruffner infers Rogers knew the man was freed, but bought him anyway.
[45] *Kanawha County Records 1791-1831*, (typed copy of original) Charleston, WV, West Virginia Archives and History Library, pp. 249-340.
[46] Ruffner Papers.
[47] Ohio did not become a state until 1803.
[48] Kanawha Records, Deeds, Bk. B, pp. 104-110; and *Kanawha County Records 1791-1831*, 249-340. The murder occurred about August 10th, 1801, on the Ohio River(Kanawha Co. VA). By August 21st, Sanders obtained affidavits concerning partnership in Smith Co., TN. By October 14th, he had arrived in Kanawha Co. to present his claim. Rogers had been in Baltimore on June 8th.

> **BILL OF SALE**
> **FILED BY WILLIAM SANDERS IN KANAWHA COUNTY, VIRGINIA**
>
> I hereby certify that on the 31th of January last I sold a negro to Colonel William Sanders and Bennett Rodgers who contracted for him jointly and became equally answerable to me for payment of the price stipulated, and that I also hold obligation against the said Saunders & Rodgers in which they jointly bound for the payment of three hundred and forty dollars for three horses-and that soon after the above Date said Rogers left this country with said Negro and horses and much other property, on a trading adventure to the Natchez and round by water to the Northern or Middle States, and that it is generally understood that the said Saunders was and is owner of one[{morety}] of all property carried on the said trading adventure by the Rogers who it is reported to have been murdered on his return some where near the mouth of the Kanawha River.
>
> T. Dixon   (Tilmon)
>
> Dixon Spring, Smith County State of Tennessee August 21th 1801[49]

Because the murder had been committed by an enslaved free man, the fate of Jack Neal was undecided. The Kanawha Court had quickly convened, convicted Neal of murder and sentenced him to hang; but the sentence was delayed because Kanawha County records never reached Richmond.[50]

About six months later, Neal was tried and sentenced a second time only to receive a reprieve on the day of his hanging, one day after he had escaped, been recaptured and dangerously beaten. The son of the county clerk was sympathetic with Neal and vividly remembered the events many years later:

> ...When the day of execution appointed by the court on his second trial approached, the last mail that could bring a pardon or reprieve arrived and brought none.......Jack decided to file off the 4 stout rivet heads........He could easily obtain from his friends without whatever tools he needed for cutting iron.......Jack was ingenious and bold in getting out of jail, but then his genius left him.......With his head all gashed and bloody, and his other injury shooting darts of fire through his nerves, he was led back to prison about 2 or 3 o'clock in the afternoon........After the governor and council heard of his unfortunate attempt to escape, and his severe sufferings in consequence, they immediately prolonged his reprieve and it be understood that he would be ultimately pardoned if he behaved well.[51] [.......indicates breaks from the original material.]

---

[49] Kanawha Records, Deeds BKB, pp 104-110.
[50] Ruffner Papers.
[51] Ibid. Ruffner was about 9 at the time of the trial and probably quite impressionable. His account was written while he was president of Washington and Lee University, around 1847. The piece begins: "Some years before Louisana came into our possession, slave traders began to carry slaves from Maryland and Virginia to the New Orleans market. This class of trader, though incidentally useful in transporting bad negroes to the cotton and sugar fields, have always been condemned among us, and have not been greatly pitied when they met with some disaster in the persecution of their trade."

Finally all the facts of Neal's case were presented to the Governor and the Assembly, and they reacted according to law:

> "An act for the punishment of persons guilty of stealing or selling free persons as slaves. January 8, 1788.
> 1. Whereas several evil disposed persons have seduced or stolen the children of black and mulatto free persons, and have actually disposed of the persons so seduced or stolen as slaves, and punishment adequate to such crimes, not being, by law provided for such offenders.
> 2. Be it enacted, That any person who shall hereafter be guilty of stealing or selling any free person for a slave knowing the said person so sold to be free, and thereof shall be lawfully convicted, the person so convicted shall suffer death without benefit of clergy.[52]

Although Neal was eventually cleared of murder charges and allowed to return East, he spent considerable time waiting on the Kanawha Court to hear his case. Some of that intervening time was spent in jail, but part of it was with the Sanders slaves.[53]

1801 and 1802 were eventful years for the Sanders family. News of the death of Colonel Williams Sanders' partner, Bennett Rogers, caused the Colonel to uproot his family in Smith County, Tennessee, and to hurry north to Kanawha County, Virginia. His claim on Rogers' property was too important to assign to some lawyer he did not know.[54] The legal proceedings lasted through several court sessions, spanning almost a year.

During the Kanawha County Court proceeding, William Sanders apparently settled his family in Teays Valley about thirty-five miles west of Charleston.[55] The Colonel and his family were well received in the neighborhood, which may have represented some of their old Loudoun County friends and family.[56] He and his sixteen-year-old son, Sampson, were certainly known and recognized about the court and the county as they attended each court session. The successful conclusion of Sanders' claim of Roger's partnership left the Sanders family quite wealthy.

Scarcely had the family settled in from their trip from Tennessee, when daughter Hetty agreed to marry a Kanawha County neighbor, Thomas Kilgore who was twenty years her senior. Kilgore, a bachelor or widower, may have followed the family about the frontier from Loudoun County, Virginia, and settled with them in the Teays Valley area.[57] Soon after Hetty's marriage and prior to September 16, 1802, Colonel William Sanders became ill and death came quickly.[58] (See Appendix 4A.)

By October 1, 1802, William's estate had been appraised and his wife Martha was

---

[52] Henning, *Statues at Large Being a Collection of the Laws of Virginia*, pp. 531-532.
[53] Ruffner Papers. Henry Ruffner stated Jack Neal returned to the coast and became a stevedore with his own company. No located records verify that statement.
[54] The Teays Valley farm was in Kanawha County, Virginia in 1801, but when Cabell County was created in 1809, the property lay in Cabell County.
[55] Kanawha Records, Deeds, Bk. B, p. 189. Martha's deed from Thomas Kilgore states "where she now lives".
[56] Several Cabell County surnames are the same as found in Loudoun County and Jeremiah Ward's wife was reported a Saunders. See Appendices.
[57] Tithable and census records in both Loudoun County, Virginia and Caswell County, Tennessee, have Kilgore families very near the Sanders family.
[58] Kanawha Records, Deeds, Bk.B, p. 176. On September 16, 1802, Martha Sanders made bond and was appointed guardian of Sampson Sanders, a minor.

required to post 4,000 Pounds (English currency) in surety as administrix of the estate and as guardian for Sampson.[59] Martha retained the widows' one-third share of the estate, but when the personal effects of Colonel Williams Sanders were sold, his minor heir, Sampson, had right of refusal at the sale.[60] (See appendix 2B.)

Colonel William Sanders' estate sale netted in excess of 700 Pounds cash. Two slave families listed among William's assets apparently were not sold. "Hannah and her children" and "Ader and her children" appear on the estate sale.[61] No information about number or ages of children was available for these women, but their mention made it possible to extend the Sanders families, both black and white, across the frontier to Cabell County, Virginia and finally to Cass County, Michigan.[62]

Figure 6. Kanawha County, Virginia 1800

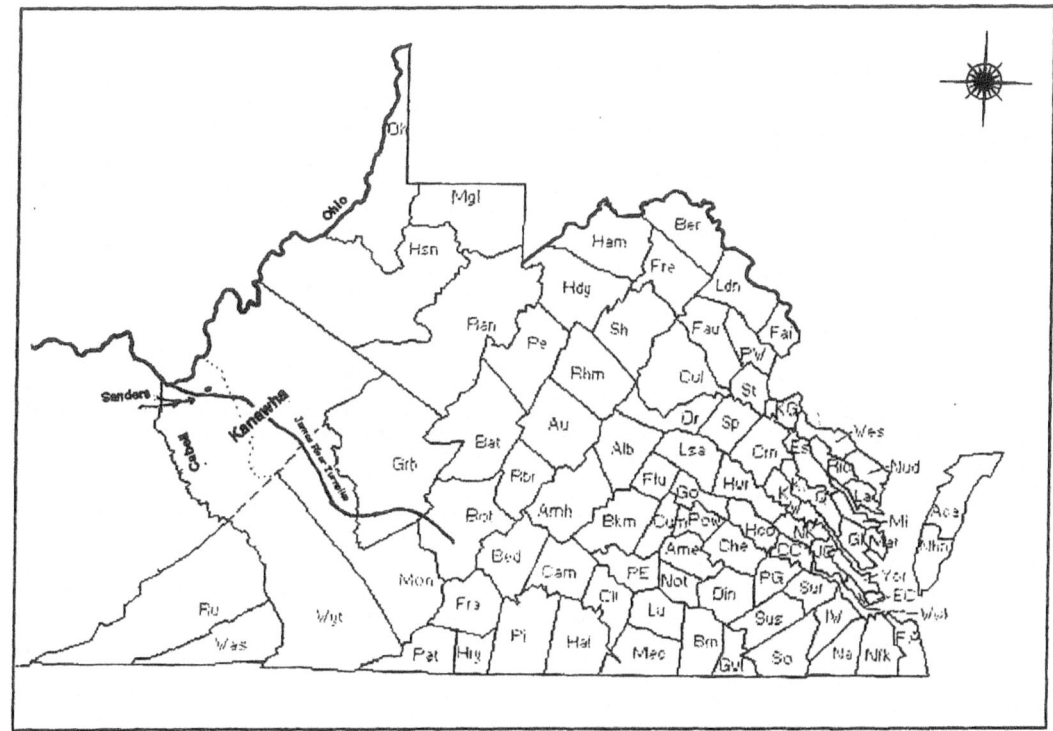

Kanawha County, Virginia, 1800, covered most of southern West Virginia. In 1809, Cabell county was created from the territory south of the Kanawha River.

---

[59] Monetary conversion for that period is difficult. If 2 1/2 dollars equal one pound, her bond was $ 10,000.00.
[60] As heir, Sampson could exempt estate items from the sale.
[61] Kanawha Records, Deeds, Bk. B, pp. 110-112.
[62] Martha's 1802 personal property tax was paid on 3 males over 16. Females and children were not taxed. (see Figure 8)

Chapter Two
Kanawha County, Virginia, 1802-1807

Martha Sanders had spent the best part of her life moving around the frontier with her husband and now the Colonel was dead. She found herself a wealthy widow at age forty-one and the administrix of the estate for her sixteen-year-old son Sampson. (See Appendix 2.) She received control, not only of her husband's property but all the property of partners Sanders and Rogers.[63] One of the first items of business Martha Sanders undertook was to purchase a two hundred and fifty acre tract of land in Kanawha County from her new son-in-law Thomas Kilgore.[64] The deed stated the tract was "below were Martha Sanders now lives" indicating Martha was already situated with a home in Teays Valley before her husband died.

The Martha Sanders property was located on the bustling James River Turnpike at the mouth of Sanders Creek on Mud River, about two miles west of the community of Mud Bridge. The property was ideally located in the fertile Teays Valley, mid-way between Mud Bridge (Milton) and Everett's Tavern (Ona). Today, the site is located just north of the highway US 60 at its crossing of Mud River, about one mile west of Milton. It is shown on Figure 7, the James River Turnpike.

During the five years between 1802 and 1807 when Sampson came of age, Martha Sanders actively purchased property and began the financial empire her son was to rule. The most important property acquired was the one thousand acre Diamond Tract in Teays Valley, originally patented by John P. Duvall in 1793. This valuable agricultural property had excellent access to markets throughout the area and to eastern Virginia via the James River Turnpike.

---

[63] Kanawha Co., Charleston, WV, County Clerk, Deeds, Bk. B, p. 175.
[64] *Ibid.*, p. 189.

Figure 7. Settlers Along the James River Turnpike

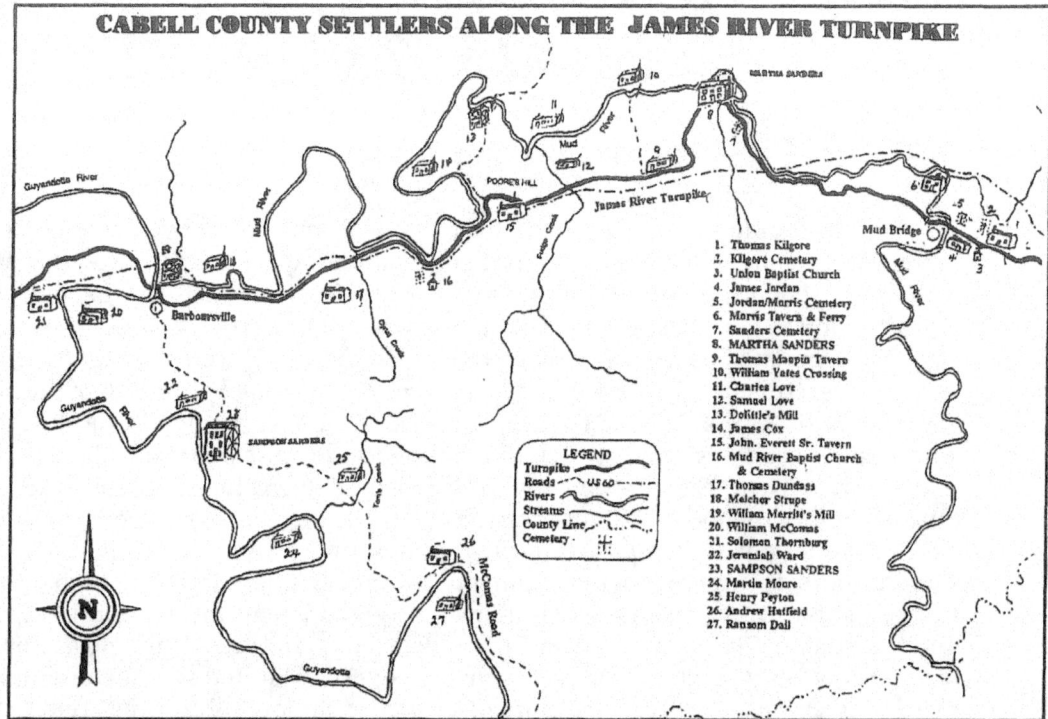

Cabell County's early settlement was in Teays Valley, a fertile valley created from a prehistoric lake. The road which became the James River and Ohio Turnpike ran through the valley as early as 1788. It cut across the big loop of the Ohio/Kanawha River route.

Martha seems to have been a dominating personality as shown by her purchase of property usually reserved to males, the administration of her husband's estate, as well as Sampson's late marriage. From the time Martha settled in Teays Valley, she expanded her acreage and developed her agricultural properties. At her death in 1831, Martha's inventory showed she had been an active farmer, owning over one hundred and eighty hogs, twenty-seven head of cattle and eleven horses. Her farm also produced corn, wheat and flax, and she had six barrels of peach brandy, which would have been made from her peach orchard.

MARTHA SANDERS INVENTORY 1831			
11	horses or mares	10	steers
4	milch cows	6	heifers
1	bull	4	calves
1	yoke work oxen & yoke	44	sheep
138	head hogs	30-50	suckling pigs
10	stacks hay	1	stack oats
1	field of corn on river below house - 50a	1	field above house 15a
		1	field-hillside above Malcombs 7a
	(Lunsford having cropped with Martha to receive 1/4 all corn)		
1	lot unrolled flax(1/4 belongs to Lewis Lunsford)		
4	oat stacks (at James Chapman's)	1	bag of cotton, in seed
4	stands of bees	1	wool bag
some tobacco		1	barrel wool
1	salt barrel	1	cotton gin
[Note: to preserve salt pork]			

Source: Cabell Co., Huntington, WV, County Clerk, Wills, Bk. 1, 101.

This may seem a small enterprise, but in the days before mechanized farming, it was an impressive affair. There were three fields, amounting to seventy-two acres in corn, an oat field, a tobacco patch; and a large area used to produce the ten stacks of hay. In addition, each group of animals was pastured in separate fields because, except in the winter months, they would forage for feed.

The farm inventory indicates good management as well. Not only does it show four milch cows but also four calves, meaning the cows were producing. The six heifers were being raised to replace or enlarge the milk stock. The flax, cotton and wool were raised to provide material and clothing. In addition to all these crops, her farm would have maintained a large vegetable garden and an orchard to provide everyday food.

Cash crops were indicated by the steers and the vast number of hogs. Some farmers herded their hogs along the James River Turnpike to eastern markets, but the Sanders butchered the animals, packed the meat in barrels and shipped it by wagon or river.[65]

It is also interesting to see not all the labor was done by slaves. Lunsford was to receive one-fourth the corn and flax crops, probably because he did the work of plowing and planting on Martha's land. James Chapman had four oat stacks at his place, indicating Martha had leased and farmed Chapman's land.

Martha's wealth and high standard of living was evident in the long list of personal possessions. (In 1815 a rich Cabell Countian paid tax on "calico curtains".)

---

[65] Note the barrels in the inventory. Later, Sampson's inventory lists pork and barrels instead of hogs (live animals).

```
12  split bottom chairs        1   arm chair
 1  pr shoe pinchers           Josephus works in 2 Vol. & sundry
 1  sugar bowl                 other books, etc.
spoon moulds                   2   large bottles with honey, etc.
 1  bread tray                 1   basket pewter
 7  counterpanes               1   pair cotton curtains
 8  coverlids                  6   sheets
 3  towels                     4   feather beds & 5 pillows
 7  bed steads
```

Not only did Martha raise and make her own cloth and clothes, but she had materials to make shoes as well.

```
 1  quilting wheel             1   small spinning wheel
 1  large spinning wheel       linen
White & blue flax thread       1   chest containing 1 pieces of jeans
 2  pieces white cotton cloth  6   pieces checked cotton cloth
 1  piece white lindsey        1   piece stripped linsey
 4  small pieces flax linen
            1 lot of leather consisting of:
 1  sheepskin                  1   deer skin
 1  piece Kip                  1   kip skin (untanned calf,kid)
 2  sides upper some remnants of upper leather
 1  side & piece side sole leather (put out to shoe the steers)
```

Finally, the inventory showed some dissension among family members, because the appraisers included the following contested items with comments.

```
1 stew kettle                  5  bed steads & pieces of cord
(supposed to belong            (3 of the beds are claimed by Mrs. Kilgore,
Sampson Sanders)               1 by Martha Kilgore, 1 by Malinda Kilgore)
                               [Hetty & her daughters]

(See Appendix 4B for complete inventory.)
```

A frontier farm in the mid Nineteenth Century was self-sufficient by need, because supplies and materials were far away and expensive. Martha's inventory shows she was beyond a subsistence farmer. She had cleared and planted enough land to be farming for profit and was making a good comfortable living. From the original "home place" base on Mud River, the Sanders, both mother and son, eventually acquired over 10,000 acres of prime Cabell County land. Most of it lay between the Guyandotte and Mud Rivers and along their rich river bottoms. It was productive farm land, noted for high crop production and quality Short Horn cattle.[66]

Martha paid taxes on about 2000 acres during her lifetime. In addition to the Diamond tract on Mud River, she owned 700 acres on Twelve Pole Creek at Trouts Hill, which later became the county seat of Wayne County. Many of the Cabell County deeds in the eastern section of the county have some reference to "Widow Sanders' line", and her name is found in assorted documents.[67]

Martha was worth $6443.78 1/2 at her death. Sampson and his sister Hetty Sanders Kilgore each received one-half of her estate or $3221.89 1/4. No bill of sale, nor property transference were listed in any Cabell County records. There was a court record, as well as the appraisal, that indicated Sampson claimed some of the property which Hetty wanted. (Possibly a share of Martha's slaves who went to Sampson.) A lawsuit filed by Thomas and Hetty Kilgore against Sampson gave no particulars. Soon dropped from court records, perhaps it was settled out of court.

Many deeds in both Kanawha and Cabell counties were made by Martha or Sampson Sanders. After 1810 the majority of property was bought and sold by Sampson (having reached age twenty-one in 1807). At various times census records show mother and son kept separate residences.[68] Figure 8 shows the frequency the Sanders appeared in local records.

---

[66] Lambert Collection, 76B-9-9. Sampson Simmons' interview states: "Raunta Pol, Uncle's Short Horn bull was known as far away as Missouri". Also note the crop production inferred in Sampson Sanders bill of sale 1849. (See Appendix 5A.)

[67] Cabell Co., Huntington, WV, County Clerk, Deeds, Bk. 1, p. 5. "Metes & bounds" describes property by naming the points where the boundary lines meet, "metes", and by surrounding property holders names, "bounds". For example: "south 14 poles to the line of Widow Sanders and Chapman corner.."

[68] Martha ceased to buy property at that time indicating Sampson became head of the family. Federal Census records on Martha and Sampson are quite frustrating because both Martha and Sampson were "skipped over" although in different years.

Figure 8. Cabell County Tax and Census Listings

CABELL COUNTY PROPERTY TAX AND CENSUS LISTINGS FOR THE SANDERS

Martha Sanders   1809 through 1848 Mud River & 12 Pole (2)
Sampson Sanders   1809 through 1831 Mud River 3mi below ferry

Federal census listings of slave holders

Thomas Kilgore(Hetty)	1820-10 slaves	1830-15 slaves	1840-13 slaves
Martha Sanders		1830- 7 slaves	
Sampson Sanders	1820-21 slaves	1830-24 slaves	1840-39 slaves

(1810 census lost and Martha not listed on 1820)[69]

Kanawha & Cabell County Personal Property Lists

	year	white male	black male 12-16	black male 16+	horses
Martha Sanders	1802	0	0	3	4
	1806	1	0	4	7
	1807	1	0	3	6
	1809	1	1	3	7
	1812	0	3	3	6
	1813	0	2	3	7
	1815	0	0	2	2
Martha & Sampson	1827	0	4	14	20
Martha	1828	0	1	3	11
	1829	0	2	2	11
	1830	0	2	2	10
	1831	0	2	2	12

No bills of sale for slaves were found.

Several Virginia county records for the 1800-1810 period were destroyed. In addition, the Federal Census for Virginia was lost in 1810 and in 1820. Cabell County had to send a duplicate copy when its original enumeration failed to reach Washington in 1820. The property tax records for Kanawha County listed Martha Sanders only once between 1802 and 1808. She paid personal taxes only three times and was listed on the census only in 1830. No slaves were named in any of these records, although the Virginia Personal Property Tax Lists did give the number of slaves over age twelve, each person held.

---

[69] National Archives, Records of the Bureau of Census, Fifth Census (1830, Virginia, Microcopy 19, Roll 190, and Sixth Census(1840), Virginia Microcopy 704, Roll 555. Hereafter cited Federal Census.

Chapter Three
Cabell County, Virginia, 1810-1850

Sampson Sanders was a complex personality. In 1809 Cabell County was formed from Kanawha County, only two years after Sampson came of age. Cabell County and Sampson Sanders began to make history together. Although very young, Sampson was exceptionally rich for the frontier, and his mother had made sure her family would be important in the new Cabell County. By age sixteen, Sampson had traveled across much of the old southwestern frontier from Virginia into North Carolina and Tennessee and back to western Virginia. He had assisted his father in business dealings, and then inherited great wealth by his father's sudden death. Sampson took over management of the family estate begun by his mother's land purchase, and over a forty year period successfully developed two high producing farms and the county's leading mill. He appeared in many of the county record books, serving on numerous county juries, appraising the property of neighbors and friends, or acting as road overseer.[70] He was nominated as a county justice about 1830, but how long he served has been lost with the Minute Book.[71] Sampson Sanders was well respected in Cabell County, Virginia, for many years.

In 1824 Sampson Sanders purchased the primary mill site in Cabell County. Situated on the Guyandotte River about ten miles from his mother's home, the mill was located at the river's first falls. The site was just three miles south of the county seat of Barboursville, where a cracker mill had been in operation before Sampson purchased the site. Under Sampson's guidance between 1825 and 1847 the Sanders Mill became the largest flour processing mill in Cabell County.[72] Sanders Mill ground corn and wheat, supported a wood lathe and loom, and had the machinery to saw timber. Sanders also operated a blacksmith shop, provided a mercantile store, and had his own whiskey still.[73] Figure 9 shows the community that grew around the Sanders Mill.

Sanders Mill was the center of a thriving community which served the area for many years. With this mill, Sampson became a frontier entrepreneur and his businesses as a gentleman farmer and a mill owner expanded through the years. All his activities required more time than he could afford for public service and would explain the dwindling entries in county records.

In 1848 plans were devised to construct a series of locks and dams to improve navigation on the Guyandotte River. Sampson Sanders, as the major businessmen on the lower Guyandotte, was one of the original planners and promoters for the Guyandotte Navigation Company. Other prosperous county gentlemen, such as John W. Hite, Percival Smith, Solomon Thornburg, Peter Dingess, and Evermont Ward joined him in

---

[70] Cabell Co., Huntington, WV, County Clerk, Deeds, Bks 1-9, and Minute Bks, 1 & 3. See Appendix 5C.
[71] George S. Wallace, *Cabell County Annals and Families* (Richmond: Garrett & Massie, 1935), p. 20.
[72] Cabell Co. Huntington, WV, County Clerk, Deeds, Bk. 9, and Minute Bk 3. Sanders sold the Mill to W.C. Dusenberry in 1848 and the Mill dam was later incorporated into the Guyandotte Navigation Company. Dusenberry was never able to return the profits that Sampson Sanders had achieved. During the Civil war the dam suffered from neglect and severe flooding. The Cabell County Court declared it a hazard to navigation and it was removed from the river. The old mill building remained standing for many years and the old community is today called Martha. The original mill site was just above the standing Martha Bridge on the east side of the river.
[73] Cabell Co., Huntington, WV, County Clerk, Wills, Bk. 2, pp. 19-29; and "William F. Dusenberry, Diaries 1854 & 1856", private collection, Huntington, WV. Hereafter cited as Dusenberry, Diaries.

the push to improve area transportation, but Sanders died before he purchased any shares of the company.[74] Lock Number 4 of the Guyandotte Navigation Company was built by raising the dam at the old Sanders Mill.[75] Although Sampson Sanders was not as visible as other county leaders, he was an important part of the growth of Cabell County. He certainly was one of the wealthiest men in the county, as shown by the fourteen people required to make a surety bond of $60,000 each, to settle his estate.

Figure 9. The Community at the Mill. Sanders' Mill Site.

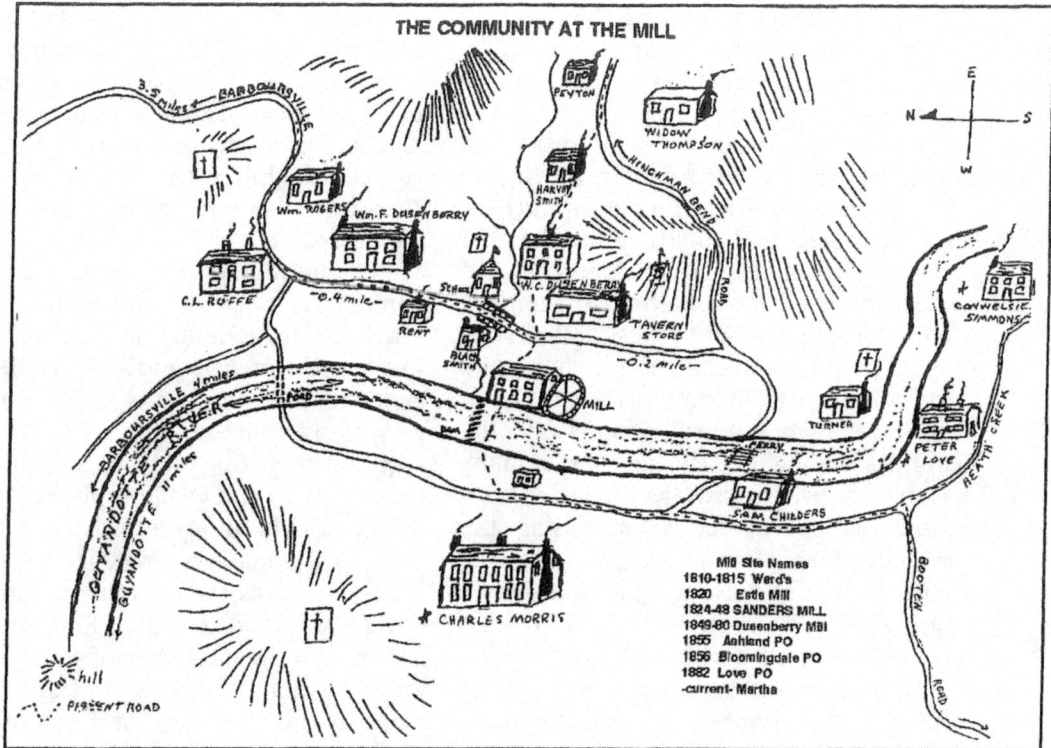

SANDERS MILL SITE, Guyandotte River, Cabell County, Virginia. Approximate home locations mentioned in Dusenberrys' Diaries. —Morris, Love & Simmons were Sanders heirs.

---

[74] Lambert Collect, 76B-4-8; and "Documents of the Guyandotte Navigation Company," Virginia Department of Public Works and the Virginia Assembly 1849-1854, Richmond. Sanders death in 1849 occurred before stock was issued for the Guyandotte Navigation Company.
[75] Dusenberry, Diaries.

Chapter Four
Sampson Sanders' Private Life, 1810-1850

Sampson seemed to have been so busy building an empire, he had no time for women, other than his mother. Most of Sampson's early manhood appeared to have been dominated by his forceful mother; Kanawha County tax records indicate he remained in his mother's home even after he was married.[76] He did not marry until age thirty-five, when his marriage was recorded in Cabell County's Marriage Book I: "Sampson Sanders to Ann Guin April 29, 1821." His wife, Ann, presented him with at least one child, but both Ann and his daughter, Rebecca, died before 1840.[77]

Ann Sanders was listed on several real estate transactions in the 1820's as Sampson's wife. Personal property tax lists seem to indicate Sampson and Ann had their own home from 1829 to 1832. (Martha Sanders died in September 1831.) Ann's death occurred after June 1835 when she signed the deed which partitioned Martha's property.[78] Cholera was especially bad along the Ohio River between 1832 and 1835, with death lists in all the local newspapers. Perhaps both women fell victim during an outbreak.

At the time of Ann's death, Sampson was about fifty years old. In the mid-nineteenth century, many a man's life was already finished. Instead of waiting to die, Sampson Sanders began rapidly expanding his businesses and acquired property until he owned more than 10,000 acres as displayed on Figure 10.[79] Records indicate Sampson accepted property as collateral or deeds of trust for mill trade. He accumulated considerable property when people were not able to meet their obligations. Through various transactions, Sampson Sanders more than doubled his property holdings after Ann's death.

Sampson may have maintained two homes and apparently lived some of the time at the "old home place" just west of Mud Bridge, originally occupied by his mother. Although Mrs. Thompson, his housekeeper, was from a family that lived near the mill on the Guyandotte River, most people's memories indicate Sampson finished his life at the "home place."[80] Contemporaries claimed the old house was made of logs and stood two stories high.[81] After a fire, a Ball nephew replaced the old house with a brick home. It still stands today very near the first house site, just below the bluff overlooking Mud River where Sampson and his mother were buried.[82]

Like his mother, Sampson Sanders recorded a will and left an appraisal of inventory, both of which reveal information about him. The bill of sale showed he was operating at least two farms at the time of his death: his mother's east of Mud Bridge and another at the mill site on the Guyandotte River. Sanders was a very successful farmer. The bill of sale listed two sets of farm equipment, livestock and crops. Like his mother, he produced cotton,

---

[76] "1827 Personal Property Tax Lists," Commonwealth of Virginia, Richmond, microfilm. The list shows Martha and Sampson Sanders as one house in 1827. Only 1828 through 1832 show Sampson and Martha in separate homes.
[77] Lambert Collection, 76B-9-9. The Sanders Graveyard is on the original Martha Sanders farm just west of Milton. Only Martha and Sampson have surviving tombstones, but it is rumored other members of the family and slaves are buried at the site. W.S. Vinson (a great nephew) stated Sanders' daughter was named Rebecca.
[78] Cabell Records, Bk. 5, p. 534.
[79] Ibid, Deeds, Bks. 1-10. (See Appendix 5B.)
[80] Lambert Collection, loose cards.
[81] Ibid. Rece interview, loose cards.
[82] Ibid., loose cards.

flax, corn, wheat, oats, and hay. His land supported at least one hundred and fifty hogs, two hundred and eighty-nine sheep, two hundred and fifty-eight head of cattle, thirty-seven geese, twenty-seven horses and ten yoke of cattle. In addition he had a large potato patch with both Irish and sweet potatoes, and a garden which sold for $2.50. Listed on the appraisal was also 4,619 pounds of bacon and the barrels to pack it in.[83] From his inventory we also learn how he improved his life after his mother's death. (See Appendix 5A.)

30	pieces of china	1	dining table
17	plates	3	side tables
10	cups & saucers	1	clock (for which he was taxed)
4	bowls & 2 pitchers	2	looking glasses
1/2 doz	silver spoons	1	large cushion chair
11	silver tea spoons	1	settie and cushion
4	silver salt cellars	11	window curtains
18	knives & forks	6	table cloths
1	Brittania Tea Pot	9	beds & bedding
3	covered dishes	1	map of the U.States & book
1	sett bed curtains	3	bureau

These were the types of items a young bride would add to a home. Considering Sampson never even pampered himself with a carriage, it seems likely his wife Ann purchased many of the above items.[84]

Sampson's bill of sale covered ten pages and included the persons who made purchases. Many items went to his relatives, but there was a large selection of farm equipment chosen by neighbors who came from all over the area. That equipment showed how difficult farming was in the Nineteenth Century, while also showing Sanders was interested in "improved" farming.[85] If one person used each plow, the inventory indicated the work force necessary to cultivate the farms, in this case his slaves.

---

[83] Cincinnati, Ohio, was already known as Porkopolis. A lot of pork was shipped down the Ohio River packed in wooded barrels banded with "hoops." The lumber was sawed, the hoop poles cut and the barrels probably assembled at the Sanders Mill.
[84] Taxes had to be paid on carriages.
[85] Both the McCormick equipment and the grass seeds indicated improved farming practices.

1	sub soil plow	5	harrows (1 & 2 horse)	1	stone mattock
1	ox plow	2	cultivators	1	stone auger
1	crane plow	1	threshing machine	5	weeding hoes
1	horse plow	1	scraper	2	sprouting hoes
1	McCormick plow	1	improved McCormick	5	mattocks
9	shovel plows(2 old)	5	wagons or parts	8	brier scythes
2	large cast plows	1	sled	8	mowing scythes
2	left handed plow	1	McCormick colter	3	flax rakes
1	right hand plow	4	blind bridles	7	cradles & scythes
1	pea cock plow	2	carts	1	wheat fan
6	corn cutters	11	axes	1	frow
	1 peck of clover seed			1	box Randal grass seed
		50	bu Buckwheat		

From the sale we also learn Sanders was engaged in several enterprises other than farming. Quite a bit of the inventory represented wood and timber from a saw mill (probably kept from the mill sale), while another section listed tools for a blacksmith shop and forge.

1	timber cart	3	pr blacksmith tongs
2	ox carts	1	billows
1	lot flooring plank	1	anvil
2	lots oak plank	1	vice
1	large sled & chain		9 3/4 lb round iron
493 ft of plank			43 lbs new bar iron
		1	blacksmith hammer

Also note that Sampson Sanders did not expect to die any time soon. All his fields were planted, many crops had been harvested, and thirteen cords of fire wood had been cut.

Sanders' mill was not listed on his inventory because it was sold in late 1848, about six months before his death.[86] Sanders apparently reserved from that sale barrels and boxes of materials which he expected to use in the near future.[87] He also kept his still and other equipment which Dusenberry, the new owner, bought back at the sale.

At the time of his death, Sampson's property covered a large section of Cabell County between the mill on the Guyandotte

---

[86] Dusenberry, Diaries. The mill was purchased by William C. Dusenberry of New York City and operated until the Civil War.
[87] Cabell Records, Wills, Bk. 2, pp. 19-29. Sampson Sanders bill of sale includes household furnishings as well as farm equipment, produce and livestock.

River and his mother's old property on Mud River. He recorded one survey for 2,300 acres on the west side of the Guyandotte opposite the mill, which ranged from the Guyandotte watershed with Davis Creek southeast to the Heath Creek watershed. Much of his property was prime bottom land along the Guyandotte River around the mill site.[88]

Part of his rapid expansion after 1830 stemmed from his mill business, but there may have been a more important explanation for Sampson's desire to make a fortune. No records were found to indicate Sanders had an overseer, but obviously, one person could not have been constantly at both farms and the mill. Nor was it possible for a single person to do the required work. Perhaps Sampson trusted his people enough to oversee themselves. How else could he have managed properties several miles apart? Sampson would have had difficulty controlling everything unless he allowed some of his slaves to act as his agents. That practice was accepted in Cabell County as will be shown in later records. Dusenberry reported several incidences when a slave arrived to collect materials or to make a delivery for his master.

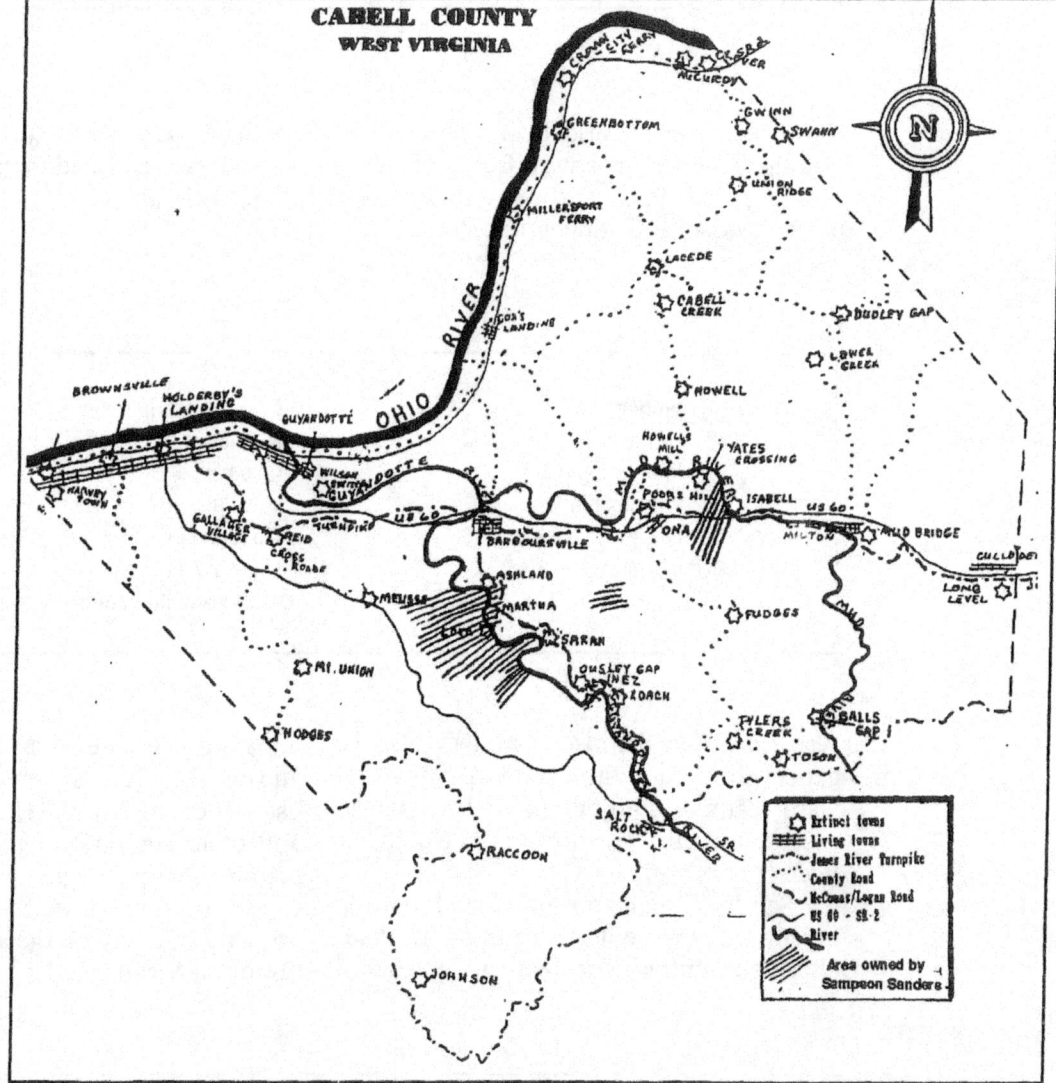

Figure 10. Sampson Sanders' Holdings in Cabell County

---

[88] Cabell Records, Survey Book 1, p. 424.

At first glance, Sampson Sanders would appear to have been a lonely man with mother, wife and child gone, but he had two other "families" to which he devoted his life. He was devoted to his sister Hetty's children. Hetty was three years older than Sampson but had married in 1802. She had grandchildren the age of Sampson's child. All her children seemed to be a joy to their "Uncle Sampson." Most of the surviving information about Sampson Sanders was written by Sampson Simmons, the youngest son of Mary Polly Kilgore and William Simmons. William Simmons died early in 1845, followed soon after by his wife Mary Polly. They left eight orphans. Sanders told those children they would never want for anything.

He left many acres of property to each of his nephews and nieces or their children by willing it to Hetty with the stipulation it be deeded to her children. Hetty died in 1853, just four years after her brother. Before her death, she transferred property from Sampson to each of her children. The largest section of property, containing 1,800 acres, went to the orphaned and particularly needful Simmons children. Martha Kilgore Morris also received more than 1,000 acres. (See Appendix 6.) After providing for all his legal heirs, he proceeded to care for his other dependents and second "family," his slaves.

Chapter Five
Sampson's Other "Family"

The Sanders family was among a small percentage of Virginians who were slave holders. The other "family" to whom Sampson was devoted was his slaves. Sampson Sanders had inherited some of the family slaves at his father's death in 1802.[89] That death was just a few short months after Sampson had witnessed a very cruel trial of a free Negro.[90] Perhaps Sampson's opinion of slavery was formed at age sixteen, or perhaps he objected to slavery on moral or religious grounds, but subsequent events definitely indicate that Sampson Sanders objected to slavery.

Although evidence exists showing Sanders maintained a housekeeper, no mention was ever made, nor did any records show he kept an overseer.[91] There were also no records to indicate Sampson bought or sold any of his slaves, while twice court records note his refusal to allow slaves to be sold.[92] Apparently Sanders either considered his slaves part of his family, or he trusted them to manage themselves.

The only remaining information about his slaves are the statistics of the Virginia Personal Property Tax Lists. Those lists enumerate only male slaves over twelve years of age, divided into categories of 12-16 and over 16. No Cabell County records show any transfer of slaves by Sampson, although Charlotte and her daughter Jane must have belonged to the Witcher family.[93] It would seem his slaves were a result of normal increase of children with Negro parents, as indicated by the large proportion of adult males with wives who registered property in Cass County, Michigan. The group of slaves seems to have been a continuation of the slave family Sampson inherited from his father in 1802.[94]

Figure 11.
Kanawha and Cabell Property Personal Tax Rate

KANAWHA & CABELL COUNTY PERSONAL PROPERTY TAX LISTS
COLUMN A NEGRO MALES 12-16 COLUMN B NEGRO MALES OVER 16
SAMPSON SANDERS (SOME YEARS SAMPSON WAS LISTED UNDER HIS MOTHER (M))

year	A		B		year	A		B		year	A	B
1810	2		3		1824	2		12		1837	2	20
1812	0	M-3	0	M-3	1825	2		13		1838	2	20
1813	0	M-2	0	M-3	1826	2		14		1839	3	20
1814	1		6		1827	4		14		1840	4	22
1815	1		6		1828	2		12		1841	3	20
1816	-		9 (all)		1829	2	M-2	12	M-2	1842	4	21
1817	-		9 (all)		1830	2	M-2	12	M-2	1843	5	22
1818	2		8		1831	1	M-2	13	M-2	1844	5	21
1819	1		9		1832	3		16		1845	7	22
1820	1		9		1833	5		15		1846	6	22
1821	1		12		1834	5		15		1847	5	27
1822	1		12		1835	2		19		1848	5	24
1823	1		11		1836	2		18		1849	4	24

---

[89] Slaves were treated as other property being bequeathed, inherited, used as collateral and to pay debts.
[90] Kanawha Records, Deeds, Kk B, pp 104-110; and *Kanawha County Records 1791-1831*, pp. 249-340.
[91] Lambert Collection, 76B-9-9.
[92] At both his father's estate sale and his mother's estate sale, Sampson refused to sell slaves.
[93] There is a Witcher deed bequeathing Charlotte, and Charlotte named Jane's father as Witcher Sanders.
[94] Lambert Collection, 76B-9-9."Hannah and her children and Ader and her children," listed in William Sanders' bill of sale, were apparently divided. Martha received one third of the estate and probably one third of the slaves. Interviews indicate Hannah's family went to Hetty.

Sampson Sanders had always been surrounded by the family slaves. It is probable that his earliest playmates on the lonely frontier were the slave children who were part of his life. Since there were few people about, Sampson would have befriended and trusted the people closest to him, the slaves. On the frontier life was hard for everyone. Although Sampson was his father's heir, many an occasion would have found Sampson working along side the slaves as they cleared land and built homes.

In 1801, Sampson, age fifteen and living in Smith County, Tennessee, would have been aware of his father's partner, Bennett Rogers. He would also have known of the business dealings in horses and slaves. When Mr. Rogers acquired one too many slaves in Baltimore and the freed man took Rogers' life on the Ohio River, Sampson would have known why the Sanders family was forced to hurry northward to protect their investment. (See Appendix 2A.)

Sampson, as son and heir, most likely accompanied his father around the court house in Kanawha County. He certainly was familiar with the plight of Jack Neal, because at various times Neal was assigned by the Court to live with the Sanders slaves on their farm.[95] The Ruffner Papers even give the impression that the local Kanawha County boys may have actually aided Neal's escape by providing him with a file.[96] (See Appendix 3A.) Researchers will always ponder the possibility that the trial, incarceration, escape and confinement of Jack Neal with the Sanders' slaves played a large part in creating Sampson Sanders' benign attitude toward his slaves. The mistreatment of an innocent Jack Neal coupled with Sampson's friendship and dependence on his family slaves, may have convinced Sampson to free his slaves. As was the common practice at that time, his sister Hetty certainly bequeathed her slaves to her family instead of freeing them.[97]

Slavery was an accepted institution in Ninetheeth Century Virginia. The antislavery movement was just getting underway when Sampson Sanders died. Many records indicate Sampson Sanders was a considerate master, and some county records show his slaves had considerable freedom. They were allowed to attend church and to go to the store unescorted.[98] They may have worked without an overseer and also may have been allowed to "hire themselves out."[99] One proof of Sampson's benevolence must be the fact that all fifty-one of the manumitted slaves kept the Sanders name after they became free and recorded property in Michigan. Although it was common practice to use the master's name, many slaves chose to use different names. Surely, that would have been the case if they were unhappy with Sanders.

Sampson did not need an empire for he had no family, and the Kilgore children and grandchildren were by no means poor. Did he make an effort to let his slaves know what he wanted to do? All his ventures were quite successful; perhaps because his slaves were diligent and hard working, with an eye to their own future. Sanders provided his slaves with a better than average life, if his inventory is an indication. The immense garden and crops for cloth and spinning wheels were not needed by one old man. Descriptions of the farm building from the Dusenberry Diaries indicate their housing was good, even though the slaves had to build it themselves. The

---

[95] *Kanawha County Records 1791-1831*, pp. 249-340.
[96] Ruffner Papers. William Ruffner, son of a Kanawha County Justice and aged 13 in 1801, states: "Jack had no trouble getting iron working tools from his friends outside the jail." Obviously no adult would help a murderer and a slave would probably not even contact Neal, so who were "his friends outside" helping Jack.
[97] Lambert Collection, 76B-9-9.
[98] *Ibid.*, 76B-9-9; 76B-12-19; and loose cards. Several interviews discuss church meetings. The two store inventories in Cabell County Will Book I list several accounts owed by slaves.
[99] "To hire themselves out", to work for other people and keep the wages, for example, a blacksmith.

conditions under which the Sanders slaves lived and worked were as good as any farmer in the county, except they did not own the land or themselves. Certainly, the slaves were apprehensive about freedom and leaving Virginia. They, as well as their parents, had been raised in slavery. Freedom was just an unknown dream, not a reality. If Sampson told them of his plans, perhaps they worked even harder knowing they were to be freed because their labor would pay for that freedom.

At his death in 1849, Sampson manumitted about fifty-one slaves. The total number will always be in doubt as Sanders did not name the slaves in his will, nor have any of the papers of emancipation survived. By studying both Cabell County, Virginia and Cass County, Michigan records, a list of those freed slaves can be compiled which corresponds to the number of slaves from the personal property lists. (See Appendix 9C for complete list.)

Figure 12
Determining the Slaves Freed

DETERMINING THE SLAVES FREED

1848 Personal Property Taxes, Cabell County, Virginia (Microfilm)

males 12-16	males over 16
4	24

1850 Deed Book, Cassopolis, Cass Cc, MI, County Clerk.

males 0-12	12-16	over 16	females 0-12	12-16	over 16
11	2	23	1	3	11

The manumitted Sanders Slaves:
    Ada and Zebeedee both 87
Solomon, his wife Phyllis and their children:
    Eli, Levi, Solomon Jr., Woodford, Jacob and Jason
    Daniel, his wife Dorcas and their children:
    Alicia, Montesque, Zebedee, Eliza, Robert, William,
    Elijah and Hamilton
Charles and his sister Mary and her children:
    Susan, Joseph, Harriet, Mahala, Charles,
    twins Theodore and Sampson
Cynthia Sanders Radford and her son Jacob
Margaret and her son Eli
Charlotte and her daughter Jane
James Sanders
Peter Sanders
Eli Sanders
Calvin Sanders (an adult who returned to the Ironton area)
Calvin Sanders (a child)
John Sanders
Luke, his wife Jane and their children
    Columbus and Mary
Moses, his wife Caroline and their children
    Albert and Robert
Hamilton Sanders (an adult)
Isom Sanders (who remained in Cabell county)

The question has been asked, "Why did Sanders wait so long?" The answer to that question lay in Virginia's law which discouraged manumission. Any slave owner could manumit by recorded deed or will, but a master who manumitted a slave must provide sufficient support for the rest of that slave's life to keep him or her from becoming a burden to the Overseers of the Poor.[100] (See Appendix 13.)

Virginia records show other manumissions for the same time period. Rarely more than one or two people were freed and usually only when the slaves were quite old. Most often they were freed at their master's death and by his will.[101] Some will manumissions delayed freedom until death of the master's wife, or until the master's

---

[100] Henning, *Statues at Large*, Vol.11, Chap. 21; and *Virginia Code*, 1849, Title 30, pp. 456-459. Although the law was revised in 1849, Sanders' death in June probably meant the estate was settled under the older law. The only addition to the Slave Code section required the slave to be responsible for any of the master's debts and that did not apply to the Sanders estate.

[101] Earl J. Prate, *The Promised Land* (New York: Vantage Press, 1964). An exception was James Twyman. He also free several slaves in 1849. His thirty-seven slaves arrived just across the river from Cabell County soon after the Sanders slaves left.

children had reached a certain age.¹⁰² John Russell of Cabell County willed the emancipation of Manuel and Patience "one year after my death and Henson to hired out to support my youngest daughter until she becomes of age then he is freed."¹⁰³

Section III of Henning's 1823 Virginia Law concerning manumissions shows why emancipated slaves were settled outside Virginia whenever possible. The law required Negroes to show cause why they should be allowed to live in an area. They could be jailed or "hired out" for non-payment of debts, for being destitute or for several other reasons. In Cabell County each year, freed Negroes had to apply to the county court for permission to remain in the county. Emancipated slaves lived under constant fear of losing their freedom.¹⁰⁴

To free fifty-one people was a massive undertaking in the Virginia of 1849, especially when their ages ranged from eighty-seven to one-year-old infants.¹⁰⁵ Not only must Sanders provide for the slaves' welfare, but also to arrange his affairs to please all his relatives thus preventing a contested will. Sampson Sanders did just that.

Sampson's legal heir was his sister, Hetty wife of Thomas Kilgore. She had already contested Sampson's right to some property at their mother's death.¹⁰⁶ To make everyone happy, Sanders had to take into account the value of his slaves, the cost of freeing them, the number of his legal heirs, and how to equally provide for both groups. To do so, Sanders acquired many additional Cabell County acres between 1835 and 1849. (See Appendix 5B.)

Sampson Sanders considered all the legal possibilities and carefully arranged his affairs so that his death would provide for all the people who had depended upon him in life. Shortly before his death, he began selling his assets for cash. He needed to accumulate the necessary funds required to fulfill his promise, either to himself or to others, of freedom for all his people. He left most of his land to Hetty's descendants, but he provided his slaves with their freedom and cash money to support themselves.

Sampson's assets reveal a very wealthy person with vast real estate holdings in addition to slaves.

---

[102] Often wills were written freeing the slave, but only after the slave had labored so many additional years to raise the master's children.
[103] Cabell Records, Will, Bk. I, p. 353.
[104] Henning, *Statues at Large*, Vol. 11, Chap. 21; and *Virginia Code*, pp. 465-468.
[105] Federal Census, (1850), Michigan, Cass Co., M555:495.
[106] Cabell Records, Superior Court, 26 Sep 1831.

Figure 13. Sampson Sanders' Assets

SAMPSON SANDERS ASSESTS			
		1849 prices	1997* prices
value real estate	5,260a x $100	$526,000	$5,260,000
estate & notes held		12,425	186,375
Mill and accessories (1848)		6,000	90,000
Value of slaves 51 (see figure 15)		30,200	453,000
cash given manumitted slaves		15,000	$225,000 [107]
		$589,625	$6,204,375
			1997 value*

value per slave -
  1849 value - $ 45,200 divided by 50 (slaves) equaled $ 904
  1997 value - $678,000 divided by 50 (slaves) equaled $13,560

Minimum value for Cabell County farm land in 1997 is $1000 per acre. Some is worth much more as it is now in housing developments and a golf course.
*The Marshall University Economics Department, Huntington, West Virginia, suggests a multiplier of 15 to reach 1997 values (except land).

To keep from having a contested will, Sampson Sanders left prime agricultural land, totaling at least 5,259 acres, to his sister to be given to her heirs.[108]

Figure 14. Sampson Sanders' Obligations - The Relatives

SAMPSON SANDERS' OBLIGATIONS - THE RELATIVES (CHILDREN & GRANDCHILDREN OF HETTY SANDERS KILGORE)	
Emaline Kilgore Ball and her 6 ch	600a
George Kilgore and his 9 ch	436a
Jeremiah Kilgore and his 5 ch	600a
8 orphaned ch of Polly Kilgore Simmons	1,800a
Martha Kilgore Morris and her 7 ch	1,612a
Malinda Kilgore Jordan and her 6 ch	211a [109]

---

[107] Amount based on the value of each slave, added to the cash left by the will. Figures can only be approximated when comparing 1849 and 1997 because of the many changes in the financial situation of the United States.
[108] Perhaps because of Hetty's age or because of a dislike for Kilgore, Sampson's property seemed to have been left to Hetty with the stipulation it go to her children. Thomas Kilgore had nothing to do with it.
[109] Frank Ball, "The Kilgore Saga Part II," *The Barboursville Bulletin* Barboursville, WV, 18 Nov 1970.

Sampson's other obligation was support for his slaves required by Virginia law. In addition to their own value, the manumitted Negroes received $15,000 cash and legal assistance. The cash amounted to about $300.00 each man, woman and child.

Figure 15. Sampson Sanders' Obligations - The Slaves

SAMPSON SANDERS' OBLIGATIONS-THE SLAVES
(SANDERS HAD TO "PURCHASE" THE SLAVES BEFORE HE COULD FREE THEM BECAUSE THEY HAD A CASH VALUE TO HIS ESTATE.)

Value of Slaves

51 slaves -				
2	over 80 - value	$100 each	$ 200.00	
5	males 50 - 80	800 each	3,000.00	
11	males 21 - 50	1,200 each	12,100.00	
8	males 12 - 20	500 each	4,000.00	
3	females 50 - 80	500 each	1,500.00	
8	females 21 - 50	800 each	6,400.00	
3	females 12 - 20	300 each	1,800.00	
12	ch under 12	100 each	1,200.00	total
				$30,200.00
			cash	$15,000.00
			total to slaves	$45,200.00

You must consider the worth of the slave as well as the cash as part of Sanders' estate, an average of $900 per slave.

Chapter Six
Life as a Sanders Slave

The first mention of any family slaves appeared in William Sanders' bill of sale. "Ader and her family" and "Hannah and her family" were listed in the appraisal and were apparently not sold, but held in trust for Sampson.[110] (See Appendix 2.) It is probable the slaves were divided among Sampson and his sister, Hetty, with mother Martha keeping one third.[111] Later records indicate Sampson kept Ader's family while Hannah and her children went to Hetty.[112] Some of these slaves were with the family through their travels from Virginia to North Carolina, Tennessee and finally to the Kanawha/Cabell County area of western Virginia.[113] Hannah possibly came into the family with Martha in Loudoun County, Virginia, about 1782 when William Sanders married Martha Green.[114] Without further records, Ader can only be placed in Kanawha County 1801 and Cass County in 1850. Of the children, the only information states: three males over sixteen. The tax lists for 1806 showed both Martha and Sampson owning slaves even though Sampson was not yet twenty-one.[115]

Life for both the white and black Sanders families would have been very similar to anyone else's on the frontier. The Cabell County area, where the Sanders settled in 1801, was a wilderness. Only a few hundred people were settled between the Ohio River on the west, the Kanawha River on the north and the Appalachian Mountains on the east. There were few existing houses when the Sanders arrived; the trees had to be cut, shaped and then laid to form their homes.

The slave homes would have been a row of cabins between the main house and the barns, if the farm layout was similar to other southern plantations. Sanders' people built all the houses and barns including the two-story log home in which Martha and Sampson lived.[116]

The labor force soon cleared fields of brush and timber and planted numerous crops. The land proved very productive and as a result the slaves had plenty to eat. Although they made their own clothing, there was an ample supply. Sanders was able to keep the slave families intact because he was rich and had no reason to sell anyone to pay his debts, nor was he forced to sell unruly slaves. Existing records show the slaves took pride in producing the best crops and livestock in the area. To be a member of the Sanders family was an important position in Cabell County.

Cabell County, Virginia, had been created in 1809 from Kanawha County and contained the Teays Valley area where the Sanders farm lay. Only two sources give any information about slaves: the Federal Census and the Virginia Tax Lists.(Tax lists have already been discussed.) The Federal Census emunerated slaves in a separate section from the household. Although the first Cabell County census has been lost, the 1820 census showed Sampson with twenty-one slaves, but failed to enumerate Martha. In 1830 Martha had seven slaves while Sampson owned twenty-four, but not until Martha's will in 1832 were any slaves named.[117] Her bill

---

[110] Children were slaves if their mothers were slaves.
[111] Kanawha Records, Deeds, Bk. B, p. 189.
[112] Lambert Collection, 76B-9-9. Ader Sanders was buried in Cass County, Michigan, in 1850, age 87. Hannah died in Cabell County, Virginia, prior to the Civil War with Sampson Simmons stating, "she came from Grandmother Kilgore's and she lived to 104."
[113] Federal Census, Michigan, Cass Co., M555:495. Various Cass County censuses list all "Sanders" born in Virginia. Ages would indicate some were born before the group arrived in Cabell County.
[114] Hiatt and Scott, *Loudoun County Tithables 1759-1790*, pp. 610,669. Sanders appeared on several tithable lists. (See Figure 4.)
[115] Lambert Collection, 76B-9-9. Hetty Kilgore probably inherited slaves from her father. Husband Thomas Kilgore was listed as owner of 10 slaves in the 1820 census. Grandson Sampson Simmons referred to different slaves belonging to either Grandfather or Grandmother Kilgore.
[116] Lambert Collection, 76B-9-9.
[117] Federal Census, 1830, Virginia, Cabell Co., Slave Census, M432:984.

of sale listed slaves Bristoe, Robin, Charles, Charlotte, Jenny, Mary and Lorry.[118] A note at the bottom of the will stated: "Slaves not to be sold by order of Sampson Sanders."[119] Another document from the same period, Love's Store Register found in Cabell County Will book I, named Sanders' slaves James, Calvary, Daniel and Charles as having accounts at the store.[120]

Records from early Cabell County give the impression slavery was considered a natural occurrence, and most slaves were treated fairly and humanely in the county. As early as 1815, Jeremiah Ward freed "his female slave, Pegalis Marget aged 60" and gave her thirty dollars a year for support.[121] There were several deed entries for purchase or transfer of slaves in Cabell County, but only one deed lists Sampson Sanders as buyer or seller. That deed of trust indicated the slaves were to be sold to pay incurred debts but those slaves were never listed as part of Sanders' family. If no new slaves were purchased, it must be assumed that all the slaves freed in 1849 were children and descendants of "Ader and Hannah" listed in William Sanders bill of sale in 1801.

Since neither the names nor the number of children were given in 1801, there is no possible way to determine how many slaves arrived with Sanders in the Kanawha/Cabell area. A comparison of census records would indicate the two women had at least three children each. The Virginia Personal Property Tax Lists show normal family increase that would result in approximately the number of slaves manumitted in 1849.(See Figure 10)

With the exodus of the Sanders slaves, Cabell County recorded three hundred and eighty-nine slaves in the 1850 census. In addition eight free Negroes were living in the county.[122] Prior to about 1856, Cabell County's slaves seem to have been completely trusted, being sent on business for their master or given permission to travel about the county without supervision.[123] Love's Store on the Turnpike near Everett's Tavern (Ona) listed several slaves other than Sanders' among its purchasers.[124]

Sampson Simmons recalled the marriage of one of their slaves, and stated: "When our Bet married Roffe's Spencer, Brother gave them the biggest wedding in all the country round about. All the Negroes from miles around came and all the white folks in the neighborhood. There was a big dinner in the 'white folk's' dinning room and they sat at the table before the white folks. Spencer begged Brother to buy him from Mr. Roffe and Brother paid $500 for him."[125] At another neighborhood wedding, William Dusenberry reported: "all the blacks stopped by our place and drank nearly three gallons of ice water."[126]

Slaves were also allowed to gather for preaching by Uncle Tom, a noted Baptist preacher. Dusenberry attended a service given by him in 1850. Uncle Tom preached the funeral of his master, Martin Moore, as well as many other events. Often the local people would gather only three or four times a year when a minister appeared.[127] At these meetings, everyone would celebrate the several funerals, the marriages and the other events which had occurred since their last meeting. For example, in June 1856, Uncle Tom preached the funeral for Peter Love's

---

[118] The tax list listed 2 males, 12-16, and 2 males over 16.
[119] Cabell Records, 368. An 1813 deed from Daniel Witcher Sr. to Daniel Witcher Jr. transferred Negroes, Jenny & Charlotte, former property of deceased son Sanders Witcher. Charlotte Sanders states on her daughter death certificate in Cass County, Michigan, that her father was Sanders Witcher. (Lambert Papers). Jenny was listed by Sampson Simmons as a slave belonging to Hetty Sanders Kilgore. Charles, Charlotte and Mary all appear in Cass County, Michigan.
[120] All appear in Cass County, Michigan, records.
[121] Cabell Records, Deeds, Bk3, p 42.
[122] Federal Census, 1850, Virginia, Cabell Co., M432:938.
[123] Dusenberry, Diaries.
[124] Lambert Collection, 76B-12-13.
[125] Ibid., 76B-9-9.
[126] Dusenberry, Diaries. Reference a wedding at Martha Kilgore Morris' across the river from the Mill. William F. Dusenberry was from New York and kept no slaves. His father purchased Sanders' Mill.
[127] Michael M. Watts, *The Teays Valley Baptist Association*, (1995), p. 31.

slave boy who had drowned the previous April. Sometimes the slave owners took the slaves to preaching as both attended the same church. Other times the slaves borrowed a buggy and drove themselves to the religious meetings.[128] Several of Cabell County's early churches reported having a balcony for the slaves.

Everything changed as the abolition movement became established. John Brown started speaking out across the country urging slaves to rebel and fear and unrest became wide spread. The situation in Cabell County may have been more unstable than other places because freedom was only a few hundred yards away across the Ohio River. In 1849, the same year Sanders manumitted his slaves, a group of thirty-seven slaves were freed in Campbell County, Virginia and settled just across the river from Cabell County at Burlington, Ohio. In 1857, a group of abolitionists lead by Congressman Eli Thayer from Massachusetts started an abolitionist community at Ceredo, Virginia. It was located on the Ohio River just a few miles below Barboursville and Guyandotte. Editorials up and down the river attacked the people of Cabell County, first for welcoming the settlers and then for failing to believe or disbelieve (according to which side you took) what the community was about.

This controversial atmosphere was spreading across the nation and was obvious in the changing attitudes in Cabell County. The slaves knew about both groups of manumitted slaves, and either from the ministers or through gossip, became aware of the abolitionists at Ceredo. The desire to attempt freedom became increasingly hard to resist, even though most escaping slaves were caught and returned.[129]

In October 1855, a disturbing event occurred: "All Roffe's niggers with a good many others started for the Ohio River with the intention of running off. It appears Ike borrowed Pat Thompson's buggy to go to Everett's for a visit. They intended to meet with a lot of others about three miles below Guyandotte and cross the river. But they failed getting together on Saturday night and yesterday (Sunday) some of them discovered Wilson Moore watching them so they all concluded to return home."[130] Several of the county's slaves were sold soon after that event, including most of Sanders' nephew, Conwelsie Simmons' slaves. Two Simmons' slaves, descendants of Hannah, were considered loyal and remained with the family even after the Civil War.[131]

In April 1856, in exchange for a hundred dollar reward, Charles Morris' runaway was captured in Ohio and jailed at Greenup, Kentucky. That same month Thorn Dusenberry tried to whip his slave woman, but she whipped him instead. Two days later Thorn sold her in Kentucky.[132] The position of the slave was in great jeopardy. Across the nation freed Negroes, caught between the proslavery and the antislavery forces, lived in fear. That situation was equally true in Cabell County.

Several manumitted slaves resided in Cabell County for a number of years after they were freed, even though they were required to petition the County Court for permission to live within its jurisdiction. Edmund and Lillie Parker, manumitted by Benjamin Brown about 1848, lived in the county through two censuses. Isom Sanders, a Sanders slave who did not go to Michigan, married a local woman and was still in Cabell County in 1860.[133] Both of these families either left the area or changed their names with the outbreak of war. Below is the Cabell County Court order concerning the residence of freed slaves.

---

[128] Lambert Collection, 76B-9-9; and Dusenberry, Diaries. Sampson Simmons notes "He was so respected the white people would take all their slaves to hear Uncle Tom." William Dusenberry states in 1855 and 1856, the slaves borrowed a buggy and traveled by themselves.
[129] Several area newspapers from the period had advertisements for runaways and articles about captures.(*Cincinnati Daily Times*, 5 Oct 1849.)
[130] Dusenberry, Diaries.
[131] Lambert Collection, 76B-9-9. "Hannah was Grandmother Kilgore's slave. Shed and Charley were kin to her. They did not leave."
[132] Dusenberry, Diaries.
[133] Cabell Records, Minute Book 3, 7 May 1861.

> "Ordered ------------ free Negroes, to show cause, if any they can, why the permission they have been granted to remain in this Commonwealth, shall not be revoked. Also any free Negroes who have been emancipated since the fourth Thursday in October 1851, and who have remained in the Commonwealth more than twelve months since their emancipation, be summoned to appear and to show cause why they have not forfeited their freedom, and why they should not be ordered sold into slavery." (Cabell County Court June 1861)

Similar Virginia rulings made residence in the state a hazard for any former slave. After the war, several references mention a black population in Cabell County, but with few details. According to census records the county black population has always remained about ten percent of the white population.[134]

---

[134] Figures based on comparison of census records.

Chapter Seven
1849 - Sanders Death and the Manumission

By 1849 Sampson Sanders was sixty-three years of age. To be sure his desires were understood, he gathered together friends, relatives and lawyers as he wrote his will.

> Know all men by these presents That (I) Sampson Sanders of the County of Cabell and the state of Virginia do make this my last will and testament in manner following: It is my will & desire that all my just debts & funeral expenses be paid by my executors out of my estate.
>
> It is my will and desire that all my slaves of every age and sex be free at the time of my death from all involuntary servitude.
>
> It is my will & desire & I hereby direct my executors hereinafter named or the survivors of them or such of them as may act do as soon as possible after my death collect so much of my estate as may be necessary to buy land for my said slaves in the state of Indiana or some one of the free states of the United States of America as may be necessary for their comfortable support of my said slaves, assigning to each head of a family their proper proportion of Lands as well as to others who have no family or families their proper proportion of lands or property binding the heads of families and the other young men for comfortable support of the old and decrepit or weakly slaves during their natural lives and for the purpose of carrying this part of my will into effect, I hereby give and bequeath to my said slaves $15,000 fifteen thousand dollars to be paid out of my estate by my executors as aforesaid and under their control & management for the use of the slaves aforesaid which may be paid by my said executors in property of mine now at its appraisal value after my death. The land will have to be purchased with money and the balance of the fifteen thousand dollars may with the consent of the said slaves be paid in property at its appraised value or part in money and part in property.
>
> Thus far I think it proper to make my will at this time and for the purpose of carrying the same into effect. I hereby appoint my friends John Samuels, John Laidley, George Gallaher and Cornwellsy Simmons executors of this my last will and testament hereby revoking all other wills by me heretofore made.
>
> Signed & sealed as and for the last will and testament of Sampson Sanders in
>
> S.SANDERS (seal)
>
> Presence of
> Wm. Paine   John Samuels
> George W. Plott   Stephen Spurlock
> Andrew Gwinn   Wm.C. Dusenbury   Cabell County Court
> Charles O. Dusenbury   July 9th 1849[135]

---

[135] Cabell Records, Wills, Bk. 1, p. 391; and Probate Orders, Minute Bk. 5, p. 329.

Section two of his will stated that his executors were to act as soon after his death as possible to collect necessary funds from his estate and to proceed to a northern state to purchase land "as may be necessary for the comfortable support of my said slaves." He directed that each slave should receive a proper proportion and that the heads of the families and other young men were to look after the old and decrepit slaves.[136]

Sanders set aside $15,000 cash, under control of the slaves and for their welfare. He also named friends and lawyers, John Laidley, John Samuels, and nephews, George Gallaher and Conwelsie Simmons, to carry out his wishes and to aid the slaves when needed. Laidley and Samuels appointed George Summers to act in their stead.

Sampson Sanders died on the 21st day of June 1849. Most of Cabell County turned out for his funeral, and many local people accompanied the coffin up the ridge overlooking Mud River. There he was laid to rest beside his mother Martha on the old "home place."[137] (See Figure 7.) By the 9th of July, his will had been probated. Immediately all the able-bodied slaves, as well as many of Sanders' neighbors, gathered to help build rafts to carry the freed slaves to their new homes.[138] All the required timber was cut and then sawed at the old Sanders Mill on the Guyandotte River. The raft keels were probably laid by raftmen from the community. While the rafts were being built, the former slaves selected livestock and materials from the Sanders estate. The estate inventory was quite extensive, but the newly freed Sanders adults carefully selected the best horses, cattle and materials they would need to start their own farms. Calvin and Peter selected left handed plows. Charlotte chose a spinning wheel and a flax wheel. Luke selected farm equipment and Solomon selected a dining table among other items.[139] (See Appendix 5A.)

By early October, everything was ready and all the neighbors gathered to see the Sanders families on their way.[140] Sampson Simmons was only six years old, but he never forgot Uncle Sanders' funeral, the multitude of people building rafts, or the way everyone in the neighborhood cried and carried on when the freed slaves left Cabell County.[141] Simmons stated, "When the boat was complete and the Negroes and all their goods were loaded into it, the whole neighborhood turned out to see them go away. My sisters and my Brother Conwelsie's wife Lizzie cried and all the Negroes cried. They did not want to go and some of them came back later."[142]

One slave, Isom, remained in Cabell County, married and had a daughter before his records ceased.[143] Another, Calvin, went to Michigan then returned to Lawrence County, Ohio, where he worked at the iron furnaces.[144] Many of the slaves probably had relatives they left behind, as well as friends and memories. Most of the slaves had been born and raised in Cabell County; leaving their home would have been very difficult. Everything familiar, from a favorite berry patch or fishing hole to the church down the lane, was being left behind for something called freedom. Apprehension for their unknown future had to concern all the adults. Although excited, everyone was surely scared to leave everything they had known and cared about.

Possibly some of the young men traveled over land with the large collection of

---

[136] Law required Sanders also to provide each slave with legal papers of manumission, but they have not survived.
[137] Lambert Collection, 76B-9-9. The Sanders Graveyard is on the original Martha Sanders farm just west of Milton. Only Martha and Sampson have surviving tombstones, but it is rumored other members of the family and slaves are buried at the site. W.S. Vinson (a great nephew) stated Sanders' daughter was named Rebecca.
[138] *Ibid*.
[139] Cabell Records, Wills Bk. 2, pp. 19-29. Sanders' Bill of Sale - The Negroes selected materials which were familiar to them: the left handed plow, the flax wheel, etc. The estate inventory was the first list to name any of Sampson Sanders' freed slaves.
[140] Cass Co., Cassopolis, MI, County Clerk, Deeds, Bk. 1848-1850, pp. 403-565. All the slaves took the Sanders name except the Radford's, John, Cynthia and Jacob. John may have been a free man who Cynthia married, as he was not listed on a deed. Hereater cited Cass Records.
[141] Lambert Collection, 76B-9-9. Simmons said one raft boat, others sources said rafts, and considering the amount of materials, were more likely.
[142] *Ibid.*; and Dusenberry, Diaries.
[143] Federal Census, Virginia, Cabell Co.
[144] Obituary, *Ironton Register*, Ironton, OH, 22 Mar 1894.

1849 - SANDERS DEATH AND THE MANUMISSION

livestock, but most of the manumitted slaves boarded the raftboats and bravely began their new lives. The party consisted of about fifty people, including seven babies under two years of age and two eighty year old grandparents. The rafts also held all their possessions, assorted supplies, seventeen horses, fourteen head of cattle, six hives of bees and the three Sanders' executors.[145]

The first part of the trip lasted several days as the rafts floated down the Guyandotte River into the Ohio River and down that river to Cincinnati.[146] At Cincinnati everyone and everything had to be taken from the rafts and loaded onto railroad cars which ran between Cincinnati and Michigan.

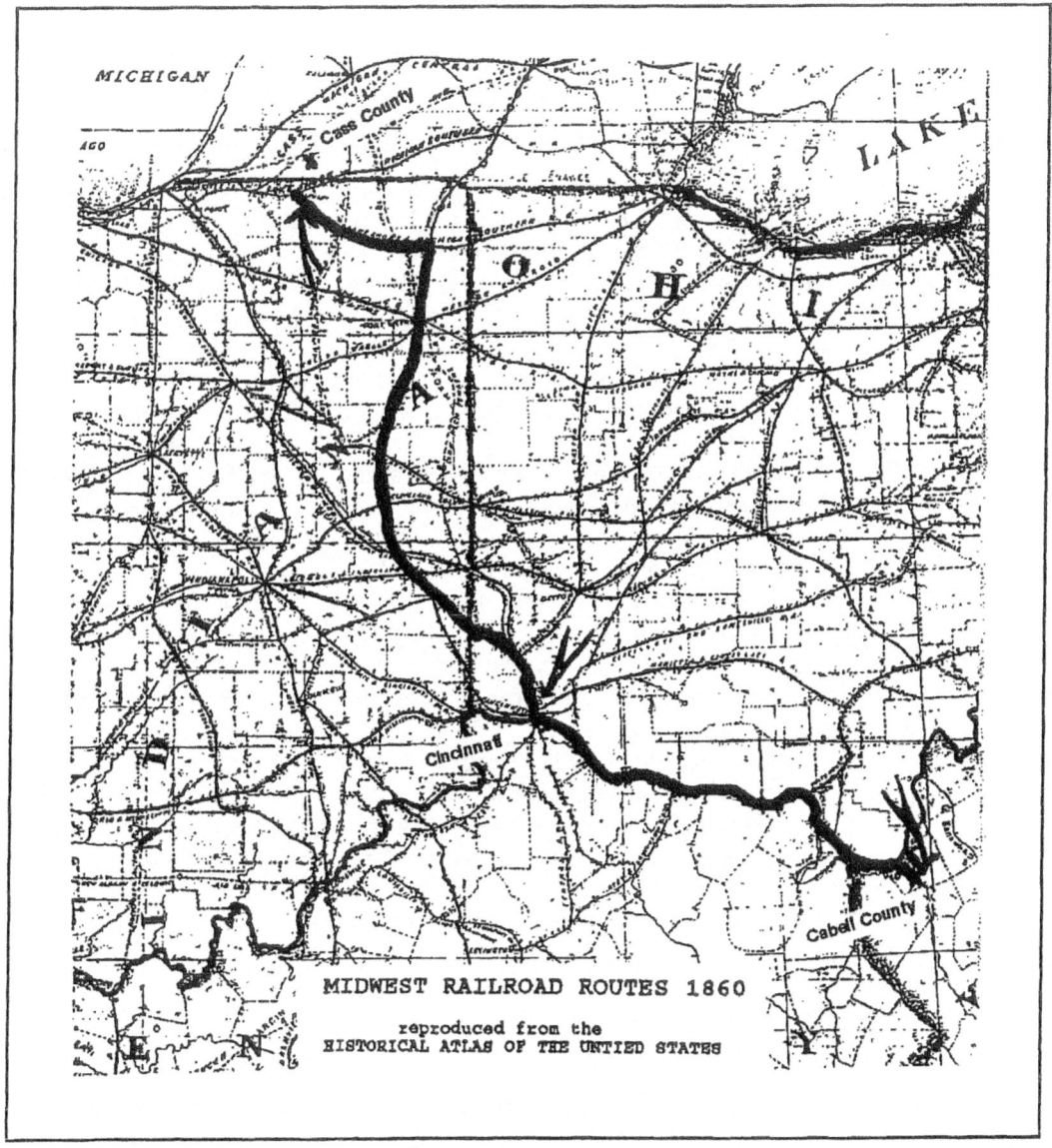

Figure 16. MIDEST RAILROAD ROUTES 1860 The heavy lines represents the most direct route for the Sanders train.

---

[145] Sanders' will required the executors to help the slaves. Travel during that period of history was very dangerous for Negroes without a white man along who appeared to be in charge.
[146] Lambert Collection, 76B-9-9.

Except for Guyandotte and its flourishing river port, the Cabell County that the manumitted slaves left behind was a rural agricultural community. Their arrival in the great city of Cincinnati must have been quite exciting and frightening for the untraveled party. The multitude of people in that city exceeded the population of most of southwestern Virginia. The crowded hustle and bustle of Cincinnati made the few wagons and carriages that traveled Cabell County's roads seem truly insignificant.

There was no railroad in Cabell County in 1849; the noise of the engines and general commotion around the railroad station was definitely a terrifying experience. Perhaps the biggest surprise for everyone was learning their train trip, from Cincinnati to Michigan a distance equal to the one they had just endured on the river, would take only one day to travel. One of the lawyers reported to all interested persons when he returned that the railroad cars moved so fast that "the corn shocks in the fields seemed to turn around as we passed."[147]

The nearest train stop to their destination was Elkhart, Indiana, about twelve miles south of the intended settlement location in Cass County, Michigan. From the end of the railroad all the goods were loaded onto wagons for the last part of an exhausting trip. That final wagon ride probably took longer than the train trip, but it also brought them to their new homes in freedom.

Sampson Sanders' will stated the settlement should be in Indiana or one of the free states. By the time the Cabell County group started west, Indiana had passed strict laws governing free Negroes. Further north, Michigan had the most lenient laws in the nation concerning former slaves. An event in 1847 brought the Cass County area of Michigan and its Quaker settlers to national attention. During a raid by Kentucky slaveholders, the Quakers lead the rest of the county, including the Negro settlers, against the invaders who were trying to capture runaway slaves.[148] The county's reputation for assisting Negroes would soon also make it a major stop on the underground railroad.[149]

Another factor for choosing Michigan for settlement regarded the price of land. Michigan land was selling for five to eight dollars an acre in 1849. Being a fairly new state, there was plenty of good land available for settlement, an excellent attraction for people wanting to buy farm land.

The final factor for settlement may have been the Negro settlements already established in Calvin and Porter townships of Cass County, Michigan.[150] Some of those settlers had come from North Carolina, while others migrated from southern Ohio, quite near Cabell County, Virginia.[151]

Although there is no evidence, it seems likely Summers, Gallaher or Simmons (the executors) had already been to Cass County looking at the land and the laws and arranging transportation from the train stop. Upon arrival, the freed slaves set up temporary shelter, possibly at the Chain Lake Baptist Church, before making their land selection. After choosing their land, each family group went to the Court House and recorded a deed. Officially, their new life had begun. Figure 17 locates their settlement in southwest Michigan.

---

[147] Lambert Collection, 76B-9-9. Lawyer George Summers got off the train for a rest break and it left without him. All three men had many stories to tell when they returned to Cabell county.
[148] Howard S. Rogers, *History of Cass County* (Cassopolis, MI: Vigilant Book and Job Print, 1875), p. 133-139.
[149] S.S. Mathews, *History of Cass County, Michigan* (Chicago: Waterman, Watkins & Co., 1882), p. 386.
[150] Roma Stewart, "The Migration of a Free People, Cass County's Black Settlers from North Carolina." *Michigan History*, (Jan-Feb, 1987): 34-38.
[151] S.S. Mathews, *History of Cass County, Michigan* (Chicago, Waterman, Watkins & Co. Cassopolis, 1882), p. 387.

Figure 17. Cass County located in southwest Michigan.

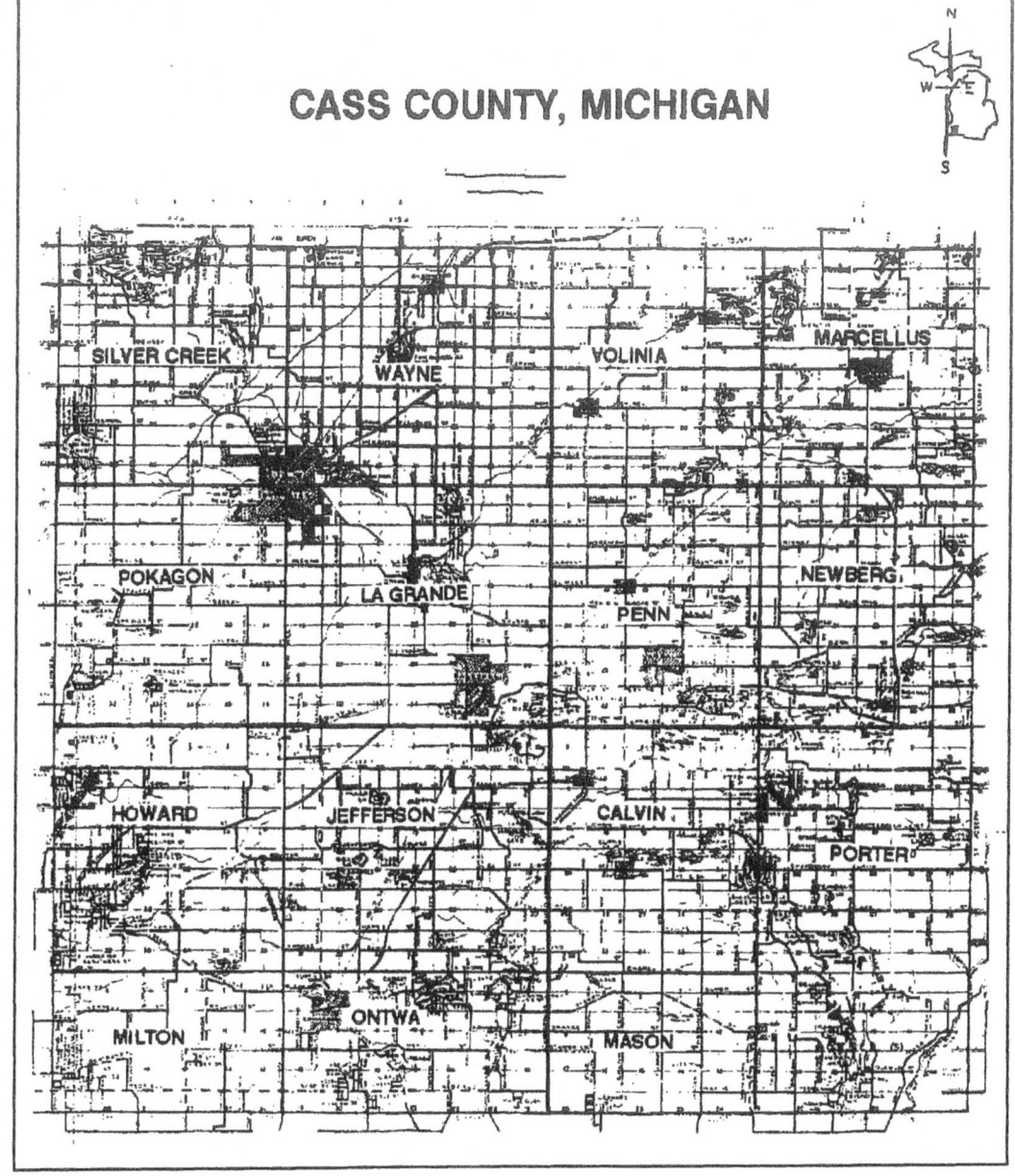

Cass County, Michigan, in the southwest corner of the state, was the junction of two underground railroad routes and had easy access to Canada. Calvin and Porter townships, in south east section, were heavily settled by free blacks.

Chapter Eight
Interlude

Traveling to Michigan with the Sanders

Maybe there were no problems, but imagine the difficulties of moving fifty people and assorted livestock, necessary equipment, personal possessions and required supplies several hundred miles. Only the very oldest members of the group had ever traveled more than ten or fifteen miles from their homes. Most of the group had never been outside Cabell County, had never ridden on a raft or even knew what a railroad was.

Can we visualize the trip they took? Everyone in the neighborhood was gathered on the banks of the river on Sunday afternoon, after a farewell church service near Sanders Mill. All the supplies had already been packed on a flotilla of rafts which swayed on their ropes in the lazy Guyandotte River. Along the shore women, children and even grown men hugged and cried as everyone said farewell. Slowly the groups broke and separated as family after family made its way aboard several twenty foot rafts. The women were uneasy as the rafts lunged and bucked beneath their feet with every step they took. The frightened, big-eyed children clung fearfully to their mothers' skirts. Slowly every raft filled, sad-eyed men and tearful women stood solemnly staring ashore with heavy hearts as they watched their familiar life slip away.

Old Solomon had made a similar trip as a child years before when the Sanders family had moved from Tennessee to Virginia. Now he moved from raft to raft assuring everyone they were safe. Several of the young men remained on shore astride horses as they herded the livestock along the riverbank. Finally everyone was aboard and the flotilla drifted away from the muddy shore into the Guyandotte River current. Although it was early October, the river was low, several of the men and a few women grasped long poles and pushed the rafts into the main stream. All along the shore from Sanders Mill to Barboursville people stood and quietly watched as the group passed by. Occasionally the bushes on the riverbank parted and the face of a friend appeared to wish them God's speed or promised to follow them.

Just before dark that first day ended as the rafts reached the community of Guyandotte, about ten miles downstream and at the mouth of the Guyandotte River. After tying up the rafts, some of the men went into town to purchase the last of their supplies while people on the rafts began to sort themselves out and to choose places that belonged just to them. Almost everyone had realized during the day that they would not fall overboard if they

moved slowly and stayed in the center of the raft. Just after sundown the women called out "supper" to end the long day.

Monday morning dawned crisp and dry. Food was quickly prepared on shore and everyone ate quietly. Shortly after daylight the group was joined by lawyer George Summers and Sampson Sanders' nephews, George Gallaher and Conwelsie Simmons. The men had ridden to town and now boarded the lead raft; and after a second round of farewells, the group was ready to leave. Shortly after 8:00 AM the lines were slipped and the rafts moved slowly into the Ohio River. There was a definite tug on each raft as the mighty river current caught them, then slewed the bound logs southwest toward Cincinnati. Momentary panic occurred as several of the women and children became frightened by the motion of the stronger current.

Soon, though, everything settled down. The water moved along calmly and after that first surge, each raft rode smoothly. While the current moved them along at a few miles an hour, the concerned travelers could catch a glimpse, now and then, of the young men herding the livestock along the Ohio shore. Sometimes poles were produced to push the rafts through some rapids. Each evening the rafts moored along the Ohio bank to find a sleeping place and to prepare food.

Surely accidents occurred. Perhaps two boys fell overboard as they tried to land a huge catfish, Momentary panic hit as swimmers leaped into the water and dragged the boys ashore, very wet, but no worse for their dunking. Maybe the lashing of one raft parted and several items fell overboard including Aunt Charlotte's spinning wheel. Everyone had to stop while the items were recovered, wet but serviceable, and the logs of the raft tightly rebound. Each day on the river was similar. Arise at dawn, prepare a meal, find some necessary privacy along the bank, load everyone aboard the rafts and float down the river until noon, stop for lunch, reboard and float until sundown. One day it rained and the rafts stayed on the river at noon while everyone ate cold cornpone. Another day the plugs worked free from one of the bee hives and there was pandemonium among the rafts until the bees all flew toward shore. Some time was required to repack overturned supplies and treat the many stings suffered by half the group.

Each evening the rafts were secured to the shore. Not only was the river dangerous to travel at night, but river pirates hid in some of the cliffs and slave catchers roamed the roads. At each stop, the young children gathered firewood while the women prepared a meal, and then everyone slept except for a couple of the men standing guard. Occasionally, the white men had to go into a river community and assure the towns' people

the travelers were free Negroes and just passing down the river.

Finally, the little bedraggled flotilla tied up to the Cincinnati wharf. The place was enormous, with more people than most of the group had seen in their entire lives. The two Mr. Georges accompanied Solomon and Daniel to the train station to make arrangements for the rest of their trip north. Mr. Conwelsie stayed with the people on the rafts to keep the local riffraff from causing trouble. The women and boys kept the long poles and paddles near to hand all through the day, to hearten themselves and to discourage the wandering hoodlums.

After several hours the waiting group was quite concerned because the men had not returned. Finally, the crowds on the docks parted and the men made their way to the impatient group. The stories they told about the streets and carriages and people were just too much to believe. Then they started talking about the Iron Horse. Those terrible railroad cars were enough to scare a body to death. Most of the children stared at the men or hid behind their mothers' skirts in fear.

None of the group, white men included, had ever ridden on a train for there was none near Cabell County. The men described the huge train cars and the loud noises they made, but not before explaining to everyone all the trouble they had trying to explain to the station master. He did not believe the size of their group, nor did he understand just how many seats and how much cargo space they needed. It had taken the men all morning, but everything was finally arranged. Everyone had seats in the day coach, and there was half a box car to store their supplies. The men had also secured wagons to transport everything from the wharf to the railroad station and had made arrangements to sell the rafts. The women almost fainted when told everything must be moved before dark and a camp set up, because their train left at 8:00 A.M. the next morning. Only one train a day went to Michigan.

Solomon and Daniel were very worried about getting everyone and everything on board in just the half hour the train stopped at the station. Several of the teenaged boys were assigned to stay with the supplies, because the older men had the livestock moving north around Cincinnati. Old Uncle Zeb was so ill, the women had made a litter for him, while a couple of the babies just would not stop crying. Mr. George Gallaher had found some paper and printed SANDERS on it and pinned a piece to every woman and child, but loading everything in the morning was still going to be a big problem. Uncle Solomon could not read, but he could count, and he knew just how many people should be in that passenger car.

8:05 A.M. The train was moving and everyone was aboard, although young Robert had been found asleep behind a box just minutes before the train was to leave. The women had gotten up at 4:00 A.M. to make breakfast and pack food to eat on the train. Then all the children had been dressed, fed and told not to move. Daniel had spent half the night helping the boys move everything from the river and loading the box car. No telling what would have happened if the railroad had not left the extra car on a siding. Solomon's job had been to herd the women, with baskets of food, and all the sleepy children aboard the passenger coach. Somehow everyone was aboard when the whistle blew.

Solomon had barely touched his seat and wiped his brow when suddenly the train lurched forward as its wheels began to turn. Bedlam broke loose around him. The children had never heard such terrifying noise. It seemed everyone was either crying or screaming and the children swarmed out of their seats into their mothers arms. Calming everyone the first time had taken twenty minutes, and they had just gotten settled down when the train slowed and stopped. Panic again. Solomon was just getting too old for all this trouble, but he had promised Mr. Sampson to look out for everyone.

Hopefully, everyone now understood the train would make several stops, and some times they would travel very fast. Soon the children and adults alike were enthralled by the scenes that passed the windows. Faces were glued to the windows until one by one the children went to sleep to the rhythm of the wheels, and even Solomon was dozing until young Calvin climbed into his lap. Mr. Sampson had told Solomon about the rail cars, but it just did not seem possible to travel so fast.

All the adults had been shown a map where they were going. Solomon and Daniel tried to understand what it said. So far the hardest part to understand was how the trip from Cincinnati to Michigan could only take a day on the train. Michigan was father away from Cincinnati than Cincinnati was from Cabell County. Riding the train was an experience none of them would ever forget. The plush seats, the lamps that hung swaying over their heads and the large coal stove at the end of the car were all so beautiful, but what the children liked most was the little wash room at the end of the car.

Solomon knew the trip would end all too soon. The conductor had told them the train would arrive in Elkhart, Indiana at 8:00 P.M. and stop for one hour. They had managed to load everything in the morning, but they knew nothing about the town they were approaching in the dark. At least all their supplies in the railcar would just be dropped to a siding.

So far the worst thing to happen had been losing Mr. George Summers. He had been left at one of the stations back down the line when he had gotten off to walk around. No one knew if he could catch another train. All the men had talked about what would have to be done when they reached the end of the train trip. Really, the only thing they could do was to unload the train and set up a camp beside the station for the night. When the train finally stopped, they found Elkhart was just a station and two or three house. The station master informed them few wagons could be found unless they could contact some of the farmers round about. A young Negro boy named Ash had been waiting for the mail on the train; and as he left, he promised to tell his father the Sanders needed wagons. Everything would just have to wait until morning. Frost covered every item they owned when everyone awoke the next morning, and there were ugly black clouds in the west that looked like snow. The women had unpacked every coverlet last night, and now left the children bundled up until they were ready to start. The group had to have shelter and soon. It seemed safe enough to leave most of the people in the camp beside the lonely railroad station. Just as quickly as breakfast was finished Solomon, Daniel, Mr. George and Mr. Conwelsie started walking north toward a Negro community the station master had told them about. The men had walked two hours before they met a buggy coming toward them. The boy from last night had brought his father, Harrison Ash, to meet the new settlers. After a brief conversation, Mr. Ash sent his son off to several neighbors requesting wagons to gather the Sanders and their goods at the train station. He said to meet at the Baptist Church on Chain Lake. Mr. Ash told them the church had been begun by the Negro community almost three years ago,

INTERLUDE

and the congregation would be happy to help the Sanders.

Mr. Ash was one of the church trustees. He promised the group could camp on the church grounds until they were able to find places of their own, and to build some cabins. Before long several of the neighbors had joined the little group by the road side. Mr. Conwelsie mounted one wagon and led the way back to Elkhart, while Solomon, Daniel and Mr. George accompanied Mr. Ash to look at some land that was for sale. The men spent the night with Harrison Ash, after he promised their people were in good hands and could not possibly arrive at the church before evening of the next day. It was fifteen miles from the train station to the church. All the wagons had to first be collected, then travel to Elkhart and load materials. Just getting the wagons there would take the rest of the day. Everything would probably not be loaded until dark the following day.

Soon after the men had left Elkhart, the women began to go through the supplies to find out what had survived the trip, and what had to be replaced. It was quite obvious most of the group needed more warm clothes. Some of the carefully packed food supplies had been damaged with all the travel, but all the tools, seeds and cuttings were safe. Late in the afternoon the wagons began to arrive. Everyone spent the evening getting acquainted; and then camped another night at the train station, with plans to begin loading at dawn.

By nightfall of their third day in Cass County, Solomon and Daniel had found several good pieces of ground for sale. They bounced along the rutted track toward the church, hoping to find their families already arrived. They were gratified to find some of the group when they reached the pretty little log church. Several wagons were already parked and several more could be seen coming down the road. It was a joyous reunion with everyone trying to talk a once. Solomon and Daniel went around meeting all their future neighbors, who had taken two days from their work to bring the Sanders families to the church grounds. Already quite late, the neighbors made their way home to worried families, after all the men promised to return the next evening. By the forth day, everyone and all their supplies had arrived and been stored at the Chain Lake Church campground. The new arrivals invited the whole neighborhood, and planned to set out a thanksgiving dinner to thank the Lord for their safe arrival.

By October 12, 1849 four families had already selected their land, and on that day entered deeds at the Cass County Court House. All their properties were in Calvin Township.

> Solomon Sanders Sr. 61, Phillis Sanders 54, Eli Sanders 24, Levi Sanders 23, Solomon Sanders Jr. 20, Woodford Sanders 18, Jacob Sanders 16 and Jason Sanders 10 all of Cabell Co.VA $1387.00 for 148a in Township 7.
> Daniel Sanders 45, Dorcas Sanders 49, Alicia Sanders 22, Montesque Sanders (20), Zebedee Sanders 19, Eliza Sanders 17, Robert Sanders 15, William Sanders 13, Elijah Sanders 11, and Hamilton Sanders 5 of VA $1125.00 for 155a in Township 7.
> Mary Sanders 40, Susan Sanders 20, Joseph Sanders 18, Harriet Sanders 15, Mahala Sanders 14, Charles Sanders 8, Theodore Sanders 1, Sampson Sanders 1, all of Cabell County, VA $725.00 for 115a in Township 7.
> Cynthia Radford 37 and Jacob Radford 1 of Cabell Co. VA $400.00 for 40a in Township 7. [152]
> (Cass Records, Deeds, Bk. 1848-1850, October 12, 1849)

On November 27, 1849, George Gallaher entered forty-two acres in Township 6 for $425.00.[153] That same day Margaret Sanders(Peggy Halistock) and Eli Sanders, her son, both of Cabell County, Virginia, recorded eighteen acres in Porter Township for $300.00. On December 1, 1849, two of the single men recorded lots they purchased in Williamsville, Porter Township. James bought lots 7 and 8 for $20.00, while Peter recorded an unknown number of lots, purchased for $50.00. All the lands selected adjoined along the Calvin Township and Porter Township boundary lines, just east of Union Road in the southeastern section of Cass County as shown on 18.

In 1849 Cass County had about fifty other Negro families already settled in Calvin and Porter Townships.[154] These families represented free Negroes and manumitted and runaway slaves. The addition of the several Sanders families helped create a core community which continued to draw other Negro settlers to the area well into the Twentieth Century.[155] The settlement was so significant that it has drawn the attention of numerous writers and researchers studying rural Negroes.[156]

---

[153] Sanders' nephew who accompanied the group. That property in Porter Township (#6) was later transferred to Daniel's family.
[154] *Stateline News Review*, Cass County, MI, 28 May 1969. Free Negroes from central Ohio were attracted to the area by the availability of land and settled the area beginning about 1845.
[155] James O. Wheeler & Stanley D. Brunn, "An Agricultural Ghetto: Negroes in Cass County, Michigan, 1845-1968." *The Geographic Review*, 59 (July 1969): 318-326.
[156] Ibid.; and Harold B. Fields, "Free Negroes in Cass County Before the Civil War." *Michigan History,*, 44 (Dec.1960): 375-383.

INTERLUDE

Figure 18. Sanders' property in Calvin and Porter Townships

CASS COUNTY TOWNSHIPS

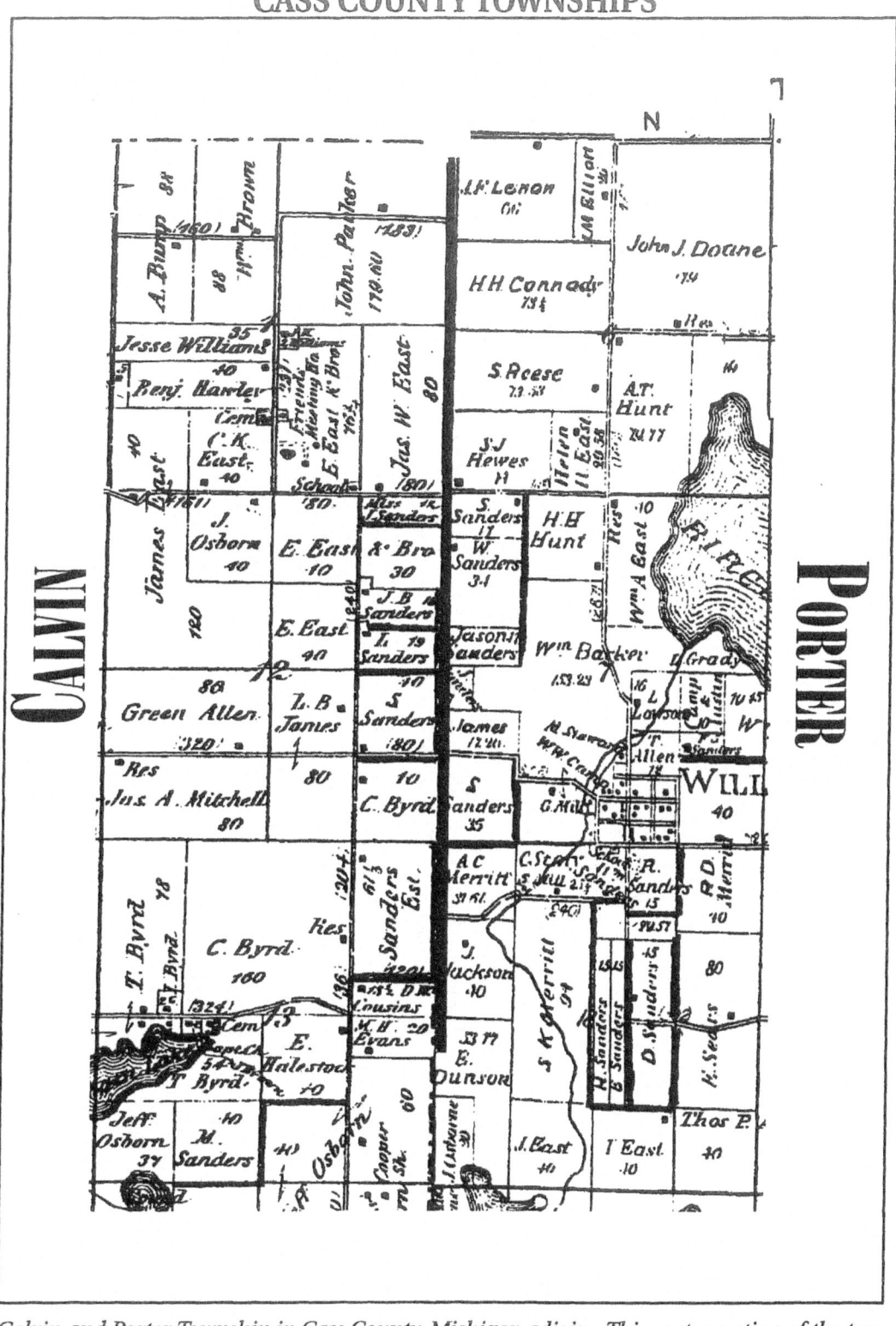

Calvin and Porter Township in Cass County, Michigan adjoin. This center section of the two townships show Sanders families in both townships. Their service center was Williamsville in Porter Township.

Chapter Nine
1850 - The New Citizens of Cass County

Living in Cass County, Michigan, was very different from life in Cabell County, Virginia. Freedom would not build houses, make clothes, plow fields or provide food. Everyone would have to work hard if the families were to survive and prosper in Cass County. They would also have to adjust their life styles and make some very hard choices. A slave received orders and did a job, but now they were free. Everyone had to decide what work needed to be done as well as provide the labor to complete the work.

The first matter of business was shelter. Fifty-one people arrived in Michigan in October with no place to live and no idea how cruel the winters were. Cass County, created in 1829, was only a generation old and very much a frontier. The land was mostly tree-covered and in some places swampy. The Sanders men had to fell the trees, remove the bark and dress the timbers, select a site for building a cabin and lay up four walls, chink the cracks, lay poles for a roof and finally, rive shingles to cover the roof. Tree limbs were piled to the side of the clearing, and the boys cut fire wood while the men worked on the cabins. Even if the neighbors all gathered for each cabin raising, the work was slowed by bad weather.

Winter usually came very early in Michigan, and it was harsh and long. Some of the families may have built a quick three sided shelter common in warmer climates, although area residents surely told the new families just how cold the winters got and helped them build snug cabins. No matter what kind of shelter they built, everything took time, and fifty people needed immediate shelter. That first winter, the cabins they managed to erect had just a dirt floor, a sleeping loft, a single door and a large fireplace. There simply was not time to cut enough timber to build solid cabins for everyone and to split the logs for floors. The severity of that first winter was indicated by the Sanders' tombstones marked "Died 1850" in Chain Lake Cemetery. (See Appendix 9B.)

That first winter must have been a real trial. In their old home by the Ohio River in the Cabell County, the families had been used to mild rainy winters. Imagine their horror as the snow piled up by feet and the temperature stayed below freezing for weeks on end. Back home in Cabell County the women had prepared preserves, pickles, and kraut. They had also dried berries and collected nuts to feed their families. Although many supplies accompanied the Sanders, there could not have been enough to feed all those people through a winter several months longer than they expected. Blankets and warm clothing would also have been in short supply. Some illness must have resulted from their limited supplies. If the reader accepts a figure of approximately fifty-one freed slaves, most of the family members lived through that first winter.[157] Only three known deaths occurred between October 1849 and October 1850. Zebedee and Charles died before the 1850 census was taken, and soon after that census in June, Ada was laid to rest beside them at Chain Lake Cemetery. (See Appendix 9B.) There may also have been children who did not live through that first year, but their records failed to survive.

When spring arrived each family set about building or finishing a home, clearing

---

[157] Lambert Collection, 76B-9-9. Interviews given fifty years later in Cabell County reported from forty-one to sixty slaves. Census and other Michigan records indicate fifty-one slaves.

and plowing their fields and planting crops. A few fields may have been cleared when they arrived, but most of the land was covered with trees four feet in diameter. Even after the trees were cut, huge stumps and roots hindered planting crops and had to be chopped out or burned. That first year's crop was pitifully small compared to the great fields of grain the men had harvested in Cabell County. Improvement came slowly. Almost all the young men stayed with their parents. After a few years the combined family labor began to improve the farms. By 1903 each yard was beautiful with shrubbery and flowers.[158]

The Sanders families purchased some of the best farm land in the area.[159] They engaged in subsistence agriculture common to America at that time. They belonged to The Ancient Order of Gleaners, a group similar to the Grange, and probably took part in the area's agricultural fairs.[160] Although their farms were small, their life was similar to farmers in any other area of the nation. They raised cows for milk, chickens for eggs, geese for feathers, and apples for cider. They produced hogs as a meat animal and cash crop, kept bees for honey and to pollinate their crops, and maintained horses to do the work. In addition each farmer raised grain and hay to put his animals through the winter and cotton and flax for clothing. Each farm was self contained, and almost every farmer could repair his own equipment. He was also a blacksmith or family shoemaker at times as well.[161]

Cass County records indicate that some of the Sanders may have moved in with families already in the area. Peggy and her son purchased land with a Sanders name; but by census time the next year, she was already married to Alex Halistock. Living in her home were Ada Sanders aged eighty, and James Sanders aged forty. Common sense would lead us to believe these people were her mother and brother, although no records support us. Perhaps some of the marriages in the next couple of years resulted from newcomers sharing a home when they arrived.

In the Cass County Will Book for 1850 is the entry:

> Jefferson Osbourn being duly affirmed I says that Charles Sanders died interstate at the town of Calvin Cass County Michigan on or about the 8th day of March 1850. Left no widow, nor children, father nor mother, left no brother, left one sister in said County of Cass, to wit. Mary Ann Sanders, aged about thirty eight years, that he left no other relatives in the state except the said Mary Ann Sanders and her children---left personal property to the value of about four hundred dollars, to the best of his information and belief.   Jefferson Osbourn
> (Cass County, MI, Court of Probate, March 23 1850)

---

[158] Louis R. Harlan and Raymond E. Smock, *The Booker T. Washington Papers* 7 Vols.(Urbana, IL: University of Illinois Press, 1972-1984), Vol.7, p. 45.
[159] *Land Use Survey for Cass County, Michigan, 1970* (Washington, D.C.: United States Department of Agriculture, 1970).
[160] *The Gleaner*, the group's magazine, had an article in the 1911 issue entitled "Colored Farmers Settle the Race Problem" by Fred J. Huntley. It told the story of the freed Sanders slaves. Although much of the information was incorrect, the hardships mentioned in the story were certainly faced by the Sanders families.
[161] Dusenberry, Diaries. The diaries record extensive information about farming in the Nineteenth Century.

There were several other Michigan records for that first year, but Charles' death record was valuable for several reasons. First, the record named two members of the Sanders family. Second, it indicated other children, unnamed. Third, it showed Charles and Mary Ann were not kin to any other Sanders, and fourth it listed personal property of $400.00. That amount was very similar to what each slave should have received from Sanders' will.[162] Charles did not buy property in Cass County in 1849, but he was listed on the Cabell County estate sale.[163] He, along with some of the other young men, may have been delayed as they brought the livestock overland. Perhaps, he arrived in Cass County so ill his death was eminent. (See Appendix 9A.)

Since the families arrived in the fall of 1849, they were in Michigan in time to be enumerated in the 1850 Cass County census. The census records gave individual names to the slaves thus providing valuable information about the families. All the families appear to have settled on adjoining lands in Calvin and Porter townships, except Peggy. Her family lived with her new husband in LaGrange Township about ten miles away. (Figure 18.)

On November 27, 1849, Margaret (Peggy) Sanders and her son Eli recorded property. The 1850 census revealed a Peggy Halistock and son Eli living with her husband Alexander, in LaGrange Township. In the same household were Ada Sanders and James Sanders. All these people except son Eli, were dead by 1860. (See Appendix 9C.) The 1860 Cass County Census listed an Eli Halistock living in Solomon Sanders home. (See Appendix 9A.) This connection to Solomon Sanders proved to be the link connecting Peggy Halistock to the Sanders, when her son Eli went to court with Solomon Sanders to collect her property.

Ada Sanders, the eighty-year old in the 1850 census in the Halistock home, was probably the same Ada Sanders, aged 87, who was buried at the Chain Lake Baptist Church Cemetery in 1850; and the "Ader" of William Sanders' will in 1802. In the cemetery beside her lay Zebedee Sanders eighty-seven, also buried in 1850, and Daniel Sanders who died in 1854. Zebedee may have been Daniel's father, considering one of Daniel's son's was named Zebedee. Daniel was the second most important male Sanders, according to his age and the number and ages of his children.

As typical of most census entries, not all the Sanders were recorded in 1850. Perhaps some of the young men had returned to Cabell County or were out looking for their own land, but several names which should be listed do not appear on the 1850 census. Those names were either found on other documents or were revealed by the 1860 and 1870 census records.

Among the missing in 1850 were the two Calvin Sanders. One Calvin, listed on the Cabell County sale, would have been an adult. He witnessed a legal document in Cass County in 1849, but returned to the Ohio Valley where he worked around the iron furnaces in Lawrence County, Ohio.[164] The other Calvin was two years old in 1848.[165] He was the son of Jane (daughter of Charlotte) and Levi (son of Solomon) whose marriage was recorded in Cass County in 1852. Calvin was descended from two Sanders lines. Later census records show this Calvin kept his Grandmother Charlotte in his home until his death. Afterwards, his son gave her a home until Charlotte's death in 1889.[166] Other

---

[162] Lambert Collection, 76B-9-9. Interviews claimed slaves received amounts due their importance and such is stated in will. Charles and Mary were not children of Ader, but when they became Sanders slaves is not known.
[163] Sanders' estate sale was the only piece of evidence in Cabell County which actually named any of the slaves.
[164] Ironton, Lawrence County, OH, was just across the Ohio River from Cabell County, VA. Calvin was never enumerated on any census. Lambert Collection, 76-9-9. Simmons interview: "Cal returned and worked at the iron furnaces." An obituary in the *Ironton Register* (Ohio) March 22, 1894, read: "Calvin Sanders, the colored man whose leg was amputated a few days ago, after being crushed in a cave-in in W.L. Ellison's cellar, died Tuesday afternoon. The deceased was about 60 years of age, and a collier by trade. He worked for years at Vesuvius and Etna furnaces and was well and favorably known in the county. In his prime he is reputed to have been one of the strongest men in the furnace regions."
[165] His birth year and birthplace are the same in 1860, 1870 and 1880 census records and his birth date is on his tombstone.
[166] Charlotte aged rapidly according to the census. She was only 50 in 1850, but she died at the age of 107 in 1889. Her death was recorded in the *Cass Vigilant*, Cassopolis, MI, 12 Dec 1889.

"missing" Sanderses included several of the young unmarried men. (See Appendix 9C.)

The 1850 census revealed three Sanders families living in Calvin Township, while three other families lived just across the township line in Porter Township. (See Appendix 11A & 11B and Figure 18) In addition to the larger families, single men James, Peter and Eli Sanders settled at Williamsville in Porter Township. James was listed in Roger's *History of Cass County* when he gave a twenty-five dollar donation to Williamsville Academy.[167] Peter married Daniel's daughter Alicia and raised a large family, but Eli was dead by 1860.

The tiny community of Williamsville was located on the township line between Calvin and Porter townships, almost in the center of the Sanders' land. Just south of Birch Lake, the town was the service center for the Sanders families, because it was several miles closer than Calvin Center. (Figure 18.)

Williamsville was laid out in 1848 and a saw mill was erected on Sam Sanders' farm on Angle Creek in the 1850's.[168] During the 1860's, Elijah and Jason Sanders volunteered for the Civil War at Williamsville and became part of the First Michigan Volunteer Militia (later the United States Colored Troops, recorded USCT).[169] That same period found, Jeff Storey the shoemaker making a pair of cowhide shoes for Cynthia Radd, with soles of three ply calfskin and fastened with hobnails.[170]

By the 1880's, the community of Williamsville had a population around three hundred. It supported a general store, a blacksmith shop, a cabinet and paint shop, two doctors, a shoemaker, a grist mill and a saw mill. The town had sidewalks in front of several buildings and had surveyed lots for a high school seminary. It was also the home of a second generation of Sanders [171]

William Radd, son of Cynthia Radford, was a teamster who hauled logs with a yoke of oxen and was known for miles around. George Sanders, son of Elijah and grandson of Daniel, operated an entertainment show in which he sang and played the guitar. Several Sanders, one being Elijah, served as mail carriers.[172] As the sons and daughters left the rural farm and its life, the size and importance of Williamsville diminished. Today, the only business still in operation is a small store.

Equally as important as the village store to the Sanders was the local church. Church membership was an important part of everyone's life in the Nineteenth Century. In Cabell County, the Sanders may have been members of the Union Baptist Church located near Mud Bridge and the Kilgores, or the Mud River Baptist Church located a few miles below Martha Sanders home. When they reached Michigan, most of the families joined the Chain Lake Baptist Church. A few joined Bethel Methodist Church near Calvin Center, while others may have joined the Quakers at Birch Lake.

Chain Lake Baptist Church in Cass County has been honored as the first African-American Baptist Church in Michigan.[173] First organized in 1839 with a creed which spoke strongly against slavery, it soon after became a member of the Michigan Anti-slavery Baptist Association. Most of the Sanders families settled within a mile or two of the church, and its membership probably offered a helping hand when the families first arrived. The Chain Lake Church must have received a real boost in membership and fellowship when nearly fifty people joined about 1850. Many Sanders took an active part in the church, and Moses Sanders was named one of first trustees when the church was officially organized in 1854.[174]

---

[167] Howard S. Rogers, *History of Cass County From 1825-1875* (Cassopolis, MI: Vigilant Book and Job Print, 1875). P. 195.
[168] There was no "Sam" Sanders. The map maker probably meant Sol Sanders.
[169] Michigan Soldiers and Sailors Individual Records (Lansing, MI: Wynkoop Hallenbeck Crawford Co. State Printers, 1915), Vol. S.
[170] Harry East and Lavon Breece, "Short History of Williamsville". Private Collection, Williamsville, MI. Cynthia Radford and her family were listed "Radd" in Dorcas' estate sale found in Cass County, MI. Probate Records, loose files.
[171] Ibid.
[172] Ibid.
[173] Green Allen, History of the Chain Lake Baptist Church. (Cassopolis, MI, undated).[Original of 2 histories]. The 1840 Cass County Census listed no Black households in Cass County, but the formation of the church in 1839 proves otherwise.
[174] Rogers, *History of Cass County 1825-1875*, p. 210.

The FORWARD of the Chain Lake Church History states:

> This is a prayful dedicated effort to record the events which founded Chain Lake Baptist Church by the influx of two general Baptist groups in our community to escape persecution and to create a better spiritual life for themselves and their posterity. Both groups searching same goals found difficult adjustments both socially and geographically. Having migrated from a warm climate it was necessary to adjust to weather, soil and crop choices. They also found customs sometimes foreign to them as they were surrounded by other communities of Quakers, Indians and blends of English, French and German descent. The Coloreds as was then known, were both helped and exploited.

The earliest church records are quite limited, but important for they include the Sanders families among the one hundred and fifty members who helped raise $1,200 necessary to build a new church in 1860.[175]

The graveyard beside the church has several rows with the names of Sanders family members, further indicating their involvement with the church.

Figure 19
Chain Lake

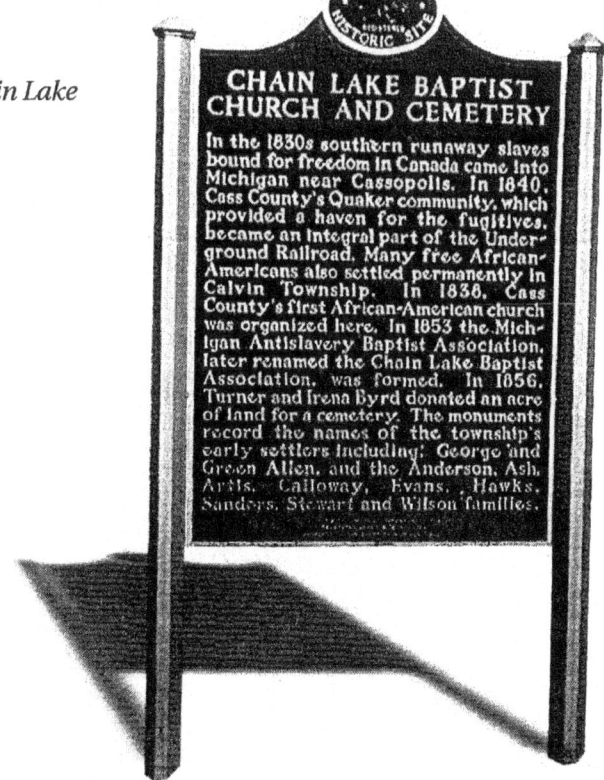

In 1986 the Michigan Historical Commission placed the Chain Lake Baptist Cemetery on the State Register of Historical Places.

---

[175] History of the Chain Lake Baptist Church. (Cassopolis, MI: undated).

Chapter Ten
The End of the Original Settlers

The age range of the manumitted slaves spread from one year to eighty-seven years. Three people, at least, died that first year; but several of the original settlers lived into the Twentieth Century. Some of their descendants still live in Cass County.

Calvin Sanders was born in Cabell County, Virginia, in 1848. Although not listed on the 1850 census, Calvin appeared on the 1860 census, "aged 12 - born in Virginia." He was the son of Levi and Jane Sanders and the grandson of two different Sanders lines: Solomon and Phyllis Sanders, who were the parents of Levi and Charlotte Sanders, the mother of Jane. Levi and Jane married in Cass County in 1852, joining the two different Sanders families. Calvin Sanders, their son, was buried at Chain Lake in 1926.

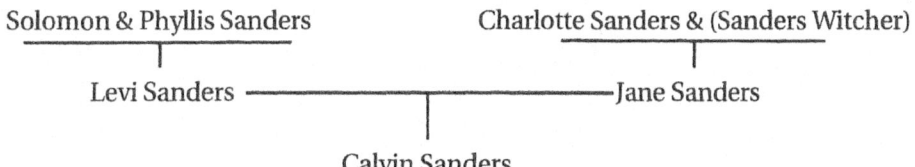

Eli Halistock was also two years old in 1850. Born in Cabell County, to Peggy Sanders, he took the Halistock name when his mother married, but he did receive her share of Sampson Sanders' will at her death.[176] Eli served in the Civil War with Company B 102nd United States Colored Troops, and although buried at Chain Lake, his tombstone was undated.

Other Sanders also lived into the Twentieth Century. Solomon Sanders Jr. was born in Cabell County in 1829. He left a will in Cass County in 1906 naming his four sons and one daughter. Mary Sanders married John Sanders in 1851, but in 1849 she took a deed for herself and seven children, including one-year-old twins Theodore and Sampson. These twins were listed on the 1860 census but then disappeared from the records. Possibly they both died prior to 1870, but more likely they lived past 1900 and moved out of the area like other members of the family. (See Appendix 9C.)

---

[176] Cass Records, Probate Records, loose files. Solomon Sanders was guardian to Eli in 1860. Eli had property valued at $700.

Solomon Sanders - Head of the Families

The primary family of the Sanders group belonged to Solomon Sanders and his wife Phyllis. Solomon was sixty-one years old at manumission, but he recorded the first deed in Cass County in 1849. That deed named his children still at home including: Eli, Levi, Solomon Jr., Woodford, Jacob and Jason. The property they purchased in Cass County, Michigan, consisted of one hundred and forty-eight acres in Calvin Township. It was purchased for $1387.00.[177] The deed was written so that Solomon and each child received an equal share of the property.[178]

KNOWN DESCENDANTS OF SOLOMON AND PHYLLIS SANDERS		
Eli	married, widowed and dead by 1860	1 daughter
Levi	married Jane Sanders/Charlotte	2 sons, 1 daughter
Solomon Jr.	married 3 times	4 sons, 1 daughter
Woodford	married Arabella Lowe	no children
Jacob	married Eliza Sanders/Daniel	1 son, 3 daughters
Jason	married Rebecca Sanders Cordia	children unknown

Some of the single males listed on the census may have been older children of Solomon. For example: Peter who married Alicia daughter of Daniel was almost certainly of Solomon's family. Solomon outlived his wife Phyllis, and remarried again in 1860 at age seventy-one. His death and burial at Chain Lake Cemetery soon followed in 1863. During his life in Cass County, Solomon witnessed marriages and deeds. He went to court to protect his children and grandchildren's share of the property. He also took different orphaned children into his home at various times.[179] Several records appear in probate records dealing with division of his property. Surviving among those records is the following receipt for his tombstone.

---

[177] Cass Records, Deeds, Bk. 1848-1850, p.403.
[178] Cass Records, Probate Records, loose files. The shares of property became evident with the death of Eli when his daughter received 1/8 share
[179] Federal Census, 1860, Michigan, Cass Co., M653:541.

THE END OF THE ORIGINAL SETTLERS

Figure 20. This bill of sale proved Solomon's death and was signed by his son.

> Bought of Moses Pettengill, One Set of VERMONT MARBLE GRAVE STONES. The Head Stone to be _3 feet_ long and of proportionate width. The following inscription to be engraved thereon, to wit: _Solomon Sanders died Aug 12 1863 aged 77 years_
> _Fin M R Panel_
>
> with suitable Foot Stones to be delivered at _Chain Lake Church_ by the _15_ of _Oct next_ unless unforeseen causes shall prevent, and then within a reasonable time thereafter. For which I agree to pay _twenty seven dollars_
>
> With use after delivery, without any relief whatever from Valuation or Appraisement Laws.
> Dated, _Calvin Aug 27 1863_   _Jeni Sanders_

The Family of Daniel and Dorcas Sanders

The second most important Sanders family belonged to Daniel Sanders and his wife Dorcas (often called Darky). According to the 1849 deed, they had the following children: Alicia, Montesque, Zebedee, Eliza, Robert, William, Elijah and Hamilton.[180] This family purchased one hundred and fifty-five acres for $1125.00.[181] Daniel died in 1854 and was buried at Chain Lake beside Ader and Zebedee Sanders. Wife Dorcas lived until 1877 and left several records.

CHILDREN OF DANIEL AND DORCAS SANDERS		
Alicia	married Peter Sanders	4 sons, 8 daughters
Montesque	married Jane Byrd	6 sons, 11 daughters
Zebedee	unknown	
Eliza	married Jacob/Solomon	1 son, 3 daughters
Robert	unmarried d 1877	
William	unmarried d 1870	
Elijah	married Laura Cousins	1 son, 2 daughters
Hamilton	unmarried d 1871	

---

[180] Property in Porter Township (#6) purchased by George Galleher (nephew), was later transferred to Daniel's family.
[181] *Stateline News Review*, Cass County, MI, 28 May 1969. Free Negroes from central Ohio were attracted to the area by the availability of land and settled the area beginning about 1845.

Dorcas Sanders had a sizable estate at her death (for that time). Her bill of sale and outstanding accounts added interesting information about the life of the Sanders' families.

```
Fan Mill & cradle              4 iron kettles           2 tea pots & contents
1 Hay knife & sheep shears     brass kettle             2 milk crocks
Hay rake                       11 gallon jars           milk safe
2 horses & mare                Lard can                 1 stand & roll pin
wagon                          4 sauce dishes           biscuit cutter
cow & calf                     3 window curtains        can fruit & 2 jars
6 chicken & 3 turkeys          9 blankets               2 pillows 7 sheet
```

Note the milk crocks and safe. It is likely that Dorcas made extra money with her cow by selling milk and butter. Her burial site was not recorded, but she probably rests at Chain Lake Cemetery near Daniel.

Her daughter, Alicia and her large family, left the county after 1880. Son, Montesque, was mentioned in few records, but he seems to have spent all the rest of his life in Cass County and fathered a large family. Of his nineteen children, four daughters died from consumption within a two year period. (See Appendices 9C and 10B.)

Figure 21. Dorcas Sanders' Settlement with W.C. Rinehart

```
1871
May  12   Repair on plow wheel         .50
Jun  18   Repair on plow wheel         .15
1872
May  10   Repair on hoes               .40
Jun  27   Sharpen 2 shovels            .25
Jul  13   Repair 2 heel wedges         .10
Sep  11   Repair on 2 forks            .25
Nov  25   4 new shoes 4 set           2.30
Dec  12   2 new shoes 2 set           1.25
                                      5.20
     interest for 5 yr 1.82            7.02

1874
Jan   2   2 chain links                .10
Feb   6   1 shoe on Bob Sleigh         .75
Mar  24   Elijah Sanders acct         9.05
Apr  15   2 shoe set                   .40
Aug   5   1 set door hinges           1.25
                                     11.55
Apr 10 Cr 1 cord wood                 1.00
                                     10.55
```

```
1873
Mar  27   Singletree hook/wedge sharp      .30
Jul  30   Repair on Wagon                  .25
Aug   5   Lenying cutter sharp spear      1.00
Aug  30   Sharp 4 shovels/singletree       .75
Sep   2   Shoe set per Elijah              .20
Nov   8   Sow & pigs                     10.00
Dec  31   3 chain links                    .15
                                         12.65
Mar   5   1 1/2 day work         1.50
Nov   8   2 bushel wheat         3.00
Nov   8   34 cabbage heads       2.04
Nov   8   1/2 bu potatoes         .36
                                 6.90     3.75
     interest to 4 yr           1.61      7.36

     interest 3 yr  2.22  12.77

                    Amount Total $27.15 against estate
```

Mary Sanders and Children

Mary Sanders arrived in Cass County with seven children and purchased one hundred and fifteen acres for $725.00. She was also listed in court records as the sister of Charles.[182] In 1851 she married John Sanders, also a Cabell County Sanders, and they had one child before Mary died prior to 1860. None of her children married other Sanders.

MARY'S CHILDREN		
Susan	married Isaac Ward both died prior to 1860	3 sons (twins)
Joseph	unknown after 1850	
Harriet	married Peter Smith died 1896	3 sons, 2 daughters
Mahala	married Thomas J. Carter 1854	unknown
Charles	unknown after 1860	
Theodore	twin-unknown	
Sampson	twin-unknown	
Mordica	(born to Mary & John in Cass County)	

The Sanders families left numerous records in Cass County, Michigan. Many of the records provided extensive information, but at times the records were as confusing as helpful. There were also other unrelated Sanders families in Cass County who added to an already complicated picture. The records show that the people set free by Sampson Sanders became a viable part of Cass County. They cleared land, planted crops and supported their church; but by about 1890 most of the old people were dying, and the young people were gone. Certainly not all the children had "died young," instead they moved away.

Booker T. Washington wrote several articles about young Negro workers in the industrial cities of Mid-America. During a trip to South Bend, Indiana, he found the factory owners there attributed some of their success to the excellent workers from Cass County, Michigan, and identified the Sanders family of Calvin Township. Washington actually made a trip to Cass County and met the people "manumitted by a Virginia slave master."[183] Obviously, some of the young Sanders did just like many other young people across the nation. They left the farm for the higher paying jobs in the factories which were springing all across the upper Midwest.

The various Sanders families all faced the same economic problems. The $15,000 allotted the manumitted Sanders did not go far or last very long. Although the combined families originally spent $4,900 for over five hundred acres in Cass County, the farms were held in individual tracts averaging less than ten acres per person.[184] As farmers across the nation shifted from subsistence farming to farming for a profit, the small Sanders units could not produce enough surplus crops to make a living and the family members were forced to find other jobs.

A second problem arose as children came along. Obviously, the men were ac-

---

[182] Mentioned earlier, Charles died in 1850.
[183] Harlan and Smock, *The Booker T. Washington Papers*, Vol.7, pp. 44,45.
[184] Cass County Deeds indicate the members of a family pooled their money to buy the farm, then divided it. Also see: Fields, " Free Negroes in Cass County."

complished farmers from their experience in Cabell County, but even a genius could not feed and cloth nineteen children on ten acres. At a parent's death, the will usually gave each child a share of their estate, dividing each small farm into an even smaller unit. Soon the only answer was to sell the land and look for a job outside Cass County. Newspaper articles and obituaries indicate individuals and families moved to Battle Creek, Flint, Ann Arbor and Detroit, Michigan; Elkhart and South Bend, Indiana; Toledo, Ohio and Chicago, Illinois. Today, of the original Sanders families, only the descendants of Solomon and Charlotte are still living in Cass County. Those people contacted are all descended from Calvin, grandson of two families. (Appendix 12B.)

Chapter Eleven
Sanders of Today

Confronted with devastating winters, an unfamiliar culture and a new way of life, the various Sanders families met the challenge and founded families that have multiplied, prospered and moved. Only one family from the original settlers has been traced to the present time. That family is actually descended from two of the original families.

Jane, daughter of Charlotte married Levi, son of Solomon. Their child Calvin married Gertrude Brown and fathered four children: Mary Jane, 1874; Oscar, 1876; Carrie, 1878; and Arthur, 1882. Oscar married Edna B. Vaughn of Cass County in 1905. Their children were: Lester, 1905; Estella, 1909; Marshall H., 1911; and Myrl 1918.

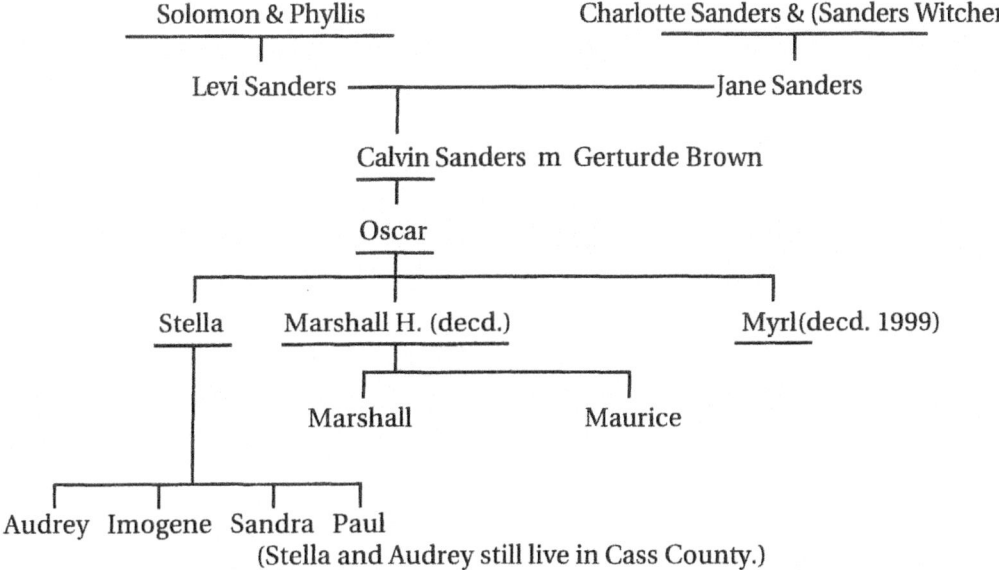

Figure 22
Geneology for Sanders of Cass County

Marshall H. Sanders, born in Porter Township, Cass County, married Esther Rosanna Wilson of Calvin Township. They moved to Detroit and produced sons: Marshall H. Jr. 1940 and Maurice W. 1942. Marshall, educated as a teacher, is now a banker in Flint, Michigan, and the father of three daughters and a son. Maurice, also an educator and a school physiologist, is the father of three daughters. Both families have twin daughters which seem to be a characteristic of the Sanders families and readily documented by census records.

Estella Sanders Lawson age 88 and her brother Myrl Sanders age 79 still live in Cass County. They are siblings to Marshall who moved to Detroit. Stella's daughter Audrey lives at home; a daughter, Imogene Brown lives in Granger, Indiana; a daughter, Sandra White lives in Kalamazoo; and a son, Paul Dean Sanders lives at Elkhart, Indiana. Stella's brother Myrl has two children in California. (See Appendix 12B for family.)

Chapter Twelve
Tracing Lost Sanders

Sampson Sanders' will of 1849 manumitted his slaves but never named them. In fact, there is little information in Cabell County, West Virginia, to indicate Sampson or his slaves even existed. The old Sanders Cemetery near modern Milton is supposed to contain "slave burials" along with the headstones for Sampson and Martha Sanders, but there is no visible evidence. Only rumor indicated that the slaves, Sampson's father William Sanders or his wife Ann and her child were buried there. The only written evidence in Cabell County of the slaves existence is Martha's estate sale and the Love's Store debt book, both of which name only five slaves, and Sampson's estate sale.

Most of the information about Sampson Sanders and his slaves in Cabell County is found in the form of interviews from relatives and neighbors collected by Fred B. Lambert many years after the event. The Lambert Collection, held by Special Collections Department of James E. Morrow Library at Marshall University, contains many personal interviews with Sampson Simmons, a namesake nephew of Sampson Sanders. Although only six years old when Sampson Sanders died, Simmons was the main source of information about the event. He and his brother and sisters were orphaned four years before Sampson Sanders' death. Of all the nephews and nieces, they received the largest share of property from Sanders' estate. Sampson Simmons had good reason to remember his Uncle Sampson.

About 1930, Simmons penned an autobiography at the request of Fred Lambert. Much of the material dealt with his Uncle Sampson and the slaves. Reading Simmons' comments led to other materials which in turn led still further. One reference concerned an article written by Booker T. Washington about Negro factory workers freed by a Virginia master. Several other national publications also mentioned a large group of former slaves in Michigan freed by a Virginia master; and eventually, the search for the manumitted slaves ended in Cass County, Michigan, where the group settled.

Cass County materials concerning the family are found in almost every book in the Court House. The Sanders first order of business was to record their deeds, but both a marriage and a death took place in 1850 and were recorded in the appropriate books. That 1850 Sanders' will left all the property of Charles to his sister because "he had neither father nor mother nor children."

Other Cass County records include an entry in the Chain Lake Baptist Cemetery report which listed eighty-seven year old Zebedee Sanders dying in 1850.[185] In all thirty-three former slaves were listed on Cass County deeds and forty-one individuals were listed on the 1850 Cass County census. Many names on both lists were the same, making it possible to verify names and families. Assorted other records supplied additional names for the list of manumitted slaves.

Some of the earliest settlers of Cass County, Michigan, were Quakers who had strong beliefs against slavery. Soon after their own settlement, the East family assisted free Negroes and escaped slaves who came to the area. By the 1840's, the Cass County Quaker community was well established and their assistance to Negroes had become well known beyond the county. When a group of Kentucky slave-holders tried to retrieve their runaway slaves in 1847, not only did they fail, but all the county rallied together and quickly spirited all the run-away slaves into Canada.[186] This event garnered national attention.

---

[185] "Cemeteries of Cass County, Michigan," (Cass Co., MI: Daughters of the American Revolution, 1933).
[186] L.H. Glover, *A 20th Century History of Cass County*, (Chicago: Lewis Publishing Co., 1906), p. 152.

The Negro community of Calvin Township organized the first antislavery African-American church in Michigan. Soon both the Quaker community and the free Negro community expanded their aid to runaway slaves. Cass County, became one of the main points on the Underground Railroad connecting both the western route from Missouri and the Ohio route before sending the runaways on into Canada.[187]

As property owners, the Sanders families, rapidly became important members of the community. In all probability, they also assisted runaways; they definitely cared for all the members of the extended Sanders family.[188] Part of Sampson Sanders' will had charged the able-bodied to care for the young, the old and the infirm. Checking Cass County records showed that they did just that. The 1850 Cass County census listed eighty-year-old Ada living with Peggy Sanders Halistock and James Sanders. Later, as death left orphaned children, those children appeared in various homes of grandparents or aunts and uncles. Occasionally older siblings cared for the younger brothers or sisters.[189]

The second half of nineteenth century was a period when contagious diseases ravaged entire communities. Although records do not show why, several Sanders families just cease to exist. The possibility exists that families moved out of the area. During that time period, it was just as likely for the whole family to have been stricken with malaria, typhus, smallpox, cholera, measles or other similar disease. The move from Cabell County, Virginia, to Cass County, Michigan, would have caused many health problems because Cabell County had a moderate climate with rainy winters, while Cass County had harsh winters with heavy snow and severe temperatures.[190] The change of climate, the severe weather, the diseases and the constant child bearing, caused many deaths.

Marriage and death records are the most commonly found records and are often the only way to trace a family. Mary Sanders had unmarried daughters when her family arrived in Cass County. Three married soon after they arrived. Susan married Isaac Ward in 1850, Mahala married Thomas Jefferson Carter in 1854, and Harriet married Peter Smith in 1856.(See Appendix 9B.) Susan Ward died before 1860, leaving three sons. Mahala Carter either died or moved from the area. Harriet Smith delivered five children of her own and cared for her two brothers, Sampson and Mordica. (See Appendix 9A.) Several census records show assorted Sanders grandchildren living in homes that were not their own. This practice made it possible to trace some families while it totally confused other families.

Sometimes, death is the only way a researcher can trace a family. Several rows in the churchyard at Chain Lake Baptist Church are devoted to Sanders and their allied families.[191] Varied surnames among those rows often represented marriages, thus offering another avenue for research. The Death Books in Cass County began soon after the Sanders arrived and those books added valuable information to the research. For example: at the death of Jane Sanders(wife of Levi), her mother was given as Charlotte Sanders and her father as Witcher Sanders, a name listed nowhere else. On re-examining the Cabell County records, a reference was found transferring slaves, Charlotte and Jennie, within the Daniel Witcher family, just after the death of son, Sanders Witcher in 1815, and about the time Jane was born.[192]

Cabell County, West Virginia, also

---

[187] S.S. Mathews, *History of Cass County*, Michigan, (Chicago: Waterman, Watkins & Co., 1882), p. 216.
[188] Cass Records, Probate Records, loose files; and Federal Census, 1850-1880 Michigan: M555:495, M653:541, M593:668, T9:575.
[189] Federal Census, 1860, Michigan, Cass Co., M653:541. Sampson Sanders, son of Mary Sanders, was living with his sister Harriet Sanders Smith in 1860.
[190] Cabell County's temperature is moderated by the Ohio River. Average winter temperatures are near freezing and most of the moisture is rainfall. Cass County, 300 miles to the north, has average winter temperatures in the teens and heavy snowfall.
[191] Chain Lake Baptist Church Cemetery grave markers.
[192] The Cass County Will book says Witcher Sanders, but other research indicates the clerk misunderstood or should have placed a comma after Witcher. Many clerks did not use commas.

yielded additional clues to the Sanders families. Family connections between Sampson's and Hetty's slaves were glimpsed when Sampson Simmons mentioned in an interview, "Aunt Jennie belonged to Grandmother Kilgore and came to live with us when Mother and Father died."[193] She may have been the "Jennie" mentioned in the transfer of "Charlotte and Jennie" in the Witcher family, because other connections seemed to exist between the Sanders, the Witcher and the Ward families. All three families were traveling across the frontier at the same time and place.[194] For some unknown reason Witcher's slaves, Charlotte and Jennie, were divided between Sampson Sanders and Hetty Sanders Kilgore.[195]

The research of this project led in many interesting directions, not all of which have been recorded here. Like any research, this project seemed to be the work of completing a giant jigsaw puzzle. There always remained at least one piece missing.

Sampson Sanders made a major impact in the beginnings of Cabell County, Virginia. By his act of manumission, Sanders' freed slaves made a major impact in Cass County, Michigan, and in the development of the Chain Lake Baptist Church. The descendants of those slaves have dispersed across the Midwest and across the nation, creating positions for themselves and their families in the American society. The act of one Virginia planter changed the lives of many people. By further examining the evidence, we may find this one man even changed our own lives.

---

[193] Lambert Collection 76-9-9.
[194] Jeremiah Ward was mentioned earlier in connection with the Mill. The Witchers were in-laws to Ward and also lived near the Mill.
[195] Lambert Collection, 76B-9-9.

Figure 23 Couple together 70 years: Forest and Estella Lawson wed 70 years ago.

STELLA SANDERS LAWSON, born 25 February 1909 - Daughter of Oscar, granddaughter of Levi & Jane, great-granddaughter of Solomon / Phyllis and Charlotte.

Figure 24
Sanders' graves in Cabell County.

The only remaining evidence of Sanders in Cabell County are these two lonely graves on a hill top overlooking Mud River near the mouth of Sanders Creek. Sampson Sanders' tombstone is intact, but his mothers' unreadable. The tiny cemetery is located on the original Sanders Property and traditions says there are slave burials here.

Chapter 12

Figure 25
Sanders' in Chain Lake Cemetery.

Chain Lake Cemetery in Cass County, Michigan is the resting place for several of the Sanders family. Vital to the strength of the Chain Lake Church, Solomon, Daniel, Ader, Zebeedee and many other family members lie in this quiet churchyard.

Appendices

1A	Loudoun County Records	80
1B	Casewell County Records	82
2	Kanawha County Records	84
3	Jack Neal Records	89
4A	Martha Sanders - Kanawha Records	91
4B	Martha Sanders - Kanawha Records	93
4C	William & Martha Sanders Genealogy	94
5A	Sampson Sanders - Inventory & Sale	96
5B	Sampson Sanders - Deeds	108
5C	Sampson Sanders - Cabell Survey	110
6	Hetty Sanders Kilgore - Will	111
7	Materials Purchased by the Manumitted Slaves	113
8	Cass County - Sanders Deeds	115
9A	Cass County - Census	118
9B	Cass County - Cemetery Records	123
9C	Known Sanders	125
10A	Solomon Sr. - Inventory & Sol Jr. - Will	132
10B	Dorcas - Apprasial & Sale	133
10C	Cass County Marriages	135
11	4 Maps - Calvin & Porter Townships 1860 & 1872	137
12A	Descendants of Hetty Sanders Kilgore	141
12B	Descendants of Cass County Sanders	147
13	Virginia Law - Act to Authorize Manumission	152

*Punctuation and spelling retained from original document.

Appendix 1A

Loudoun County, Virginia Records
Source: *LOUDOUN CO. VA TITHABLES 1758-1786* 3 volumes

VOL 1	1761	James, Thomas, William SANDERS		(Jas. Hamilton-list)
	1761	Daniel, William		(Richard Coleman)
	1762	James, James, William SANDERS		
		Aaron, Sarah, Isaac		(James Hamilton)
	1762	James SANDERS		Cameron Parrish
	1762	(James Green next door)		
	1765	James, William, John, George SANDERS at Nicholas Manor		
	1765	William 180a & another SANDERS		(Wm. Carr)
	1766	James, William, John SANDERS		(Phil Nolan)
	1767	William 180a, SANDERS		
	1767	Philip, Philip Jr., SANDERS		
		William, Benjamin, James, Isaac		(James Hamilton)
	1767	James, John, Gunill, SANDERS		
		James, William, William Jr.		(Powell)
	1768	Philip, William, Benjamin, Philp, Thomas		SANDERS
	1768	James, William, John, Gunill, Jas. Jr.		SANDERS
	1769	James, William, John, James, Presely, Gunnill		SANDERS

note: 1767 near Wm. Sanders- Francis George Summers, Thos. Lewis, Thomas Donaho, George Kilgore, Sampson Turley

VOL 2				
p610	1772	William & Samson	SANDERS	Shelburn Parrish
	1772	Phil	SANDERS	
	1772	Benjamin	SANDERS	
p669	1773	William & Samson	SANDERS	Cameron Parrish
	1773	Benjamin	SANDERS	
p756	1774	James Green		Cameron Parrish
p809	1775	Wm., Benj., Sampson	SANDERS	Shelburn Parrish
p861	1777	James Green		Cameron Parrish
p891	1778	James Green, Gerrard		Cameron Parrish

VOL 3   many Sanders, Saunders 1780 lists by George Summers, Samuel Love
                (Cabell County neighbors)

p1082	1780	William SANDERS,	Benja., Jas.	&	Negro	Hannah
p1104	1780	William SANDERS,	Benja., Jas.	&	Negro	Hannah
p1105	1780	James Green, Gerrard 5 Negroes				
p1156	1781	William SANDERS,	Benj.	&	N	Hanna
	1781	James Green, Garred 5 Negroes				
p1190	1782	William SANDERS,	Benja., Jas.	&	N	Hannah
p1281	1783	William SANDERS 5w 1n				
p1326	1784	William SANDERS, Jarrett Green,			N-Hannah	
	1784	(next house) James Green, Thos.			& 4N	
p1359	1785	William SANDERS, Garret Green, John Vincent,			N-Hannah	
	1785	(next house) James Green, Thos.			4n	

Note: Should have married Martha prior 1783 (2nd wife ?) (At no time is a Hannah listed as a Green slave.) (William has possession of Hannah from 1780 at least) (Both Summers & Turley, among others, owned a "Hannah")

Appendix 1A

Loudoun County, Virginia, Will Bk E 1788
pp237-238

In the name of God Amen, the Twenty-third of April in the year of our Lord one thousand seven hundred & eighty-eight, I *James Green* of Loudoun County in the state of Virginia; being very sick &----- in body but of perfect mind & memory thanks be to God, therefore calling to mind the mortality of my body & knowing that all men by appointment must die, Do make & ordain this my last will and testament that is to say principally & first of all I give & recommend my soul into the hands of the Almighty God gave it & my body to the Earth to be buried in decent Christian burial at the direction of my executors, not doubting at the general resurrection I shall review the same again by the Almighty Power of God. and as touching such worldly estates wherewith it has pleased God to bless me in this life; I give demise and dispose of the same in the following manner & form Viz: First, I leave to my beloved wife *Frances* the full possession & enjoyment during her life of my Plantations houses & Negroes, with all my movable effects, stock & cattle--- also all my open accounts Bonds Debts or other property, belonging to me to be peaceably & entirely enjoyed by her & my three youngest children, That is my two sons *William & Fielding* and my youngest daughter *Frances* whom I wish should continue with their Mother during her life, I also constitute & appoint my wife *Frances*, to be sole and principal executrix during her life and at her decease, then the whole of my effects and property to be equitably & equally divided among all my children in the most exact & truest manner. I also desire that my son, *Thomas* may continue with his mother as long as it is convenient to them both, to my son *George*, I leave one shilling, to my son-in-law *Elihu Harding* and his children by my daughter *Ann*, I also cut off with one shilling, the remainder of my property to be disposed of as above mentioned Ex, during my wife *Frances* living a widow, but in case she shall marry another, then my entire property and effects to be divided in this manner; My wife Frances, to a third part of all my estate & property, and the remainder to be equally divided between my children, namely my son *Gerrard Green*, my sons *Thomas, William & Fielding*, also my daughters, *Elizabeth Shelton, Mary Bennett, Polly Saunders*, & my youngest daughter *Frances Green*, each of the aforementioned children to have and equal part or share of all my worldly estate & property whatsoever, also I do hereby entirely revoke & disannul all & every other forms, testaments and wills, legacies & bequests or executors, by me any ways beforenamed, therefore I ratify & confirm, this to be my last will & testament-For witness whereof, I have hereunto set my hand & seal this 23rd day of April Anno 1788

Signed & Sealed   his
In presence of us   James X Green [{SEAL}]
William Fox   mark
J.R.Bordridge (Bosdridge)

At a court held for Loudoun County December 12th 1796, This last will & testament of James Green deceased was proved by the oath of William Fox one of the witnesses thereto & ordered to be recorded and on the motion of Frances Green, the Executrix therein named, who made oath thereto according to the law together with Thomas *Blincoe* & John *Turley* (Logarland) (??) her securities entered into and acknowledged their bond in the penalty of three thousand pounds with condition as the law directs certificate is granted for obtaining probate.   Teste; Chas. Binns

Appendix 1A

NOTE: Martha Green Sanders'- first daughter Hetty FRANCES Sanders (after her mother?) Shelton, Bennett and Turley named in Sanders deed with Blincoe.

sons	George	daughters	Elizabeth Shelton	wife	Frances
	Gerrard		Mary Bennett		
	Thomas		Polly Saunders (not a Mary)		
	William		Ann Harding (decd)		
	Fielding		Frances Green		

1796   when probated- Martha was already in NC or TN.

Appendix 1B

Caswell County, North Carolina Records
Source: *State of North Carolina Census 1784-1787*

Caswell County, North Carolina is directly south of Pittsylvania County, Virginia and at Virginia's southern end of Carolina/Piedmont Road

Residents of Caswell county, North Carolina
Tilman & Wayne Dixon -- founders of Dixon Springs, Tennessee

William Saunders	1 white males 21-60 residence near Dixon Springs
	5 white males under 21-over 60
	2 white females
	4 blacks 12-50
	6 blacks under 12-over 50
Thomas Kilgore Jr.	1 male 21-60, 1 female
Lydda Kilgore	2 males under 21/over 60,1 female, 1 slave under 12/over 50

Also Cabell county surnames: George Summers, Thomas Swann, James & William Chapman, Chas. & Reuben Hanie, Thomas Poor, James Walker and all listed below.

1790   Census NC - Hillsborough District, Caswell County (from tax lists)

Caswell Dist.	Gloucester Dist.	Richmond Dist.
Black, Sarah	Burton, Henry,	James Atkins, Thomas
Burton, Jane	Bryant, James	Bennett, Thos., John
Clarke, Solomon	Barnett, John	Barnett, John
Chapman, James	Donoho, William	Burke, James
Dixon, Henry, Charles,	Davis, Henry Sr.	Burton, John
Dixon, Martha, Roger	Everet, Samuel	Cox, Phillip
Dixon, Tilmon, Wynn	Hearndon, Larkin	Carter, Jesse
Dickerson, Nathaniel	Kilgore, Thomas	Dameron, Joseph, Christopher
Dameron, Joseph	Love, Samuel	Donoho, Maj.Thos., Patrick
Martin, Joseph, Bailey	Moore, Robert., Geo.	Farley, Geo.
Payne, John	Payne, John	Farley, James, Sarah
Roberts, Vincent	Ray, James	Kiles, James, Elizabeth
Swan, Thomas	Simmons, Thomas	Merritt, Benj.,Sol.,Daniel
Sommers, George,	Yates, Thomas	Roberts, Absolum, Thomas
Sommers, James, John		Sanders, Richard, Col. James
Walker, James	Nash Dist.	Sanders, Wm. (2)

Appendix 1B

St. Davids Dist.	Barnett, David, John	Sanders, Col. Adam
Burton, David	Gwin, John	Stewart, Hezekiah
Brown, Leonard, Wm.	Sanders, Richard	Swan, Joseph, Edward
Ballard, Dudley	Walker, Jese	Sheltonn, David
Brown, Carter, Davis,	Walker, Moses, Burkley	Stokes, Man
French, Gwin, Payne,	Wilson, James	Yates, Wm., John
Roberts, Walkers, Williams		Johnson, Ball, Black, Fuller,
Hix, Hughes, Hews, Stuart, Aldridge		Bryant, Pogue

================================

Gerrard Green who appeared in William Sanders home in 1782 was brother to Martha (Polly) Green Sanders and son of James Green of Loudoun County, VA

================================

Will Book E p284 Harrison Co. KY (Cynthiana)
    GERARD GREEN (pensioner) wife/ Virlinda, sons: James, William,
    Fielding, George, Lilburn; daughers: Mildred Holliday, Elizabeth
    McLoney, Parentha Kenney. written 23 mar 1845-probate aug 1845
    Ex: James Green. Wit: Burwell N. Carter, Jacob Rennecker
SOURCE: Kentucky Records Julia Hoge Ardery. Lexington, 1926.
reprint Genealogy Publishing Co.Inc. Baltimore, 1977.

25 jul 1789   Caswell County, North Carolina, Deed Book 1 - p315
    This indenture this twentififth day of July in the year of our Lord one thousand seven hundred and eighty seven, Between *William Sanders* of Caswell County & State of North Carolina of the one part & *Robert Matheriel* of the county & state aforesaid of the other part witnesseth that the said *Sanders* for consideration of the sum of one hundred pounds good and lawful money to him in hand paid by the said *Matheriel* at or before the sealing & delivery of these presents----etc: Land lying and being in the county of SUMNER on the waters of Collins River near Bradbys Licks begining---etc
signed Joseph Motherel, John Gambell, William Sanders, J.Winchester(reg.)

8 jul 1797   Sumner County, Tennessee, Bond Book 1 - p205
    Know you of an agreement entered into this 11th November 1785 between *William Sanders* and *John Marshall* of the one part and James Sanders Jr. of the other, the said William Sanders and John Marshall have delivered into the hands of *James Sanders Jr.*, forty seven (47) land warrants containing twenty-six thousand nine hundred and ninety three acres, granted to soldiers of the continenal line of this state, which said lands the said James Sanders is to locate and survey at his expense, for which expense the said William Sanders and John Marshall doth each oblige themselves and each of their heirs -etc-to make the said James Sanders a lawful right to one third part--etc.etc. signed: Thos.Donoho, Alanson Tragg, James Sanders, William Sanders, John Marshall, James Sanders Jr.

Appendix 1B

1 dec 1784
Sumner County, Tennessee, Bond Book 1 - p247 (Caswell County Dec.1st,1784)

Dear Sir
     The Assembly has passed a law that the officers shall survey their lands together which makes it necessary to make some alterations of my locations. You will lay the warrant for the heirs of *Isaac Hancock* decd for one thousand acres on the place I surveyed on the East Fork of the Station Camp Creek with *Lt. Col. Henry Dixon's* which warrant is in the name of *Charles Dixon* in trust for the legates, you will have surveyed where it is located. *Lt. William Sanders* lands to be surveyed where Jimmy Sanders surveyed 1840 arces for him to include 1000 acres joining to it which was surveyed for Lt.Wynne Dixon, the remainder of the thousand acres there will be a small warrant ready before the works are returned, my own warrant you will have surveyed at my lick above Goose Creek, etc.etc.-------------
To Major Isaac Blesoe   from   Tilman Dixon

Sumner County, Tennesee - Executor and Administrator Bonds 1796 - 1816 (3 oct 1798)
State of Tennessee Sumner County - Know all men by these presents that we William Sanders & George Smith are jointly ans severally held and firmly bound unto this Justices of the Court of the said county in the sum of twelve hundred & fifty dollars to be paid to the said justices--etc.etc-- this 3rd day of October 1798. The condition above obligation is such that whereas the above bounden William Sanders has obtained an order of court to keep a ferry on Cumberland River at Bledsoesborough---etc.etc---

Appendix 2

Kanawha County Deed Book B

Kanawha B-104
Know all men by these presents that we William Saunders, William Sterrett, John Reynolds, Allyn Prior, Robert McKee,(Jr.) & James Caruthers are heald & firmly bound unto Leonard Morris, John Rousch, George Alderson, & Obadia Fugua Gentm. Justices for Kanhawa County in the Penal sum of Five Thousand Dollars, to which payment well & truly to be made we bind us our joint & several heirs & In witnesss thereof we have hereunto put our hands & seals this 14th Day of October 1801.
     The Condition of this Obligation is that if the said William Saunders Administrator of the Goods Chattle & creadits of Bennett Rodgers decd. which have or shall come to the hands or knowledge or possession of him the said William Saunders or in the hands or possession of any other person or persons for him & the same so made do exhibit unto the Kanhawa Court when he shall be thereunto required by the said court & such Goods Chattles & Creadits do well & truly administer according to Law & further do make a just & true account of his acctings & doings therein thereto required by the said Court & all the Rest of the said Goods & Chattles & Creadits which shall be found remaining upon the accounts of the said administrator the same being just examined & allowed by the Justices of the Sd Court for the time being shall deliver & pay unto such persons respectively as are intitled to the same by law & if it shall hereafter appear that any Last Will & Testament was made by the Decd & the same be proved in Court & the Executors obtain a Certificate thereof and the said William Saunders do in such case being thereto required, Render & deliver up his letters of Administration then this Obligation to be void else to remian in full force & virtue

Sealed & Acknowledged	William Saunders	(SEAL)	Robt.McKee (Jr)	(SEAL)
In Presence of	William Sterritt	(SEAL)	Jas.Caruthers	(SEAL)
Acknowledged in Court	John Reynolds	(SEAL)		
John Reynolds CKC	Allyn Prior	(SEAL)		

Appendix 2

I Thomas Banks do Testify and say that Bennett Rodgers who is said to be lately murdered on the Ohio River was a near relation of mine by afinity that he made my house his home aboute two years (Towit) in the year 1798 & 1799 and that he lived afterwards at the house of Colo William Saunders which is in the same neighborhood until last February chiefly, & then left this country on a trip to the Natchez with property which I understood belonged to said Rodgers & Saunders in Connection, I also understood by letters from him afterwards that he went from the Natchez around to New York.   Thomas Banks

I hereby certify that on the 31th of January last I sold a negro to Colo.William Sanders and Bennett Rodgers who contracted for him jointly and became equally answerable to me for payment of the price stipulated, and that I also hold an obligation against the said Saunders & Rodgers in which they jointly bound for the payment of three hundred and forty dollars for three horses-and that soon after the above Date said Rogers left this Country with said Negro & horses and much other property, on a trading adventure to the Natchez and round by water to the Northern or Middle States, and that it is generally understood that the said Saunders was and is owner of one [{morety}] of all the property carried on the said trading adventure by the Rogers who it is reported has been murdered on his return some where near the mouth of Kanhawa River.
Dixon Spring Smith County State of Tennessee   August 21th 1801   T.Dixon
                                                                                      S.Williams   (SEAL)

Kanhawa County October Court 1801
Motion of William Saunders ordered all affidavits and letters respecting the partnership between Saunders and Bennett Rogers who was murdered on the Ohio, be entered as a Copartnership of the said Rogers   Teste John Reynolds   CKC

Kanawha B-106
I Willis Jones testify that on the day before Mr.Bennett Rodgers set oute for the Natchez being the first of last February I was with said Rogers & in conversation respecting the terms of his partnership with Colo.Saunders said Rogers told me they were to share equally in the proffits as they were equal owners of the property which he should carry, or words to this purport. I also testify that I was acquainted with most of the purchases they made of horses all for said trip and I understood that they made their Contracts jointly.

Willis Jones

Kanawha B-108
Dear Sir
        Having heard the Meloncholly fate of our friend Rogers, I hope you will take measures to secure the property that business properly belongs as his partner Tho I am the only Heir he has left in this State yet I conceive I have no write to interfer in the management of it until the copartnership Debts are paid, But if it were my business I could not leave home on such a journey and should relinguish it to you.
Douglas Creek August 28th 1801   Thos.Banks
Colo.William Saunders
        Kanhawa County October Court 1801
This letter presented in Court by Colo.Wiliam Saunders & ordered to record.
Kanawha County Deed Book B-110

Appendix 2

Agreeable to an order of Court of Kanhawa County to us Allyn Prior, Nehemiah Wood and William Sterritt directed we have proceeded to appraise the property of Bennet Rogers decd. having been first sworn do appraise the said property as followeth (Viz) D C

Item	Value
One negro man named Tom Lyle	300.00
One do named Sam(now sick)if he recovers	300.00
One do named Dick	300.00
One do named Bob	333.33
One do named Tom	300.00
One gold watch	60.00
One hundred & fourteen Rings	114.00
One case of pocket pistols & holster & belt	10.00
One great coat $10.00 one strait Coat $10.00	20.00
Two waist Coats $10.00 two pr small cloaths $10.00 2 pr pantalon $3.00 two pr silk stocking $6.00 five pr cotton hose $5.00	34.00
One pr half boots & shoes $6.00 To sundres $18.00	24.00
	1795.33

The property in the hands of William Sterrit, Nehemiah Woods has agreed to rest his judgement upon the judgement of William Sterrit and Allyn Prior as he has not seen it. Sworn before me Obadiah Fugua a Justice of the Peace for Kanhawa County this 14th oct 1801

Kanhawa County November Court 1801
This Appraisement of the estate of Bennet Rogers decd was presented in Court by the apprasiers amounting to Seventeen hundred & ninety five dollars and thirty three cents which is order to record. teste John Reynolds

Kanawha B-110
*do = ditto
At a public auction at Point Pleasant on Saturday the 24th of October 1801 William Saunders Administrator of the property of Bennet Rogers deceased and Surviving partner the following property was exposed for a sale as followith (to wit) --*do = ditto

buyer	item		dol cents	
William Saunders	a Negro named	Tom	$200.00	
do	do	Dick	225.00	
do	do	Bob	236.00	
do	do	Little Tom	200.00	
do	do	Samuel	200.00	
William Sterret	wearing apparel of the deceased		34.25	
William Saunders	one shirt		.50	
do	one brace of pistols		1.75	
Walter Newman	one silk handkerchieff		1.00	
Samuel Longan	one neck do		.50	
Andrew Donnally	one neck handkerchief		.51	page B-111
Charles Lewis	one Great Coat		12.00	
William Saunders	one wool hat		.25	
do	one powder flask $1.25 one ink stand $.32		1.37	

Appendix 2

William Sterrett	one pair of slips	.51
John Allen	hair powder bag	.51
Charles Donally	one cotton handkerchief	1.37
William Saunders	one do do bandana	1.27
Charles Donally	one do do do	1.26
Robert Slaughter	one iron spoon	.25
Polly S. Donally	one pocket handkerchief	.04
William Saunders	one Lathery Hatchet	.17
William Sterret	one pair worsted hoes	1.30
William Sanuders	8 yards tow linen at .25 pr yd	2.00
James Tylor	one pair cotton hoes	1.50
Allyn Prior	one do	.25
Samuel Longan	one do	.30
Robert Slaughter	one pair silk hoes	3.25
Andrew Donnally	one pair do	4.57
William Sterrett	2-yards Hair ribband	.53
Lewis Newton	night cap & cravat pd .30 silk handkerchief $1.50	1.80
William Sterret	one Raisor & stick of sealing wax	.45
William Saunders	one Shaving box & soap	1.00
Walter Newman	Black silk handkerchief	.12
William Clendinen	one horse whip	3.00
Andrew Donnally	6 Gold rings	3.61
William Saunders	6 do	3.00
Andrew Donnally	2 do	1.03
William Saunders	3 do	1.50
Charles Lewis	Indian Wampam Necklace	.75
William Sterret	pair short boots	2.50
Alexnader Henderson	one gold watch	42.50
William Saunders	6 gold rings	3.00
Jesse Bennett	4 do	1.50
William Saunders	5 do	2.00
John Henderson	6 do	2.08
Robert Slaughter	5 do $1.25 6 -$1.55	2.80
Allyn Prior	4 do	1.20
John Allen	3 do	1.00
Robert Slaughter	5 do	1.39
Charles Lewis	4 gold rings	1.15 page B-112
William Saunders	6 do at $2 3 do at .80	2.80
Andrew Donnally	4 do	1.07
William Clendinen	4 do	1.09
Goouch Slaughter	5 do	1.35
Richard Slaughter	4 do	1.10
George Tylor	4 do 1 broken	.81
Andrew Donnally	4 do	1.16

Appendix 2

Robert Slaughter	2	do		.59
James Tylor	2	do		.56
Peter Hogg	6	do	one pair horse locks	1.76
				$1228.58

I certify that the above is a fair statement of the property as aforesaid
Attest   Anselum Tupper   Will Sanders Adm & Co
           Clerk of the auction   Part.with said Rogers

Kanhawa County November Court 1801
This vindue sale of the estate of Bennet Rogers decd was presented in Court by William Saunders Administrator of the estate aforesaid which is examined by the Court & the same is ordered to be recorded

teste   John Reynolds CKC

Kanawha B-86
do=ditto
A List of property belonging to the Heirs of Bennett Rodgers now in my possession To wit. One gold watch, One hundred and seven Rings, one broad cloth straight coat(London Brown) one pair Breeches of the same, one pair of catton slips, one pair of nankeen Pantaloons, one do of cloath, two waistcoats, two pair white silk stockings, two do of white cotton stockings, two do of mixed cotton, four Silk Handkerchieffs, four do of cotton & one do of Bandana, three shirts, two neck handkerchieffs(plain white) & pad two yards & three quarter of hair ribbon one raizor & shaving box, one Powder bag & puff, one beeded stock, one night cap, eight yards of coarse tow linen doubled & sewed together, one pair of half boots, one pair shoes, one ink stand, one piece of sealing wax, one belt one Holster & two pistols & powder flask, one riding whip, one old wool hat, one spoon, one hatchet, one Great Coat, part of skean of corse thread, piece of pomatom & one syringe.

William Sterrett

Kanawha County Deed Book B-181,182
October 1st 1802
Agreeable to an Order of Kanawha Court bearing date September Court, We the Subcribers hath appraised the estate of William Sanders decd as follows the articles brought forward (Viz)

&=pound   /=pence   (&=pound)   pence

No.1 Hannah & children &200 Cash in hand &191.24p	&391	2	4 1/2
One Bay Mare &25, Sorrell Ditto &6	31	0	0
One bed & furniture &12 Alsburys Bond &22	34	0	0
Pewter Bason 6/ Do 6/ 3 Plates 3/		15	0
One Iron kettle 21/6 Pott 21/10p	2	3	4
Frying Pann 7/6 Bake Hoe 9/ Tin Kettle 6/	1	2	
Trunk &1,10 Whipsaw & file &3 Weedg Hoe 7/6	4	17	0
Spade 9/ mattock 9/ parcel of nails 18p	1	16	
Plain 18/6 4 earthen plates 8p Dish 2/	1	8	6

Appendix 2

Pewter Tea Pott 6p/3 Box of glass 16/8	1	2	8
Sickle 6/ Leather straps 12/ Swingleing trees & hangings	1	6	0
Table-cloth 3/ 37 lb Iron 27/9	1	10	9
Pewter Dish 10/ pools ax 4/	0	14	0
Set of Candle moles 6/ stock lock 6/ potrack 10/	1	2	0
20 lb old Iron 6/ Tankard 6/ 2 lines 9p	0	11	9
claw hammer 1/6 Smoathing 4/ Copper Coffee Pott 4/	0	9	6
Notched Clevis 3/ 2 ditto & pines 3/ 2 Bridles 5/	0	11	0
wheel 18/ old hoe 3/ 2 knives & forks 4/6	1	5	6
old Bagg 2/ 2 wine sifters 5/	0	7	0
Cow & Calf &3,12 one steer 36/	5	8	0
No Sampson Sanders agrees	&482	13	5
Ader & her children &170 Cash in hand &35	&205	0	0
Bed & Furniture &12 G mare &15	27	0	0
Small bed &3,12 coffe mill 20p Pew Bason	5	0	0
3 pew Plates 4/ I kettle &1,6,10	1	10	10
Dutch oven 12/ Pott 6/ Tea kettle 15/		33	0

Appendix 3

Jack Neal

information from LDS microfim entitled
" Kanawha County Records 1791-1831" V150-92. West Virginia Archives and History Library. This is a typed copy of the original records.
(probably Court Minutes but not so identified)

Entries to the arrest and trial of Jack Neal and five other black men accused of killing Bennett Rogers, trader 1801 at the mouth of the Kanawha River. - Other material is found in Kanawha County Deed Book 1

p249

At a Court of Oyer & Terminer held at the Court House of Kanawha County on Monday the 17th day of August in the year of our Lord, one thousand eight hundred & one, & of the Commonwealth of Virginia the Twenty Sixth for the Trial of Jack Neale, Bob, Sam Robinson, Tom Lyle and Dick Rollans, Negro slaves, who belonged to a certain Bennett Rodgers late & c, who stand committed to the common Jail charged with feloneus Killing and murdering the said Bennett Rodgers & Ralph Elliott.

Present: Leonard Morris, Andrew Donnally, Samuel Shrewsbury, George Alderson, Thomas Rodgers & Obediah Fugua. Gentlemen.

p250
comm vs Tom Lyle, Negro man slave an indictment
    Prisoner held not guilty. Discharged.
comm vs Jack Neale an indictment
    for the murder of Bennett Rodgers in the first degree
    Bob, Sam Robinson, Tom Hecks & Dick Rollans as guilty of murder

Appendix 3

of Bennett Rodgers in the second degree Plea not guilty
comm vs Dick Rollans Negro slave an indictment- not guilty, Acquited.
comm vs Sam Robinson Negro slave an indictment- not guilty, Acquited.
comm vs Tom Hicks-not guilty, Acquited.
comm vs Bob, Negro slave- not guilty, Acquited.
comm vs Jack Neale an indictment

p251
The said Jack Neal being seized an in the custody of the sheriff of this county, and it being examined whether he was guilty of the murder wherewith he now stands charged or not guilty. He said he was in no wise guilty thereof. Where upon divers witnesses were produced, sworn & examined against said Jack Neale & he was fully heard as well by himself as the Counsel assigned by the Court in his own defence. Whereupon it seems to the Court here that the said Jack Neal is guilty of the murder aforesaid & it being demanded of him if anything he had to say for himself why the Court should not procede to Judgement & Execution against him. Said he had nothing to say but what he had already said. Therefore, It is considered by the Court that he (be) hanged by the neck untill he is dead. And it is said to the Sheriff of this county that he cause the execution thereof be done on Saturday the Nineteenth day of September next, precisely at two o'clock in the afternoon. Which said slave was valued at One hundred pounds.

Ordered that Thomas Dobbyns be allowed his jailers fees out of the hire of said Negroes.

Ordered Joseph Ruffner & Thomas Rodgers, Gentlemen: be appointed to superintend the erection of a gallows where they shall think most proper. Court adjourned.

p270 10 nov 1801
By Council of William Sanders (Adm of Bennett Rodgers - murdered by a certain Jack Neal now in prison, a Negro slave under sentence of death.) And whereas the said Jack Neal was not executed on the day appointed, It is ordered that Tom Lyle, a Negro slave, the only witness against the said Jack Neal be detained in custody of the sheriff of this County until a return from executive authority of the Commonwealth.

p304 10 aug 1802
At a Court of Criminal Jurisdiction specially summoned and convened at hte Court house of Kanawha County on the 10th day of August 1802 for the purpose of identifying and awarding execution------- against Jack Neal, a Negro man slave, who is now in custody of this County & who has been legally tried and condemed by a Court of Oyer and Terminer summoned and convened at the Court House on Monday the 17th day of August 1801.

p328 4 apr 1803
On the petition of Jack Warner(alias Jack Neal) who is detained in slavery by William Sanders, he is allowed to sue his said master in this Court for his freedom, in forma pauperis and the said Jack Warner (alias Jack Neal) gives Francis A. Dubois, Gilbert Christian, Angus Daggs, Zachariah Estill, Thomas Ray and Thomas Dobyn for his security, the sum of $500.00 unto George Alderson, David Ruffner, Thomas Rodgers and William Morris, Gentlemen

Appendix 3

Justices of the County of Kanawha, and their successors in the sum aforesaid, for the said Jack Warner's (alias Jack Neal) appearance at the next quarterly Court and then abide by the judgement of the said Court. And it is ordered that the Sheriff hire out the said Jack Warner (alias Jack Neal) for the benefit of William Sanders the legal representative of Bennett Rodgers,decd. until the decision of the aforesaid suit according to Law.

p335   15 Jun 1803

Ordered that the petition of Jack Warner (alias Jack Neal) brought against William Sanders, adm of Bennett Rodgers decd., at the April Court last for the purpose of proving his freedom, be dismissed, no vouchers being produced to prove the same and that the sheriff of this county take him into his custody as the property of William Sanders, to be delivered up when proper application is made.

Appendix 4A

Martha Sanders Records
" Kanawha County Records 1791-1831" V150-92. West Virginia Archives and
History Library. This is a typed copy of the original records.

p309   15 Sep 1802

On motion of Martha Sanders, widow and Relict of William Sanders decd, who made oath thereto, and together with Thomas Ward, James Jorden entered into and acknowledged their bond in the Penalty of three thousand pounds conditioned as the Law directs certificate is granted her for obtaining letters of Admininstration of the estate of the deceased in due time.

Ordered that Thomas Ward, Jeremiah Ward, John Russell & Henry Hampton or any three of them being first sworn before a justice of the Peace for this county do appraise in current money the slaves (if any) and personal estate of William Sanders deceased and return the appraisement thereof to the next Court.

p310

Sampson Sanders, orphan of William Sanders decd., made choice, with approbation of the Court, of Martha Sanders for his guardian who together with H.(Cammaick- McCormack?), Nehemiah Wood, Joseph Ruffner Jr., and James Jordin, his securities entered into and acknowledged their bond with penalty of one thousand pounds with conditions according to Law.

p334   (14 Jun 1803)

This day Martha Sanders widow and relict of William Sanders decd comes into & acknowledged herself satisfied with the division which was made by the appraisers of the descendent estate & takes the part No. 3, a childs part, and the same is ordered recorded by the court.

Kanawha B-175
Know all men by these presents that we Martha Sanders, Joseph Ruffner Jr., James Jorden, Nehemiah Woods, & W.H.Cavendish are held & firmly bound unto Francis Walker, David Ruffner, John Rousch, Obadiah Fuqua Gentlemen Justices of Kanawha County & their sussessers in the just & full sum of one thousand pounds, to which payment well & truly to be made, We bind ourselves our heirs, executors & administrators jointly & severally firmly by these presents sealed with our seals & dated this 16th day of September 1802(two).

Whereas the above bound Martha Sanders hath been this day appointed Guardian of

Appendix 4A

Sampson Sanders a minor until he shall attain the age of Twenty One years, now the condition of this obligation is that if the said Martha shall take good care of such estate of the said Sampson as has or may come into her hands & possession & the same to use & employ to and for the benefit of the said Sampson according to law & a time account of her actings & doings therein shall render when legally called on & finally when the said Sampson shall attain to the age of Twenty One Years shall account with settle & pay to him his heirs & whatever monies or other property which may remain in her hands belonging or due to him then this obligation to be void and of none office otherwise to remian in full force & c.

Duly Acknowledged in Court		Martha Sanders	(SEAL)
Teste John Reynolds CKC	Joseph Ruffner Jr. (SEAL)	James Jorden	(SEAL)
	Nehemiah Wood (SEAL)	W.H.Cavendish	(SEAL)

Kanawha County Deed Book B-176

Know all men by these presents that we Martha Sanders, Thomas Ward & James Jorden held & firmly bound unto Frances Walker, William Clendinen, John Rousch & Joseph Ruffner Gentlemen Justices in commission of the Peace of the County of Kanawha in the State of Virginia in the penal sum of Three Thousand pounds lawful money of Virginia which payment well & truly to be made unto the said Francis Walkers(Watkins), William Clendinen, John Rousch & Joseph Ruffner-We bind ourselves our heirs, Exors, Administrator and assigns firmly by these presents In Witness whereof we have hereunto affixed our hands and seals the 16th day of September in the Year 1802

      The condition of this obligation is, that if the said Administration of all the Goods, Chattels, Credits of William Sanders deceased do make a true & perfect Inventory of all & Singular the Goods, Chattels & Credits of the said deceased; which have or shall come to the hands, possession or knowledge of the said Martha, or into the hands or possession of any other person or persons for her & the same so made do exhibit unto the County Court of Kanawha at such time as she shall be hereunto required by the said Court and the same Goods, Chattels & Credits do well & truly administer according to Law & make a just & true account of her acting & doing therein when thereunto required by the said Court & shall deliver & pay unto each persons respectively as are entitled to the same by law; and if it shall hereafter appear that any last will & testament was made by the deceased and the same be proved in Court & the executor obtain a Certificate of the Probate thereof, and the said Martha do as such case being required render & deliver up her letters of Administration then this obligation to be void.

Signed Sealed & Acknowledged	Martha Sanders (SEAL)
in Court	Thos.Ward (SEAL)
John Reynolds CKC	James Jorden (SEAL)

Kanawha County Deed Book B-95

      This indenture made this fourteeth day of September in the year one thousand eight hundred and two between Thomas Kilgore of the County of Kanawha & state of Virginia and Hetty his wife of the one part & Martha Sanders of said County of the other part. Witnesseth that the said Thomas Kilgore for and in consideration of the sum of two hundred pounds lawful money of Virginia in hand paid to the said Thomas Kilgore the expect whereof he doth hereby Acknowledge & confess he the said Thomas Kilgore that garanteed bargained sold & delivered & by these presents doth grant Bargain sell & deliver unto the aforesaid Martha Sanders one certain tract or parcel of land containing two hundred & fifty acres being part of two certain tracts or parcels of land granted to John P. Duvall by patent which said Duvall deeded to Thomas Kilgore lying & being in the county of Kanawha & on Mud River & bounded as followeth, Beginning at & elm & mulberry on the west bank of Mud River at the mouth of a small creek below the house of the said Martha Sanders thence up the river according to

Appendix 4A

several small meanders & bending thereon two hundred & twenty sight poles to a beech on the edge of the river bank & two white oaks in the narrows thence South thirty two degrees West one hundred & fifty four & three quarters Poles to three Maple together from one rock about ten poles East of a branch, thence North fifty eight degrees West one hundred & ninety eight Poles crossing said at ten poles & other branches to a sour wood, Beech, Popular & White Oak on side of a flat hill about six poles north of a wet drain thence North thirty two degrees East two hundred & eleven Poles to the Begining. To have and to hold the said two hundred & fifty Acres with the appurtenances unto the said Martha Sanders her Heirs & Assigns forever & said Thomas Kilgore & Hetty his wife, for themselves and their heirs by these presents Covenant to & with the said Martha Sanders her heirs & assigns, That they the said Thomas Kilgore & Hetty his wife the aforesaid two hundred & fifty Acres of land, the the appurtenances unto the said Martha Sanders her heirs & assigns will warrant & forever defend against all persons whatsoever, In Witness whereof the said Thomas Kilgore & Hetty his wife to these presents have set their hands & Seals the day & year first written.

Witness Present		Thomas Kilgore (seal)
Thos. Ward	Martin Hull	her
Henry Hampton	Michael Holland	Hetty Kilgore (seal)
John Russell	Jeremiah Ward Jr.	mark
Joseph Chenwith	Kanawha County Dec. Court 1802 Clk John Reynolds	

Appendix 4B

Martha Sanders - Cabell County

Martha Sanders inventory Will Book 1-101

11	horses or mares	10	steers
4	milch cows	6	heifers
1	bull	4	calves
1	yoke work oxen & yoke	44	sheep
138	head hogs	30-50	suckling pigs
10	stacks hay	1	stack oats
1	field of corn on river	1	field above house 15a
	below house - 50a	1	field-hillside above Malcombs 7a

(Lunsford having cropped with Martha to receive 1/4 all corn)

	plows, plows gears	2	scythes & cradles
1	old barshear	1	ox cart & body
	pr wagon wheels	1	flax brake
	barrels		wash kettle
1	salt barrell	1	ax (at Jeremiah Kilgore's)
1	dutch oven & broken lid	3	dutch scythes, hangers & threads
#1	skillet & lid	2	iron bakers
1	funnel	1	old coffee pot
1	bread tray	1	stew kettle (supposed to belong
12	split bottom chairs		to Sampson Sanders)
1	arm chair	4	stands bees
1	rifle gun	1	lot unrolled flax(1/4 belongs to (Lewis Lunsford)
1	grind stone	5	bed steads & pieces of cord
1	small spinning wheel	2	beds & bedding (3 of the beds are claimed by Mrs. Kilgore, 1 by Martha Kilgore, 1 by Malinda Kilgore)
1	pr traces		
1	basket of pewter		
3	weavers reeds & 1 basket		
4	counterpanes	1	chest containg 1 pieces of jeans

Appendix 4B

2 pieces white cotton cloth
1 piece white lindsey
3 towels
5 sheets
linen
8 coverlids
3 counterpanes
some spun cotton
white & blue flax thread
table cloth
1 man's saddle
1 quilting wheel
1 piece pot rack
1 lid of wagon box
1 hammer strap for wagon
1 large spinning wheel
1 half bushel measure
1 pr shoe pinchers
1 sugar bowl
spoon moulds
1 small bag country sugar
4 stacks oats at James Chapman's
5 barrels supposed to be peach brandy
2 ditto 1/2 full
1 cotton gin

6 pieces checked cotton cloth
1 piece stripped linsey
some tobacco
1 wool bag
1 barrel wool
1 chest containing 1 sheet
1 pr cotton curtains
4 small pieces flax linen
1 small chest containing
1 basket with gourd inclosed
1 bag of cotton in seed
4 English grass scythes
1 German grass scythes
1 iron slider for wagon
1 pr old cards
4 feather beds & 5 pillows
1 churn
Josephus works in 2 Vol. & sundry other books, etc.
2 large bottles with honey, etc.
1 pr steel yards
1 lot of leather consisting of:
1 sheepskin
1 deer skin
1 kip skin (untanned calf,kid)
1 piece kip & some remmants of upper leather
2 sides upper
1 side & piece side sole leather put out to shoe the steers

Solomon Thornburg, Adm. of estate of Martha Sanders decd.

Appendix 4C

William and Martha Sanders Genealogy
William Sanders (17)-1801   Kanawha will
    m Martha Green(Gwinn) 1761-1831   Cabell will
        (possibly Loudoun County,   VA @1782)
  1 Hetty 27 feb 1783-1852   Cabell will   age 70
  2 Sampson m 1821 Ann Gwinn (Cabell) one girl both died young @1836-40
        1786-1849   Cabell will

Thomas & Hetty Sanders Kilgore m ? probably Kanawha 1801/2
    1 SHetty   b 27 feb 1783 VA (lived VA, NC, Sumner and Smith Co. TN)
d 8 apr 1852 (aged 70) buried Kilgore Cem. Milton, Cabell Co. VA

children
11 Emaline (Linie-)@1802-(1849)   m   Harry Ball Cabell Co.
    111. Telitha 1827
    112. Lafayette 1834   m   1856 Mary Gwinn   CCM
    113. Marietta
    114. Hetty Ann 1838
    115. Martha Ann 1841   m   1866 James Rece   CCM
    116. John D.S. 1849

Appendix 4C

```
12  George 1803-af1880              m  Elizabeth Margaret Newman  Cabell Co.
    121. Matthew inf                   (Geo d Boyd Co. KY)
    122. Eliza 1827-           m   1847 James Jordan
    123. Malinda 1828-         m   1856 (John Hatfield) or James Riggs
    124. James 1830-1912       m   1850  (1) Malinda Riggs
                               m         (2) Lucretia Alexander
    125. William 1831-         m   1854 Rachael McCune          CCM
    126. Martha 1834-          m   1878 James Jordan (sister)
    127. Mary 1836-            m   1854 Isaac Blake
    128. Sarah 1838-           m   1854 John Heath
    129. Elizabeth Margaret 1841-m 1856 (?) Geo.W.D.Williams
                               m   (2) Nancy Riggs pr 1850
13  Jeremiah (?) 1803-@1847       m   1821 Nancy Fullerton Law.Co.OH
    131. Mary Ellen            m   Rogers
    132. Eliza Jane            m   Samuel Johnson
    133. Hetty                 m   John Gwinn
    134. Julia                 m   James McKeand
    135. Thomas Gwinn 1822     m   Mary Jane Rogers
         (1860 CCcen)
14  Mary (Polly) 1806-1845        m 1823 William Simmons(d 1846)  Cabell Co.
    141. William
    142. Elizabeth 1822
    143. Conwelsey 1824            unmarried
    144. Ann  1834                 m   1853 Peter E. Love         CCM
    145. Malinda 1838
    146. Naomi 1841            m   George Gallaher
    147. Sampson 1842          m   1870 Agnes Ruffner             CCM
    148. Mary Frances 1844     m   Dr. Bennett Clay Vinson
15  Martha Green 1819-1897        m   Charles K. Morris       Cabell Co.
    (given in Dusenberry)
    151. Mary 1839             m   1855 Dr. V. R. Moss            CCM
    152. Ellen 1842            m   1880 Arthur Williams           CCM
    153. John A. 1845          m   1866 Emily Gwinn               CCM
    154. James J. 1847
    155. Edna E. 1849          m   1870 T. Heven Rece             CCM
    154. Ida K. 1855           m   1880 T.S. Berkely              CCM
    155. Charles R. 1859       m   Myrtle Ayers
16  Malinda    1822-1855           m   Thomas Lee Jordan
    161. Ella
    162. John
    163. Charles
    164. Mary
    165. Martha
```

Appendix 5A

Cabell county Will Bk 2 pg 19-29
page 19 Appraisment bill and bill of sale of the personal estate of Sanders

	SAMPSON SANDERS(decd)		February 25th 1850	Sale
30	pieces of china appraised	$ 3.00	sold to John L. Everett	$3.00
5	dishes	1.00	Sidney Bowden	.80
17	plates	1.00	Milton P. Spurlock	.75
3	covered dishes	1.50	Sidney Bowden	1.30
10	cups & saucers			
	4 bowls & 2 pitchers	1.50	Thomas Kyle	1.30
6	ps glass ware	.75	Chas. Morris	.85
1/2	doz silver spoons	9.00	Wm. C. Dusenbury	7.85
11	silver tea spoons	6.00	same	4.80
4	salt do & tongs	4.00	same	2.30
18	knives & 4 forks	1.50	Milton J. Spurlock	1.40
9	ps tinware, 5 iron spoons			
	Brittania Teapot	2.50	P. H. M. McCullough	1.90
1	tin safe	3.00	Armstead Howell	4.25
2	candle sticks			
	2 rea waiters & snuffers	.75	Joseph W. Roffe	.31
4	sad irons	1.00	John Hensley	.90
1	dining table	4.00	Joseph Foster	3.95
1	stand	.50	same	.62
1	pr side tables & covers	10.00	Charles Morris	8.25
1	stand table	1.00	Daniel (at appt)	1.00
1	clock	3.00	Oliver Fuller	2.25
1	looking glass	1.25	John A. Everett	.70
1	large cushion chair	1.00	Sidney Bowden	1.00
3	calico widow curtains	.75	Elizabeth Like	.75
1	bedstead & bedding	18.00	Cynthia (at appt)	18.00
1	" "	15.00	Emberson Turley	12.13
1	Map of U.States & book	3.00	George Kilgore	2.50
1	Gilt Mirror	5.00	George K. Morris	4.25
1	2 drawer stand	2.00	Elizabeth Like	2.00
1	Settie & Cushion	3.00	same	3.00
1	bureau	8.00	CASH	9.70
1	bureau	6.00	Theodore Adkins	6.62
2	fenders	5.00	Chas. Morris	2.00
1	sett Andirons	.75	same	.65
1	lot of books	10.00	H. J. Samuels	3.50
1	split box & s barszine	.50	CASH	.50
4	white window curtains	2.00	Elizabeth Like	2.00
1	carpet	4.00	same	4.00
6	table cloths	4.00	Chas. Morris	3.00
4	wondow curtains & 4 towels	2.50	Chas. Collins	1.12
rosin		.40	would not sell	.00
1/4 bbl vinegar		1.00	Chas. Morris	1.00
2	bbl vinegar at $3.00 each	6.00	same	2.31
1 1/2	keg 4d nails	9.00	same	5.00
1 1/2	keg 8d nails	7.50	James Gallaher	5.00
1/2	keg 10d nails	2.50	same	1.38
1	pr steelyards			

Appendix 5A

	Item	Price	Buyer	Price
	paint keg & belting	.75	sold - George Gallaher	.60
1	bedstead & bedding	18.00	Emilly Butcher	15.00
1	" "	15.00	Mary (at appt)	15.00
1	bedstead & bedding	15.00	Rowland Bias Jr.	13.00
1	" "	15.00	Daniel (at appt)	15.00
1	trundle bedstead & bedding	10.00	Wm. C. Dusenbury	8.25
1	tick & feathers	7.00	Elizabeth Like	7.00
1	looking glass	.25	Chesley B. Davis	.55
1	chest	.25	same	.25
	pg 1	$255.15		$214.79

page 20

	Item	Price	Buyer	Price	
2	little wheels	5.00	CASH	2.75	
2	bbls, bow * harnis leather	1.00	George Gallaher	.75	
2	cotton window blinds	.12	Chesley B. Davis	.10	
1	lot of old carpet	1.00	Luke (by appt)	1.00	
1	bedstead & bedding	18.00	Emberson Turley	16.87	
1	" "	16.00	Thomas Kyle	16.12	
2	yds lindsey	.50	Chesley B. Davis	.31	
8	pieces linen	7.00	T. L. Jordan		
			at $.13 yd	6.59	
1	sett bed curtains	1.00	William Messinger	.50	
4	quilts	12.00	George Kilgore 2	3.00	
			Thomas Kilgore 1	2.00	
			Mathew Thompson 1	3.00	
1	white counterpane	1.50	George Kilgore	1.00	
2	blankets	5.00	Zachariah Nicely	3.30	
3	coverlids	6.00	same 1	1.00	5830
			Mathew Thompson 1	2.25	
			CASH	3.00	
2	comforts	5.00	P.L. Keller	3.00	
1	large chest	.50	Samuel Scott	.75	
1	bureau & mirror	15.00	Thos.W. Kilgore	18.12	
12	bales cotton yarn & sack	10.00	W.C. Miller	9.60	
2	new hats	6.00	John G. Miller	2.25	
2	leather trunks	1.50	George Killgore	1.75	
2	parts of sacks of coffee	10.00	Robt.B.Thompson	9.22	
			105 1/2 lb at 8 3/4		
	part of barrel of sugar	3.50	H.J. Samuels	1.50	
1	barrel such & peaches	.50	J.L. Everett	.25	
1	box 5 jars honey	3.50	Chas. Everett	1.50	
1	keg tallow	.62	John A. Everett	.70	
7	weavers reads & temples	.25	Andrew Sexton	1.25	
1	old shot gun leather	.50	George W. Plott	.50	
1	pc carpet	.25	Charles Morris	.37	
	about 70lb. rolls	20.00	Chas.L. Roffe	20.00	
1	lot picked wool & coverlid	6.00	George. W. Plott	4.72	
	4 bbls. unpicked wool	3.00	Mrs.Dolen 3 bbl	2.02	
			Emily Butcher 1 bbl	.12	1/2
1	peck clover seed & barrell	1.00	Milton P. Spurlock	.62	1/2

Appendix 5A

3	empty barrels & 3 boxes	.50	Chelsey B. Davis	.37	1/2
1	lot venetian blinds	1.00	Charles Morris	1.50	
1	new saddle (man's)	8.00	William Childers	8.75	
20	chairs	5.00	Chesley B. Davis .31	6.20	
1	home made carpet	5.00	George Kilgore	5.50	
1	cot	.50	Emily Butcher	.12	1/2
1	still & apparatus	10.00	Wm. C. Dusenberry	16.75	
3	kitchen tables	1.50	Samuel Hensley 1	1.00	
			Mrs. Dolen 1	.18	
			Rolan Bias 1	.13	
1	hackle	.50	Charles Morris	.25	
1/2	of cleaver	1.00	Charles L. Roffe	1.00	
1	coffee mill	.12	Zachariah Nicely	.19	
	shovel & tongs	.50	Mathew Thompson	.25	
	Tea Kettle, griddle, skillet, frying pan	1.00	Roland Bias	.55	
1	barrell of lime & wash tub	1.00	Charles Morris	.50	
1	water bucket & 2 cups	.12	R. N. B. Thompson	.26	
1	pr. andirons	.50	James Gallaher	.25	
				185.58	

page 21

1	knife box	.12	Mrs. Dolen		.05
1	crow bar & sledge	3.00	Luke (at appt)		3.00
13	axes	8.00	John A. Everett	1	.50
			Green Harrison	10	1.50
			Daniel (at appt)	1	.62
1	broad ax	1.00	Thomas A. Childers		1.20
5	mattaxe & 1 sprouting hoe	5.00	Royal A. Childers	1	1.05
			Charles Morris	2	1.68
			Zachariah Nicely	1	.60
			Hy Hawkins	1	.50
			Conwesley Simmons	1	.75
1	briar scythe	.50	Thomas A. Childers		.25
5	weeding hoes	2.50	Charles Morris	2	.77 1/2
			R.N.B. Thompson	2	.15
2	shovels	.50	William Morris		.50
5	bull tongues & 2 shovel plows	4.50	Charles Morris		4.12
1	dog wedge & iron wedge	1.00	Henry Smith iron wdg		.50
			Wm. Gallaher dog wdg		1.00
1	pr. stretchers	1.00	Luke (at appr)		1.00
1	lot of chain in barrell	4.75	William Morris		1.75
1	post boxes & bar	1.50	Watson Davis		.62
1	lot of old iron	10.00	same including 1 ax-1 hoe		4.50
1	big clevis & bell	1.00	Charles Morris		.50
1	lot of Mowing scythes	10.00	George Kilgore	2	2.66
			James Newman	2	1.42

Appendix 5A

			Samuel Scott	1	.35	
			Pat W. Thompson	1	.87	1/2
			R.N.B. Thompson	1	1.25	
			Zach Nicely	1	1.35	
			William Smith	1	.75	
4	old scythe blades	.50	Watson Davis		.55	
1	stone hammer, 2 picks, chisel	1.00	Luke (at appt)		1.00	
1	griindstone	1.50	Emberson Turley		.81	
1	spinning machine	1.00	Charles Morris		.50	
1	reel	1.00	Nutton Childers		.62	1/2
2	large spinning wheels	2.00	same		1.75	
1	cannon stove	2.00	Luke (at appt)		2.00	
2	grain shovels & spade	1.00	(no spade) R.B.N. Thompson		.40	
	Grass seed & bathing tub	1.50	Henry J. Samuels		.50	
1	lot of hoop iron	2.00	William Morris		.75	
1	lot of corn	8.00	Samuel Scott		3.05	
	can & oil	.50	Charles Morris		.50	
1	well bucket & chain	1.00	same		.37	
1	wooden churn	1.00	Samuel Scott		.30	
	Stone ware	4.24	Charles Morris		2.75	
1	barrel sugar	15.00	F.G.L. Beuhring		11.12	
4	large kettles & bales	7.00	Watson Davis	1	1.31	
			Charles Morris	1	1.00	
			Richard McCallister	2	2.94	
1	wheelbarrow	3.00	Charles Morris		2.50	
3	tubs	1.50	F. G. L. Beuhring		.80	
1	copper kettle	3.00	John L. Everett		2.25	
1	brass kettle	1.00	Thomas Kilgore Sr.		1.00	
4	ovens	2.00	Rowland Bias Sr.		1.75	
2	skillets	.50	Alex McCallister		.50	
1	stew kettle & pot	.75	Charles Morris		.87	1/2
					77.66	1/2

page 22

1	pot rack, 2 ladles, big fork, 2 shovels, 1 large frying pan, gridiron, hone(horn), & strainer	1.50	Richard McCallister	1.25	
1	lot old (jowls ?)	.25	Charles Morris	.06	
1	large salt kettle	5.00	Alex. Johnston	1.87	
3	1/2 bbls salt	8.00	William Morris 1 bbl	2.25	
			Charles Morris 1 bbl	2.25	
			M. J. Spurlock 1 1/2 bbl	2.60	
1	bbl lard	12.00	Charles L. Roffe	12.00	
	part bbl of grease	.50	Samuel Hensley	.10	
46	new pork barrels	30.00	Thomas A. Childers	20.12	
4	log chains	8.00	Thos. R. Hope 1 at	2.00	
			Chas. Morris 1 at	1.62	
			J. S. Everett 1 at	.87	
			Edmund McGinnis 1 at	.38	
1	timber cart	15.00	Charles Morris	19.25	

Appendix 5A

1	ox cart No.1	10.00	W. C. Dusenbury	6.00	
1	" " No.2	8.00	Wm. Morris	10.50	
1	lot of flooring plank	10.00	George W. Plote	10.00	
1	" oak plank	3.00	Chas. Morris	1.50	
1	" " "	3.00	Geo. F. Miller	3.50	
1	lot locust post	1.00	same-27 posts-3 1/2c	.95	
1	lot plank	8.00	John T. Hibbins	7.00	
12	Bee Stands & Hives	24.00	Peter 2 (at appt)	4.00	
			Daniel 2 (at appt)	4.00	
			Luke 2 (at appt)	4.00	
			Rowland Bias 1 at	1.75	
			Chas. Morris 2 at	2.75	
			John Samuels 1 at	3.00	
			Chas. Morris 2 at	3.12	
7	empty gums	1.75	same	.25	
1	subsoil plow	6.00	James Gallaher	4.00	
1	ox plow	4.00	Luke (at appt)	4.00	
1	crane plow	1.00	John Guinn	1.25	
1	horse plow & singletree	2.00	George Killgore	1.75	
1	McCormick plow	1.50	Henry Medley	.75	
4	shovel plows & singletrees	6.00	Chas. Morris	3.37	
1	harrow(small) & singletree	1.50	Wm. Morris	.87 1/2	
1-2	horse harrow	4.00	Chas. Morris	3.25	
1	scraper	3.00	Luke (at appt)	3.00	
1	old cultivator	.75	Theodore Adkins	.25	
1	old waggon	10.00	Chas. Morris	8.25	
1	left handed plow	6.00	Calvin (at appt)	6.00	
1	shelling machine	2.50	Samuel W. Johnson	6.87	
2	hay & 1 dung fork	1.30	Wm. Morris 1 at	.15	
			Mathew Lusher 1 at	.15	
			Alexr. Newman 1 at	.20	
1	pair brickbands	3.00	R. N. B. Thompson	.75	
4	blind bridles	2.00	Isaac Blake 2 at	1.87	
			Conwelsy Simmons 1	1.75	
4	setts single gear entire	8.00	Wm. Morris 1 sett	1.15	
			Conwelsy Simmons 1	1.25	
			Jesse Martin 1 at	1.25	
			Chas. Morris 1 at	2.75	
1	collar line & brush	1.25	Isaac Blake	.63	
2	bakets & 2 hipstraps	1.25	J.T. Hibbins(baskets)	.18 3/4	
				185.39 1/4	

page 23

1-4	horse waggon	50.00	Conwelsy Simmons	35.00	Sanders
1	stone crane and apparatus	5.00	W. C. Dusenbury	5.00	Sale
1	threshing machine	10.00	Luke (at appt)	10.00	
1	box Randal grass seed	1.00	W.C. Dusenbury	.75	
1	lot of plank at barn	1.00	Chas. Morris	1.13	
1	" " " " "	5.00	J.T. Hibbins	1.50	
1	mans saddle	5.00	Peter (at appt)	5.00	

Appendix 5A

1	watch	10.00	Isaac Blake		9.50	
1	stone mattock, vice, hoe, clevis & sundries	3.50	Johnson Lusher		.30	Lusher
			Chas. Morris clevis		.50	hoe & c
			Wm. Morris stone, iron		2.10	mattock
			Philip Bumgardner		.50	vice
			James Gallaher		.25	sundries
1	log chain	2.00	Alexr. Johnston		1.75	
9	stacks hay	90.00	John Garrison 3 at		29.00	
			Chas. K. Morris	2	9.12	
			Martin Moore	1	7.00	
			Conwelsy Simmons	1	4.00	
	Field of corn below house	275.00	Charles Morris		155.00	
1	bar iron	2.00	Alexr. Johnson		2.00	
2	large & 2 small oatstacks	25.00	George Gallaher		13.00	
4	oat stacks	35.00	George Gallaher		29.00	
8	" "	70.00	Chas. Morris		48.00	
1	field corn (R. Bottom)	150.00	George Gallaher		105.00	
4	hay stacks	30.00	Wm. C. Dusenbury	1	5.00	
			George Gallaher	1	6.50	
			James Morris	1	7.25	
			Wm. C. Dusenbery	1	3.00	
			" " "	2	1.50	
4	hay stacks	20.00	Conwelsy Simmons	3	5.50	
	Corn in pond	4.00	Andrew Dotson		5.25	
1	vice	8.00	Watson Davis		7.75	
3	pr blacksmith tongs	.75	cash		.75	
	about 40 lbs spun yarn at 44 cts per lb.	17.60	Thos. Killgore		3.80	
			10 1/4 lb at	.37 1/2		
			St. Mark Russell		4.72	
			11 1/2 lb at	.41		
			Thomas Ward		6.36	
			16 lb at	.46		
			Isaac Blake		5.97	
			13 1/4 lb at	.45		
			Saml. Childers		4.16	
			9 1/4 lb at	.45		
	Hay in stable	2.00	Chas. Morris		1.00	
	Hay in Cow House	9.00	same		3.00	
	Clover hay in barn	7.50	same		3.00	
1	stone auger	1.00	Luke (at appt)		1.00	
	Garden	2.50	Charles Morris		5.50	
	Buckwheat at 50	6.00	Luke -31pr Bush	12	3.75	
2	clothes brushes	.25	Peter Martin		.50	
1	billows	12.00	L.S. Keller		8.00	
1	anvil	12.00	same		8.88	
	9 3/4 lb round iron	.45	same		.35	
	43 lbs new bar iron	1.72	Johnson Lusher		1.00	
1	large pr of wheels & c	30.00	Wm.C. Dusenbury		30.50	
	Brick	80.00	George Gallaher		42.75	

Appendix 5A

Lot of flax		2.50	James Gallaher	7.00
Grindstone			Wm. Morris	1.15
				659.29

page 24

2	barrels salt	5.00	Henry W. Shelton	5.10
1	barrel wool	1.50	John T. Hibbins	.80
1	cart & chain	25.00	George Gallaher	16.00
1-2	horse harrow	5.00	George Killgore	4.50
1	old cart	6.00	James Bumgardner	3.25
1-1	horse harrow	1.75	Henry W. Shelton	1.25
1	" "	1.00	" "	.75
1	" "	.50	" "	.25
1	painted plow	2.00	George Kilgore	1.10
2	old shovel plows	3.00	Wm. Morris	1.30
2	large cast plows	2.00	same	1.00
1	dung & 1 pitch fork	1.00	Chas. L. Roffe	.75
2	old double trees	1.00	Alexr. Newmaan	.75
5	weeding hoes	1.50	James Shelton	1.35
2	new axes	1.50	James Gallaher 1 at	1.25
			Johnson Lusher 1 at	.75
2	sprouting hoes	1.00	Peter Blake	.70
5	old axes	3.00	Charles (1 at)	.50
			Moses (1 at)	.63
			James Shelton 3 at	.45
4	mattocks	3.00	G.Killgore & C.Simmons	2.62
1	Flax Hackle	.75	Danl. Love	.45
1	shovel	.25	James Gallaher	.50
3	iron wedges		same	.81
4	bull tongues, 3 shovel plows, 1 barstrin	2.00	Irvin Lusher	1.05
1	old shovel & single tree	.50	James Shelton	.37
1	lot of old iron & steel	5.00	William Morris	3.75
1	pr sheep shears	.25	James Bumgardner	.37 1/2
3	brier scythes	1.50	Henry W. Shelton	1.35
3	mowing scythes & sneads	1.00	George Killgore	.37 1/2
1	cradle Blade	.50	James Bumgardner	.18
1	sett of gears entire	3.00	Irvin Lusher	2.30
1	" " "	3.00	Chas. Morris	1.62
1	" " "	2.50	Chas. Collins	1.81
1	" " "	3.00	James Shelton	1.25
3	sycles	.50	James Bumgardner	.12 1/2
3	flax rakes	.50	James Shelton	.25
1	large left hand plow	6.00	Peter (at appt)	6.00
1	wheat fan	10.00	James Gallaher	15.50
1	large right hand plow	9.00	Wm. Morris	9.00
1	cradle & scythe	1.00	Wm. Gallaher	1.00
1	" "	2.00	Chas. Collins	1.75
1	" "	1.75	George Gallaher	1.75
1	" "	1.75	Jehu Martin	1.25

Appendix 5A

1 " "		1.75
1 old wheat fan		1.00
1 old 1 horse harrow		1.00
1 new waggon		30.00
2 large spinning wheels		1.00
3 flax wheels		3.00
1 reel		.50
80 acres of corn		300.00
(p25)		
1 lot old iron		.25
7 stacks of oats		70.00
Hay in Barn		1.00
Wheat in Barn		1.00
15 sides upper leather		35.00
1 side of harness leather		3.00
2 -2 horse harrows		8.00
1 - 1 horse harrow		1.00
1 cultivator		1.00
1 ox wagon & body		25.00
1 large sled & chain		3.00
2 lead chains		1.50
1 ox cart		20.00
1 old waggon hind part		5.00
1 flax brake		.75
4 setts plow gears entire		4.00
1 lot of brick		10.00
1 lot of plank, scoutting, joists & laths		30.00
1 wheat fan		8.00

James Gallaher		1.00
James Bumgardner		2.00
Irvin Lusher		.80
Alexr. Johnston		25.00
Thos. Book 1 at		1.25
Chas. Collins 1 at		1.45
David Thornburg 1 at		.50
Robt. Stewart 1 at		.25
James Gallaher 1 at		2.25
Robt. Stewart		.75
Irwin Lusher 1 field		45.25
George Gallaher	1"	163.00
William Morris		.20
O.S. McGinnis 5 at		30.50
I.Lusher & G.Killgore	2	15.50
E.M. Underwood		1.00
Irvin Lusher		1.00
Chas. Collins 1 at		1.75
Solomon Thornburg	1	1.80
William Howard	1	1.70
Charles Collins	1	1.90
Rowland Bias	1	1.25
Chas. L. Roffe	1	1.30
Alexr. Johnson	1	2.00
Thos. S. Childers	1	1.15
Armstead Howell	1	1.15
Thomas McCallister	1	1.45
Henry Knight	1	1.65
James Files	1	1.85
Alexr. Johnson	1	2.05
Thos. J. McComas	1	1.70
Thos. Hatfield	1	1.85
Sidney Bowden		3.00
Vincent Newman	1	2.50
James Miller	1	3.50
Daniel Love		.75
John A. Everett		.75
George Gallaher		25.00
same		2.37
Thos. W. Killgore	1	.50
Jno. A. Everett	1	1.10
George Killgore		16.00
Sampson Hanley		3.00
Daniel Love		.40
Johnson Lusher	1	.55
James Newman	1	1.75
Daniel Love	1	1.30
Samuel Everett		6.40
Thos. W. Killgore		30.00
John Morris		11.00

Appendix 5A

3	large iron kettles	3.00	Charlotte (1 appt)	1.00	
			James Newman 1 at	.50	
			Absalom Biaas 1 at	1.62	
2	scythes & cradles	3.00	Eli (1 at appt)	1.50	
			Jehu Martin 1 at	1.25	
1	pea cock plow	1.50	Andrew Sheff	1.62 1/2	
1	improved McCormick	5.00	Levi (at appt)	5.00	
1	McCormick & colter	1.50	Absalom Bias	2.05	
1	new ground colter	.75	Thomas Scales	.50	
3	shovel plows 2 singletrees	5.00	Conwelsy Simmons	2.37	
1	old shovel plow	.50	Andrew Sexton	.25	
3	iron wedges	1.50	Mathew Thompson	1.25	
1	double 2 single trees	1.00	George Gallaher	.62 1/2	
1	double tree	.50	John M. Rece	.25	
3	bull tongues	1.50	Samuel Everett	1.00	
5	hoes	2.00	George Gallaher	1.50	
1	mattock	.75	John A. Everett	.75	
				207.645	
6	axes	3.00	George Gallaher	2.25	
1	shovel & a dung fork	1.25	Absalom Bias	1.70	
5	brier scythes	2.00	James Gallaher	1.50	
6	corn cutters	.75	David Harshbarger	.25	
1	lot of old iron & 2 sneads	2.00	P. Roushe	2.75	
1	wheat shovel	.12	St. Mark Russell	.12	
1	coffee mill	.12	Dr. P.H. McCullough	.25	
1	large still cap & worm	20.00	John Morris	18.12	
1	small still cap & worm	15.00	same	10.00	
2	large spinning wheel	1.00	Charlotte (1 appt)	.50	Sanders
			G.W. Simmons 1 at	.30	Sale
1	flax wheel	.75	Charlotte (at appt)	.75	3734
1/2	bu table salt	2.00	E.W. Hite	1.05	
1	grindstone	.50	George Gallaher	1.05	
1	blacksmith's hammer	.25	Solomon Thornburg	.25	
5	mowing scythes	6.00	Absalom Bias 1 at	1.20	
			George Gallaher 3 at	3.38	
			Thos. W. Killgore 1	1.37 1/2	
1	hogshead picked wool	5.00	Rowland Bias	5.35	
1	lot of wool	12.00	same	15.87	
1	wheat sive	.75	James Newman	.25	
5	old barrels	.25	Thos. W. Killgore	.10	
1	large spinning wheel	1.00	James Newman	1.65	
2	flax wheels	2.00	George Killgore	3.00	
1	frow	.37	J.T. Hibbins	.45	
1	dining table	.50	Solomon (at appt)	.50	
1	crosscut saw	2.00	Thos. W. Killgore	2.25	
1	potatoe patch	10.00	C. Morris & others	8.75	
1	loom	4.00	Amrstead Howell	3.00	
5	stacks oats & 40 shocks	45.00	Jacob Harshbarger	50.00	
8	wheat stacks	13.00	Thos. W. Killgore	27.00	

Appendix 5A

21 shocks oats	1.50	
crops of corn - Mud Farm	260.00	
7 hay stacks		
6/7 of unstacked hay	38.00	
1 stack of hay	6.00	
2 stacks of hay	20.00	
230 bush of oats	41.76	
129 3/4 bush wheat	84.33	
13 cords of wood $1 cord	13.00	
493 ft of plank	5.66	

Mat Thompson	1.25
Thos. Scales 1 field	27.50
John Morris 2 fields	41.00
John M. Rece 1 field	126.00
same 2 at	13.37
O.A. McGinnis 3 at	24.50
John Guinn 1 at	8.13
Warren Rece 1 at	9.37
John M. Rece	18.50
Jno. A. Everett	5.10
John Guinn	9.75
F.G.L.Beuhring 18ct	41.76
Alex. Johnson & others 65ct per bu	84.33
F.G.L.Beuhring	13.00
A. Laidley $1.15 per hundred	5.66
	394.18 1/2

1 mare "Flora"	85.00	
1 " "Sophia"	35.00	
1 grey mare "Kit"	5.00	
1 pr.young horse "Bells" at $45 each	90.00	
1 sorrel mare "Nancy Dawson"	10.00	
2 yearling colts $15 & $10	25.00	

page 27

1 mare "Pats"	15.00	
1 horse "Old Bill"	35.00	
1 bay horse "Paddy"	75.00	
1 mare "Dandy"	60.00	
1 bay stud colt	75.00	
17-2yr old steers & heifers	170.00	
8 cows & heifers	160.00	
5 dry cows at 14 each	70.00	
2 cows $17 & $13	30.00	

Cynthia (at appt)	85.00	
George Gallaher	30.00	
Conrad Beyel	7.75	
Calvin (at appt)	90.00	
John (at appt)	10.00	
Chas. Morris 1 at	7.12	
James Gallaher 1 at	17.50	
Zeb (at appt)	15.00	
Jehu Martin	34.00	
Luke (at appt)	75.00	
Peggy (at appt)	60.00	
Calvin (at appt)	75.00	
L.L. Jordan 1-6.25 16 at 8.50	152.50	
Charles L. Roffe	15.00	cow-calf
Rufus Baltzell	12.25	" "
William Peters	16.87 1/2	"
O.A. McGinnis 2	30.50	"
cash	29.00	"
L.L. Jordan	21.00	"
F.G.L.Beuhring	40.00	"
same at 1	26.00	
L.L. Jordan	13.50	
Levi J. Hampton	14.25	
Alexr. Johnson	12.00	
Melchor Merritt plus calf since ap	31.50	
Andrew Guinn 1 at	9.70	

Appendix 5A

18 yearling calves at $7		126.00
4 - 2yr old heifers $14.10		36.40
1 grey mare "Hollenbeck"		40.00
1 yoke steers "Polk & Dallas"		60.00
1 " "Bright & Firm"		60.00
1 " "Buck & Berry"		50.00
1 " "Charley & c"		50.00
1 " "Jim & Pete"		35.00
1 " "Tip & Bill"		75.00
1 " "Turk & Pad"		75.00
1 " "Pip & Tyler"		75.00
1 " "Mark & Gabriel"		55.00
1 " "Buck & Redmond"		55.00
1 lot hogs		60.00
1 lot hogs		71.00
1 lot hogs		291.00
5 - 3yr old steers $12		60.00
1 calf		10.00
about 212 sheep		212.00
(1st-2nd-3rd-choice)		
sheep (con't)		
37 geese		6.00
1 largest cow & calf		20.00
4 cows & calves best at $20 each		80.00
3 cows & calves		45.00
1 stripper cow		12.00
1 bull		20.00
1 bay mare "Nelly"		35.00
1 sorrel horse "Snaps"		35.00
1 sorrel mare "Suze"		45.00
1 yellow horse "Tom"		20.00
1 bay colt "Dave"		50.00
1 " " "Scott"		30.00
1 mare "Fan"		35.00
67 sheep		67.00

L.L. Jordan 1 at		10.00
Geo. F. Miller 2 at		7.00
Geo. Gallaher		83.25 9 - $9.25
O.A. McGinnis		70.35 7 - 10.05
John Morris	2-14.95	
2 at 10 & 13		52.90
Charles Collins		30.25
John Laidley		69.00
Thos. R. Hope		70.00
Chas. L. Roffe		45.00
Levi J. Hampton		42.50
O.A. McGinnis		32.06
Charles Beale		80.50
Thos. R. Hope		76.00
Charles Beale		66.00
James Martin		64.50
Levi J. Hampton		47.50
John Morris		60.00
David Harshbarger		205.00
William Jenkins		450.00
Thos. L. Jorden $9		45.00
James Shelton for Vickers		10.00
Samuel W. Johnson		15.00 - 20 1st
Joseph W. Roffe		13.00 - 20 2nd
Wm. C. Dusenbury		12.00 - 20 3rd
James McKeand		9.00 - 20 4th
Wm. C. Dusenbury		6.75 - 20 5th
Rufus Baltzell		7.00 - 20 6th
Rowland Bias		7.75 - 20 7th
John Dolen		6.29
		2694.545
Solomon (at appt)		20.00
Phillis a (at appt)		20.00
Charlotte (1 appt)		20.00
Cash	1	19.40
George Gallaher	1	15.25
Calvary McCallister		14.00 - 1
Edmund W. Hill	1	12.50
R.N.B. Thompson	1	12.12
George Gallaher		20.00
Eli (at appt)		20.00
Eli (at appt)		35.00
L.L. Jorden		71.00
George Gallaher		26.50
Solomon (at appt)		20.00
Levi (at appt)		50.00
Charley (at appt)		30.00
O.A. McGinnis		35.00
John Morris		29.99 20 1st

Appendix 5A

			same	21.25	20 2nd
			George Killgore 10	8.50	
			same 17 at .68 3/4	11.68	
1	white face red cow	15.00	Solomon J. Richard	25.00	
1	bull	20.00	Charles Roffe	25.00	
1	large cow & calf "Popeye"	20.00	Charley (at appt)	20.00	
1	cow	10.00	James (at appt)	10.00	
1	spayed heifer	16.00	Peter (at appt)	16.00	
1	cow & calf "Riley"	18.00	Levi J. Hampton	21.62	
1	" " short horn	15.00	Solomon J. Richard	17.00	
1	young short horn	13.00	Moses (at appt)	13.00	
1	horse colt "Bill"	65.00	James (at appt)	65.00	
1	old grey horse "Jolly"	10.00	Moses (at appt)	10.00	
1	sorrel mare "Coaly"	20.00	Luke (at appt)	20.00	
1	bay horse "Doctor"	20.00	Daniel (at appt)	20.00	
1	grey filly	45.00	Moses (at appt)	45.00	
65	head 4yr old cattle at $14.10 per head	916.50	Chas. K. Morris		
			7 steer at 12.62	88.37	1/2
			7 heifers 6.62 1/2	45.37	1/2
			1 yoke of steers	25.31	1/2
			John Morris		
			2 heifers	18.12	1/2
	115 head cattle $16 per	1840.00	Charles Beale		
			164 head-13.10	2148.40	
	potatoes sweet & Irish	8.50	Charles K. Morris	8.50	
	1/2 bu & spade	.75	cash	.75	
			George Killgore 1 steer found since sale	10.00	
				3164.64	3/4

page 29

4619 lb. bacon at 5ct per lb		230.95	Charles L. Roffe	230.95
1	lot unpicked wool	25.00	same	36.59
amt of appraisal Beech plank		4.00		
2	stacks of hay	20.00		
1	small harrow	1.00		
33	bu corn sold not apprsd. at Stribbling farm	6.27		
4	bu rye same	1.00		
		299.81		

Appraisal & sale given under our hand 12 nov 1849
Solomon Thornburg
H.J. Samuels
John Everett
Daniel Love
C.L. Roffe

Cabell Court 25 feb 1850 John Samuels

Appendix 5A

Deed Bk 2-29 Commissioners settlement of estate of Sampson Sanders
1849 July Bill of sale of estate $8325.61 1/4
            cash received of Sheff   60.00
            "   William Love   200.00
            "   on hand at death   5.70
            "   Henry Peyton   266.65
        cash mortage of C.B. Riggs   1444.41
        cash   Jubel Henly   2.17
        cash note   Will Love   27.50
            "   Wolcott   187.00
            "   J & S Miller   409.00
            "   Charles T. Beale   500.00
            "   Henry H. Wood   542.32
        Rigg mortage on H.W. Shel   220.00
            "   William Irby   42.55
                          Evermont Ward   20.00
                          James Reynolds   25.00
                          James Shelton   51.00
                          George Kilgore   84.64 ---- total $12423.58 1/4

    cash to emancipated negroes $10399.31
         additional pd negroes   451.05
                                    _____
    25 feb 1850 total expenses $13483.38 1/4

Appendix 5B

Will Bk 2-29 25 feb 1850		Will Bk 2-78 26 mar 1851	
value of estate sale $	8325.61	cash receipts	$9636.82
cash receipts	4097.97	expenses	
		to emancipated slaves	3357.92
Will Bk 2-102 27 sep 1852		total expenses	$10241.42
cash receipts	993.50		
expenses	778.60	Will Bk 2-229 22 oct 1855	
		receipts	520.00
Will Bk 2-162 20 may 1854		expenses	5064.15
receipts	3155.90		
expenses	3515.19	Will Bk 2-255-25 oct 1856 (last entry)	
		receipts	320.00
		expenses	839.80

Sanders deeds Cabell County

	grantor	grantee	sold
1824	Martha Sanders	Abraham Trout 500a 12 Pole 4/87	500
1826	Ann & Sampson Sanders	John Merritt 31a Guyan River	31
1832	Sampson Sanders	William Simmons etal 109a Mud	109
1846	"	Mathew Knight 50a Heath ck	50
1846	'	John Ward 105a & 75a Davis Ck	180
1846	"	George Chapman 216a Guy Riv	216
1848	"	William C. Dusenberry 5 tracts Guyan R	mill
1849	"	Malchor Merritt 6a Mud	6
1849	"	Samuel W. Johnson 211a lot 36b Savage	211
1849	"	Benjam F. Drown 160a 4 Pole	106

Appendix 5B

Sanders deeds Cabell County

Book		grantor	grantee	bought
1-152	1811	Arch Bennett etal	Sampson Sanders 300a Mud	300
1-207	1812	Chester Howe	Martha Sanders 160a Mud	160
1-130	1810	Martha Piggott	Martha Sanders (P of Atty)	
3-707	1824	Joel Estes - mill	Sampson Sanders 700a Guy R	700
4-15	1824	Abraham Trout	Martha Sanders 100a Mud	100
4-140	1826	John Cookus	Sampson Sanders 133 1/2 Guy	133+
4-141	1828	John Cookus & etal	Sampson Sanders 50 Ohio (bene)	50
4-156	1826	John Cookus etal	Sampson Sanders 133 1/2 Guy	133+
4-458	1830	John Peyton	Sampson Sanders 150 Swamp Ck	150
5-64	1832	Joel Estes atty	Sampson 48 & 75 Guy R	123
5-241	1833	Wm. Hite	Sampson 400 lot 45 Savage Guy R bene	400
5-266	1833	Willis Mckeand	Sampson 414 1/2 Grays Branch	414+
5-267	1833	Joseph Malcomb	Sampson 300 Mud bene	300
5-288	1832	Richard Brown	Sampson 200 1/2 OH	200+
5-380	1834	John Bryant	40a Mud	40
5-534	1835	T. Kilgore	26a Mud	26
6-15	1835	James Reynolds	34 Dry Ck	34
6-64	1835	Nath.North etal	133 1/2 3/4 interest Guy R	133+
6-197	1836	Edmund McGinnis	part lot 45 Savage	
6-481	1825	Jacob Black	83 Sanders Ck	83
6-563	1838	Henry Clark	211 1/2 1/2 lot 36	211+
7-249	1839	Charles B.Riggs	200a Russells Ck	200
7-302	1839	Henry Peyton	personal	
7-417	1840	Luther Richey	1/2 near B'ville	
7-474	1840	Charles Peyton	160a	160
7-485	1840	Laidley comm	400a lot 56 Savage	400
7-486	1840	Laidley comm	133 lot 55 Savage	133
7-527	1840	Martin Moore	400 Frying Pan on Guy	400
7-535	1840	Joel Walters	personal	
7-604	1841	Jacob Harshbarger	34 1/2a Mud	34+
8-172	1841	Willis McKeand	105a	105
8-196	1842	Charles B. Riggs	200a	200
8-259	1842	John R. Porter Sr.	150a Guy	150
8-261	1842	Joseph Newman	50 & 60 Toms Ck	110
8-262	1842	Wm.R. Seamand	350 4pole	350
8-331	1843	Alex.R. McKeand	160 4 pole	160
8-332	1843	Chas.L. Roffe	75 Davis Ck	75
8-344	1842	John Samuels	414 Guyan	414
8-462	1843	Henry Clark etal	211 1/2 lot 36 SAvage	211+
8-511	1844	John Seashol	50 Mud 6 Guy	50
9-78	1845	Judith Anstice	211 1/2 lot 36 Savage	211+
9-80	1845	Wm. Carson etal	450 Sugar Camp Branch	450
9-130	1846	Jeremiah Witcher	120 Swamp /Ck	120
9-205	1846	D.Witcher	75 & 64 2 lots Dan.Witcher estate	139
9-223	1846	Thos. Ward etal	75 & 105 Davis Ck	180
9-238	1846	George Chapman	217 Guy	217
9-245	1847	Andrew Sheff	3 tracts Mud	

Appendix 5B

9-278	1847	Alex Johnson	715a 8 tracts Smith & Merrits ck	715
9-302	1847	John Samuels	217 a Guy	217
9-410	1848	Robert Ross	7 tract Smith Ck	
9-479	71848	Jacob Black	90a	90
9-483	1848	Joel Estes estate	119a Guy	119
9-484	1848	Jon Burton	75a Guy	75
9-538	1848	Wm.C.Dusenberry	217a + 5 tract guy	222
10-16	1848	James Reynolds	34+ Dry creek	34

---at least 9075a in Cabell most around Martha toward Milton---see map

Appendix 5C
Sampson Sanders Survey

Figure 24

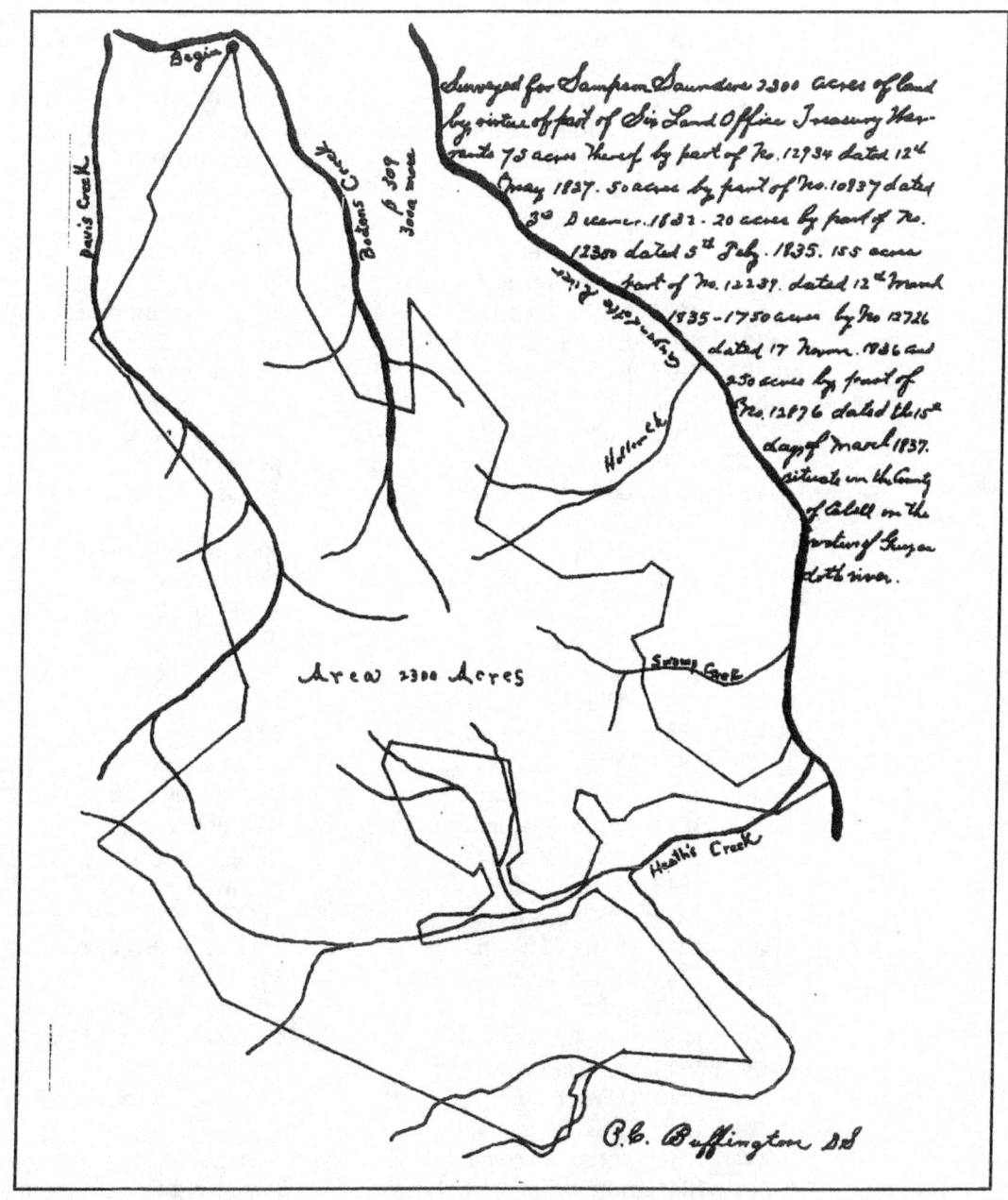

Sampson Sanders survey of 2300 acres - Cabell County Survey Book I

Appendix 6

Cabell Will Bk 2 p133

Will of Hetty Sanders Kilgore

In the name of God Amen, I Hetty Kilgore of the County of Cabell and the State of Virginia being weak and feable old and infirm knowing the certainty of human life and the certainty while in the possession of my facutlies and senses do hereby make ordain and publish this my last will and testament in form as follows:

First: I will and desire that at my death my executor who hereafter named give my body a Christian burial by the side of my late husband Thomas Killgore and that he erect over my grave tombstones as such as has been placed over my husbands body.

Second: After my said eecutors has pay my debts and funeral expenses the (residue) of my personal estate I will and bequeath to my three grandchildren William Killgore, James Killgore and Malinda Killgore, children of my son George Killgore share and share a like.

Thirdly the real estate that I possess I will and bequeath as follows to wit: The farm containing about three hundred acres on Mud River adjoining the lands of Messrs Summer, Newman and Duncan I will and bequeath absolutely to my son George Killgore and his heirs forever, the farm George Gallaher now lives on called the Simmons farm containing about 241a I will and bequeath to my two grandsons Conwelsy Simmons and Samspson Simmons theirs heirs and assigns forever, I also will that Conwelsy shall hold the land hereby bequeathed until Sampson Simmons becomes 21 years of age without charge against said Conwelsy and at that time when said Sampson comes of age that then the said Conwelsy shall divide said land by metes and bounds and said Sampson chose his mority.

Lastly I hereby appoint my beloved son George Killgore executor of this my last will and testament hereby revoking all other will by me heretofore made in whitness whereof the said Hetty Killgore has heretofore set my hand and seal this 7th day of March 1852.

Signed sealed and acknowledged
in the presence of
George W. Summers Jr.
Andrew Jordan
William Jorden
29 March 1853 John Samuels CCC

          her
Hetty X Killgore {seal}
         mark

Note: Hetty's death has various recorded dates.

Appendix 6

Hetty Sanders Kilgore

Cabell County Deed Book 10 pp71-72

Indenture 23 July 1849 from Thomas & Hetty Killgore to George Killgore, Martha Morris (wife of Charles K Morris), Malinda Jordan (wife of Thomas Lee Jordan) Thomas W. Killgore, Julian McKeane, James Duncan and Hetty Killgore (ch of Jeremiah) Marietta Ball, Lafayette Ball, Jeremiah Ball, Hetty Ann Ball and Martha Ball (ch of Emaline & Harry), Cornwellsy Simmons, Naoma Simmons, Mary Francis Simmons and Sampson Simmons (ch of Mary Polly Frances & Wm.) grandchildren all, lands which they inherited in right of Hetty Killgore as the heir at law of SAMPSON SANDERS.

George Killgore (their son) all land on west side Guyandotte held by Sampson Sanders' being 436 acres

Martha Morris (daughter & wife of Charles K. Morris) all Sampson Sanders property on the west side of Guyandotte opposite the Guyandotte mills now owned by William C. Dusenberry north & below following lines and along lines of Sampson Sanders 2300a survey being 1612 acres

Cornwellsey Simmons, Naoma Simmons, Ann Simmons, Matilda Simmons, Mary Francis Simmons and Sampson Simmons, grandchildren (children of Mary Polly & William both decd) residue of all Sampson Sanders' land on west side of Guyandotte above Martha Morris and including Rich Bottom, the Witiker farm and the Peyton farm and 1127 acres of the 2300a survey being 1500 acres plus a tract on east side of river 1 1/2m below Barboursville known as the King place a total of 1800 acres

Marietta Ball, Lafayette Ball, Jeremiah Ball, Hetty Ann Ball and Martha Ball grandchildren (children of Emaline Killgore and Harry Ball) all land on SW side of Mud River 8 miles east of Barboursville including home place of Martha Sanders (decd) and the Harshbarger farm being 600 acres.

Thomas Killgore, Julian McKeane (wife of James T. McKeane), Eliza Johnson (wife of Samuel Johnson), Mary Duncan (wife of James Duncan) and Hetty Killgore, grandchildren (children of Jeremiah) tract on the NE side of Mud River 8 miles east of Barboursville opposite land conveyed to Emaline Ball's heirs and adjoining Andrew Gwinn Newman being 600 acre

Malinda Jordan (daughter & wife of Thomas Jordan) tract on Ohio 3 miles below Guyandotte adjoining Albert Laidley & Samuel W. Johnson being 211 1/2 acres

Appendix 7

Materials purchased in Cabell County by manumitted slaves

Qty	Item	Price	Buyer		Amount
1	stand table	1.00	Daniel	(at appr)	1.00
1	bedstead & bedding	18.00	Cynthia	(at appr)	18.00
1	" "	15.00	Mary	(at appr)	15.00
1	" "	15.00	Daniel	(at appr)	15.00
1	lot of old carpet	1.00	Luke	(at appr)	1.00
1	crow bar & sledge	3.00	Luke	(at appr)	3.00
13	axes	8.00	Daniel 1	(at appr)	.62
1	pr. stretchers	1.00	Luke	(at appr)	1.00
1	stone hammer, 2 picks, chisel	1.00	Luke	(at appr)	1.00
1	cannon stove	2.00	Luke	(at appt)	2.00
12	Bee Stands & Hives	24.00	Peter 2	(at appt)	4.00
			Daniel 2	(at appt)	4.00
			Luke 2	(at appt)	4.00
1	ox plow	4.00	Luke	(at appt)	4.00
1	scraper	3.00	Luke	(at appt)	3.00
1	left handed plow	6.00	Calvin	(at appt)	6.00
1	threshing machine	10.00	Luke	(at appt)	10.00
1	mans saddle	5.00	Peter	(at appt)	5.00
1	stone auger	1.00	Luke	(at appt)	1.00
50	Bu Buckwheat at 31pr	6.00	Luke 12 Bu	(at appt)	3.75
1	large left hand plow	6.00	Peter	(at appt)	6.00
5	old axes	3.00	Charles 1	(at appt)	.50
			Moses 1	(at appt)	.63
3	large iron kettles	3.00	Charlotte 1	(at appt)	1.00
2	scythes & cradles	3.00	Eli 1	(at appt)	1.50
1	improved McCormick	5.00	Levi	(at appt)	5.00
1	flax wheel	.75	Charlotte	(at appt)	.75
1	dining table	.50	Solomon	(at appt)	.50
1	mare "Flora"	85.00	Cynthia	(at appt)	85.00
1	pr. young horse "Bells" at $45 each	90.00	Calvin	(at appt)	90.00
1	sorrel mare "Nancy Dawson"	10.00	John	(at appt)	10.00
1	mare "Pats"	15.00	Zeb	(at appt)	15.00
1	bay horse "Paddy"	75.00	Luke	(at appt)	75.00
1	mare "Dandy"	60.00	Peggy	(at appt)	60.00
1	bay stud colt	75.00	Calvin	(at appt)	75.00
1	largest cow & calf	20.00	Solomon	(at appt)	20.00
4	cows & calves best at $20 each	80.00	Phillis 1	(at appt)	20.00
			Charlotte 1	(at appt)	20.00
1	bull	20.00	Eli	(at appt)	20.00
1	bay mare "Nelly"	35.00	Eli	(at appt)	35.00
1	yellow horse "Tom"	20.00	Solomon	(at appt)	20.00
1	bay colt "Dave"	50.00	Levi	(at appt)	50.00
1	" " "Scott"	30.00	Charley	(at appt)	30.00
1	large cow & calf "Popeye"	20.00	Charley	(at appt)	20.00
1	cow	10.00	James	(at appt)	10.00
1	spayed heifer	16.00	Peter	(at appt)	16.00
1	young short horn	13.00	Moses	(at appt)	13.00
1	horse colt "Bill"	65.00	James	(at appt)	65.00

Appendix 7

1 old grey horse "Jolly"		10.00	Moses	(at appt)	10.00
1 sorrel mare "Coaly"		20.00	Luke	(at appt)	20.00
1 bay horse "Doctor"		20.00	Daniel	(at appt)	20.00
1 grey filly		45.00	Moses	(at appt)	45.00

	Calvin	Cynthia	James	Luke	Peggy	Solomon
Purchasers:	Charley	Daniel	John	Mary	Peter	Zeb
	Charlotte	Eli	Levi	Moses	Phillis	

Sampson Sanders' will gave blacks right to buy from his estate at "appraised value". Total purchased amounted to $1046.00 to be taken from the $15,000.

Cass County - Sanders Deeds
Sanders Slaves listed from deeds Cass Co.MI (Most took Sanders name.)

Deed Bk 1849 Cass Co. MI

p403   12 oct 1849 Solomon Sanders Sr, Phillis Sanders, Eli Sanders, Levi Sanders, Solomon Sanders Jr., Woodford Sanders, Jacob Sanders and Jason Sanders of Cabell Co.VA $1387.00 w 1/2 NW 1/4 S7 TWP7 R13 and E 1/2 NS 1/4 S12 TWP7 S R14 W both 148a

p404   12 oct 1849 Daniel Sanders, Dorcas Sanders, Alicia Sanders, Montesque Sanders, Zebedee Sanders, Eliza Sanders, Robert Sanders, William Sanders, Elijah Sanders, and Hamilton Sanders of VA $1125.00 N 1/2 W 1/2 SW 1/4 S7, SW 1/4 NE 1/4 S18, NW 1/4 SE 1/4 S18, NW 1/4 NE 1/4 S18,TWP 7 S R13 W 155a

p405   12 oct 1849 Mary Sanders, Susan Sanders, Joseph Sanders, Harriet Sanders, Mahala Sanders, Charles Sanders, Theodon Sanders, Sampson Sanders   all of Cabell County, VA $725.00   115a E 1/2 NE 1/4 S13 TWP7 S R14 W, S 1/2 W 1/2 SW 1/4 S7 TWP7 S R13 W

p407   12 oct 1849 Cynthia Radford and Jacob Radford of Cabell Co. VA $400.00 40a being S end W 1/2 NW 1/4 S18 TWP 7 S R13 W

p465   27 nov 1849 George Gallaher (lawyer and friend who accompanied slaves) $425.00 22a E side NE 1/4 SW 1/4 S36 TWP6 S R15 W, E 1/2 NE 1/4 SE 1/4 S23 same range & twp 20a (total 42a)

p466   27 nov 1849 Margaret Sanders and Eli Sanders her son of Cabell Co.VA $300.00 for 18a W side NE 1/4 SW 1/4 S36 TWP6 S R15 W

p515   1 dec 1849 entered 2 jan 1850 James Sanders $20.00 lots Village of Williamsville Blk1 R1 E lots 7 & 8

p625-6 1 dec 1849 entered 19 mar 1850   Peter Sanders (Porter town Cass Co.MI) lots Williamsville $50.00

Book 1850 Cass Co. MI

p296   12 mar 1850 entered 6 jan 1851(50) Eli Sanders $100.00 lots 5 &6 Williamsville

p411   Sanders, Daniel & wife Dorcas Sanders, Hamilton & wife Sarah Sanders, Peter & wife Letia 22a $220 sold to Jacob (Price)

p483   sheriff's sale to Solomon Sanders $150 (blurry)

Appendix 7

p552   7 jun 1851   Daniel Sanders (quardian of Eliza Sanders, Robin Sanders, William Sanders, Elijah Sanders and Hamilton Sanders minor heirs and Montesque Sanders

p553   Sanders, Daniel & wife Docas Sanders, Montesque Sanders, Peter & wife Alicia to Edward Graham (Alitia)

p554   (jun 1851)
Sanders, Daniel (guardian for) Eliza, Robin, William, Elijah, Hamilton to Edward Graham

p565   3 feb 1850 recorded 17 feb 1851 George Gallaher & wife Naomi of Cabell Co. VA to Daniel Sanders and Dorcas Sanders and their children Montesque, Eliza, Robin, Elijah, Hamilton and Alicia Daniels daughter of Cass Co. (Alicia Daniels or daughter of Daniel??) $425.00 (see above)

Appendix 8

Cass County - Sanders Deeds

Cass County Surveyors Book I

1853 - page 41
surveyed 22 Sep   1855 for Eli Saunders 39'94 acres   S12 T7 R14

page 42
surveyed 17 Oct   1853 for M. Saunders & heirs 34 62/100 a   S7 T7 R13

page 43
surveyed 17 Oct   1853 for Daniel Saunders & heirs 34'42 a   S7 T7 R13
surveyed 19 Oct   1853 for Mary Saunders & heirs 8 62/100 a   S13 T7 R14
surveyed 19 Oct   1853 for Mary Saunders & heirs 14 40/100 a   S13 T7 R14
surveyed 19 Oct   1853 for Mary Saunders & heirs 14'40 a   S13 T7 R14

page 44
surveyed 19 Oct   1853 for Mary Saunders & heirs 43 20/100 a   S13 T7 R14
surveyed 20 Oct   1853 for Mary Saunders & heirs 5 84/100 a   S14 T7 R13

page 47
surveyed 22 Oct   1853 for Solomon Saunders & heirs 18'44 a   S12 T7 R14

page 48
surveyed 24 Nov   1853 for Solomon Saunders & heirs 18'44 a   S12 T7 R14
surveyed 24 Nov   1853 for Solomon Saunders & heirs 36 84/100 a   S12 T7 R14
surveyed 24 Nov   1853 for Solomon Saunders & heirs 6'34 a   S12 T7 R14
surveyed 24 Nov   1853 for Solomon Saunders & heirs 18'44 a   S7 T7 R13

page 49
surveyed 24 Nov   1853 for Solomon Saunders & heirs 18 44/100 a   S7 T7 R13
surveyed 24 nov   1853 for Solomon Saunders & heirs 18'44 a   S7 T7 R13
surveyed 24 Nov   1853 for Solomon Saunders & heirs 12'12 a   S7 T7 R13

Appendix 8

1854 - page 55
surveyed	10	Mar	1854	for Robert Saunders 15 a	S18 T7 R13
surveyed	10	Mar	1854	for Montique Saunders 15 a	S18 T7 R13
surveyed	10	Mar	1854	for William Saunders 15 a	S18 T7 R13

page 56
surveyed	10	Mar	1854	for Daniel Saunders 30 a	S18 T7 R13
surveyed	10	Mar	1854	for Darkey Saunders 15 a	S18 T7 R13
surveyed	10	Mar	1854	for Elijah Saunders 15 a	S18 T7 R13
surveyed	10	Mar	1854	for Hamilton Saunders 15a	

page 57
surveyed	21	Mar	1854	for Peter Saunders 17 26/100 a	S7 T7 R13

page 58
surveyed	21	Mar	1854	for Eliza Saunders 17'24 a	S7 T7 R13

Cass County - Sanders Deeds
original deed of Solomon Sanders and family
    pg 403 - 1849 Deed Book Cass County, MI

John Butler & wife to Solomon Sanders & others
Entered for record October 12, 1849 at 3 O'clock PM

    This indenture made the twelth day of October in the year of our Lord One Thousand and eight hundred and forty nine Between John Butler and Mary Jane his wife of the County of Cass & state of Michigan of the first part and Solomon Sanders Senior, Phillis Sanders, Eli Sanders, Levi Sanders, Solomon Sanders Junior, Woodford Sanders, Jacob Sanders & Jason Sanders of Cabell County, Virginia of the second part Witnesseth that the said parties of the first part for and in consideration of the sum of thirteen hundred and eighty seven dollars to them in hand paid by the said parties of the second part, the receipt whereof is hereby confessed and acknowledged, have granted, bargained, sold, re-----, released, al----- and confirmed and by these presents do grant, bargain, sell, re--ise, release, al--- and confirm unto the said parties of the second part and to their heirs forever, All those certain pieces or parcels of land situate, lying and being in the County of Cass and the state of Michigan known and described as follows to wit: The West half of the North West quarter of Section number seven(7) in Township number seven(7) South of Range number thirteen(13) West and also the East half of the Northeast quarter of Section number twelve(12) in Township number seven(7) South of Range number fourteen(14) West, containing in both pieces one hundred and forty eight acres be the same more or less. Together with all and singular etc.,etc.......

Appendix 8

pg 404
Jesse Williams & Larkins Williams to Daniel Sanders & others
Entered for record October 12, 1849 at 3 O'clock PM

    This indenture made the twelth day of October in the year of our Lord one thousand eight hundred and forty nine Between Jesse Williams and Maritta his wife and Larkin Williams and Sarah his wife of Cass County Michigan of the first part and Daniel Sanders, Dorcas Sanders, Alicia Sanders, Montesques Sanders, Zebedee Sanders, Eliza Sanders, Robert Sanders, William Sanders, Elijah Sanders & Hamilton Sanders of Virginia of the second part. etc......

North half of the West half of the Southwest quarter of Section seven(7), the Southwest quarter of the NOrtheast quarter of Section eighteen(18) and also the Northwest quarter of the Northeast of Section eighteen(18) all in Township number seven(7) South of Range number thirteen(13)West containing in all one hundred and fifty four acres etc.etc............

pg 405
Larkin Williams & Jesse Williams to Mary Sanders & others
Entered for record October 12, 1849 at 3 O'clock PM

    This indenture made the twelth day of October in the year of our Lord one thousand eight hundred and forty nine Between Larkin Williams and Sarah his wife and Jesse Wiilam and Marietta his wife of Cass County Michigan of the first part and Mary Sanders, Susan Sanders, Joseph Sanders, Harriet Sanders, Mahala Sanders, Theodore Sanders & Sampson Sanders of Cabell County, Virginia etc.etc................................

Appendix 9A

Cass County - Census - 1850 census Cass County, MI

Sanders - Cass, MI   * named deed
CALVIN Township. - 8 Aug 1850

HH#	Surname	Name	Age/Sex	Color	Birthplace	*	Notes	Location	
607-615	Saunders,	Solomon	62m	M	VA	*	(m Francis Oglesby 1861 Penn Twp) d1863 77y	Chain Lake	
		Lillis	55f	B	VA	*	d186- 55y (NOT ON 1860 CENSUS)	Chain Lake	
		Eli	25m	M	VA	*			
		Levi	24m	M	VA	*		Chain Lake	
		Solomon	21m	B	VA	*	(24 m Phymuda McCullon 1859-Calvin Twp)	Chain Lake	
		Woodford	19m	B	VA	*	m by 1860 w/A.	Chain Lake	
		Jacob	17m	M	VA	*	(21 m Eliza Sanders 1855 Calvin Twp)	Chain Lake	38y?
		Jason	11m	B	VA	*	102 USCT	Chain Lake	
	Sanders,	Lelia	23f	B	VA	*	(m Peter Sanders dec 1850 Porter Twp ?) (Daniel's see will) where's Peter ?		
608-616	Saunders,	Luke	39m	B	VA				
		Jane	23f	B	VA				
		Columbus	4m	B	VA				
		Mary	2f	B	VA				
615-623	Saunders,	Mary	41f	B	unk	*	(m John Sanders 1851 Porter Twp)(Mary d 1860)		
		Susan	21f	B	VA	*	(by Solomon's will wife/Isaac Ward)m 1850 d by 1860		
		Joseph	19m	B	VA	*			
		Harriet	16f	B	Va	*	(21 m Peter Smith 1856 Calvin Twp)	Chain Lake	
		Mahala	15f	B	VA	*	(18 m Thomas Jefferson Carter 1854 Calvin Twp)		
		Charles	9m	B	VA	*			
		Theodore	1m	B	VA	*	twin		
		Sampson	1m	B	VA	*	twin		

(Mary in Solomon's will is she sister to Charles who died 1850 interstate only sis & ch)

660-668	Saunders,	Charlotte	50f	M	VA		(d 1889 age 107 Jefferson Twp)(b 1782 VA)	Chain Lake
		Jane	35f	M	VA		(32 m Levi Sanders age 34-1852 Calvin Twp) Levi ?	
							(d 1870 age 50 d/Witcher & Charlotte Sanders)	
							(d 1870 Mary J. d/Levi & Jane)	Chain Lake

1850 PORTER Township 29 Jul 1850

358-365	Sanders,	Moses	37m	B	VA		(78 in 1860 census) (1875 Moses 63 m Martha J.Keith)	
		Caroline	28f	B	VA		(dead by 1875)	
		Albert	7m	B	VA		Co H 102 USCT Civil War	
		Robert	1m	B	Va		dead by 1860)	
363-370	Gray,	Daniel W.	37m	W	miller			
	Saunders,	Susan	19f	B	VA		(is this Susanna who married Ward- census twice?)	
364-371	Radford,	John	54m	B	VA		(not on deed)	
		Cynthia	38f	B	VA	*		
		Jacob	2m	B	VA	*		
381-388	Saunders,	Daniel	46m	B	VA	*	d 1853 44y	Chain Lake
		Dorcas	50f	B	VA	*		
		Zebedee	20m	B	VA	*		
		Eliza	18f	B	VA	*		
		Robin	16m	B	VA	*	(d 1877 Robert age 43 s/Daniel & Dorcas-both dead)	
		William	14m	B	VA	*	(d 1870 Porter Twp age 37 s/Dan & Dorcas)	
		Elijah	12m	B	VA	*	Co H 102 USCT Civil War	- Chain Lake
		Hamilton	6m	B	VA	*	(d 1871 age 27 s/Daniel & Dorcas	Chain Lake

(dau Alicia in Solomon's house m Peter)
(where is Monticue listed on deed)

LaGRANGE Township 31 Jul 1850

820-828	Halistock,	Alexander	24m	M	VA			
		Peggy	29f	B	VA	*		
		Eli	2m	M	VA	*		Chain Lake
	Saunders,	Ada	80f	B	VA			Chain Lake
	Saunders,	James	40m	B	VA	*		
	Halistock,	Elizabeth	6/12f	M	MI			

not shown   Hamilton & wife Sarah (on one deed)
               Calvin (witness in 1849)
               Peter who marries Alicia/Daniel and has lot in Williamsville   Chain Lake
               James with lot in Williamsville
               John who marries Mary/Mary in 1851
               Montecue son of Daniel listed on deed   Chain Lake
               Levi who marries Jane/Charlotte(1860 says Eli)
               Eli who has lot in Williamsville
               Charles who dies 1850 only family sister Mary Ann & her children
               Zebedee who died in 1850   Chain Lake

ISOM REMAINS IN CABELL   Other possibles -Sarah named as adult Hamilton's wife--Who is Hamilton?

Appendix 9A

Cass County - Census - 1860 Cenus Cass County, MI

CALVIN Township 20 Jun 1860

623-623	Sanders,	S.	29m	B	VA	
		S.	72m	B	VA	
	Halestalk,	Eli	11m	M		s/Margaret m Alex Halestock(Was Solomon son of Ada)
624-624	Sanders,	Eli	29m	B	VA	(Levi?) s/Solomon
		Jane	33f	M	VA	Charlotte's daughter did she marry both Eli & Levi
		E.	11m	M	VA	(Calvin)
		M.F.	6f	M	MI	Mary Jane 17 dies 1870
		Elihu	7m	M	MI	
		Charlotte	70f	M	VA	(only 50-1850 but 107 by 1889(Charlotte,Jane Mulatto)
						Jane d1870 d/ Witcher & Charlotte
625-625	Sanders,	Jacob	29m	B	VA	s/Solomon m Eliza/Daniel 1855
		Eliza	27f	B	VA	d/Daniel
		Chilen(?)	10/12m	B	MI	
	Ward,	Joseph	5m	B	MI	child of Susan/Mary & Issac Ward ?
629-629	Sanders,	John	66m	B	VA	Widower of Mary
		Charles	16m	B	VA	
		Theodore	13m	B	VA	should be 10/11 and twin to Sampson (see Smith)
630-630	Byrd,	C	78m	M		
grch (?)	Sanders,	C.A	5f	M		s/Montcue/Daniel married Jane Byrd 1851
	Roberts,	Stewart	--			(Maybe Robert Stewart- Martha Jane married Wm.Stuart 1855
631-631	Smith,	Robert	25m	B	OH	maybe second name for Peter Smith m Harriet 1856
		Harriet	27f	B	VA	dau/Mary m Peter Smith 1856
		W.	7m	B	MI	
		J.E.	2m	B	MI	
	Sanders,	S.	10m	B	VA	(Sampson twin to Theodore)brother to Harriet-s/Mary
		M.	6m	B	M	Mordicai
761-761	Sanders,	Moses	78m	B	VA	(37 -1850)(m2 Martha Keith 1875 lost 2 ch before 1870)
		C.	38f	B	VA	dies prior 1875
		Albert	17m	B	VA	102 USCT
		J.	7m	B	VA	102 USCT
		E.F.	3f	B	MI	
	Ward,	Wm.	8m	B	MI	s/Susan/Mary & Issac Ward

PORTER Township

1504	Saunders,	W.	27m	B	VA	(Woodford)/Solomon
-1514		A.	21f	B	NC	
	Ward,	Nathan	8m	B	MI	s/Susan/ Mary & Issac Ward
1605	Sanders,	Peter	39m	B	VA	
-1616		Lucy	36f	B	VA	(Alicia/ Letha/ Elissa)d/Daniel-lost son 1879 Jesse
		L.A.	8m	B	MI	
		G.	7f	B	MI	(Gerturde 1852-1921 Ch Lk
		Mary	5f	B	MI	
		Newton	1m	B	MI	twin
		Jasper	1m	B	MI	twin
1615	Sanders,	M.	29m	B	VA	(Montecue)/Daniel m2 Sarah lost 2 dau 1878
-1626		Jane	26f	B	NC	(m Jane Byrd (Is one child with her father?)
		M.J.	8f	B	MI	
		Samuel	6m	B	MI	
		Charity	4f	B	MI	
		Mary	3f	B	MI	twin
		Martha	3f	B	MI	twin
1616	Sanders,	Wm.	23m	B	VA	s/Daniel (died 20 sep 1870 dc)
-1627		Dorcas	65f	B	VA	widow of Daniel d 1876 will
		Elijah	22m	B	VA	
		Robert	26m	B	VA	dies 1877 dc
		Hamilton	19m	B	VA	dies 1871 dc
1619	Radford,	John	63m	B	VA	
-1630		Cynthia	42f	B	MI	
		John	7m	B	MI	
		Wm.	4m	B	MI	

PENN Township 355-355 Jones,Wm-   Elijah Sanders 20m B VA laborer -s/Daniel
PENN Township 520-520 Jones,Nathan   William Sanders 27m B VA border -s/Daniel (also with mother)
(Are they listed twice?)

Appendix 9A

Cass County - Census - 1870 Census Cass County, MI

1870 Cass census CALVIN Township   BC=Birth Certificate

#	Surname	Given	Age/Sex	Race	Birthplace	Notes		
80-83	Sanders,	Jacob	23m	B	WV	s/Solomon		
		Eliza	37f	B	VA	d/Daniel		
		Elihu	10m	B	MI	1860-1912	m 1896- Book	D-123 Martha Ash
		Mary J	8f	B	MI			
		Fannie A.	6f	B	MI			
		Martha E	1f	B	MI	BC 1868	m 1898	D-153
81-84	Saunders,	Jason	31m	B	VA	s/Solomon		
82-85	Saunders,	Levi	42m	B	VA	s/Solomon		
		Janie	50f	B	VA			
		Cavlin	22m	B	VA			
		Mary F.	17f	B	MI			
		Elihu	14m	B	MI		m 1894	D-94
**		Charlotte	70f	B	VA			
87-90	Saunders,	Solomon	38m	B	VA	s/Solomon		
157-162	Smith,	Harriet	30f	B	VA	d/Mary	d 1896 Toledo	
		Mordica	18m	B	MI	works hotel (brother - youngest ch of Mary)		
		James W.	15m	B	MI			
		Mary J.	10f	B	MI			
		John W.	7m	B	MI			
		Elizabeth	4f	B	MI			
	Ward,	Nathan	16m	B	MI	1 of 3 Ward sons of Susan & Isaac Ward - nephew		
	Morgan,	Beth	23f	B	NC	?		
		Lucinda	14f	B	IN	twin		
		Marinda	14f	B	IN	twin		
163--168	Hailstock,	Eli	21m	M	VA	s/Margaret		
		Elmore M.	24f	M	VA			
		Coravida	11/12f		VA			
	Brown,	Melissa	8f	M	MI			
		Zachariah	6m	M	MI			
		Margaret C.	6/12f	M	MI			
164-169	Sanders,	Moses	58m	B	VA	/Moses	m2 1875 Marth Keith	
		Caroline	50f	B	VA			
		Eliza	13f	B	MI	d 1870 Ch LK (DC says Moses & Martha) (DC - Death Certificate)		
		Hezekiah	10m	B	MI	d 1871 Ch Lk (DC says Moses & Martha)		

PORTER Township

#	Surname	Given	Age/Sex	Race	Birthplace	Notes	
118-120	Saunders,	Montaque	39m	M	VA	s/Daniel	
		Sarah J.	35f	M	NC	Sarah Jane	
		Samuel	16m	M	MI		
		Mary	13f	M	MI		
		Martha	13f	M	MI		
		Daniel W.	10m	M	MI		
		Josephine	8f	M	MI	d 1878 Cass Vigilant	
		Charlotte E.	6f	M	MI		m Frank Coleman of Williamsville
		Charles	5m	M	MI	BC	
		Susan E.	3f	M	MI	BC	
		Ida	1f	M	MI		
120-122	Saunders,	Dorcas	76f	B	VA	w/Daniel	
		Robert	35m	B	VA		
		Elijah	29m	B	VA		
		Hamilton	26m	B	VA		
	Hailstock,	Elizabeth	20f	B	MI	d/Margaret (Peggy)	d 1877 buried Ch Lk
		Eliza	16f	B	MI	d/Margaret	
	Dunger,	James	10m	M	MI		
121-123	Radford,	John	70m	B	VA	/John	
		Cynthia	45f	B	VA	/Cynthia	
		William	13m	B	MI		
		Frederick	8m	B	MI		
		Rosetta	6f	B	MI		
	Saunders,	Frederick	1m	B	MI		
126-128	Saunders,	Woodford	35m	B	VA	s/Solomon	
		Arbillion	28f	M	NC	(Lowe from Cass Vigilant)	
127-129	Saunders,	Peter	50m	B	VA	/Peter	
		Leicia	42f	B	VA	d/Daniel	
		Amanda	18f	B	MI		
		America V.	16f	B	MI		
		Jannetta A.	14f	B	MI		
		Newton	12m	B	MI	twin	m 1899 D-162
		Jasper	11m	B	MI	twin	
		Philis	9f	B	MI		
		Jesse	7m	B	MI		
		Arbillion	2f	B	MI		m 1888 D-16

Appendix 9A

Cass County - Census - 1880 Cenus Cass County, MI

CALVIN TWP

177-177	Sanders,	Solomon	47m B WV VA VA		(not married 1870)	*
		Fred	11m B MI WV IN		married 1889 D-21
		Willis O.	8m B MI WV IN	BC Sol & Mary
		Melvin	6m B MI WV IN	BC Sol & Mary
180-180	Sanders,	Peter	58m B WV VA VA
		Alissia	53f B WV WV VA
		Arbella	13f B MI WV WV		married 1888	D-16
		Alice	9f B MI WV WV	BC 1871 (Peter & Marlisa)
	Sanders,	Minnie	6f B MI MI MI	gr-daughter married 1889	D-22
183-183	Sanders,	Elihu	26m M MI WV WV
		Sarah Jane	18f M MI OH OH
		Jacob	2m M MI MI MI	BC
		(Rolla(M))		1883 BC
		(son)		1885 BC
	Sanders,	Charlotte	93f M VA VA VA
186-186	Sanders,	Moses	68m B WV VA MD	*Cass Vigilant* 20 Feb 1890 very ill dying
		Martha	42f M VA VA VA	(2nd wife)
		David	18m M OH WV WV
		Emily V.	12f M OH WV VA
		Albert	6m M OH WV VA
	Keith,	Nora	6/12f B MI MI OH	step gr dau

PORTER TWP

124-126	Sanders,	Montacue	48m B VA VA VA
		Sarah J.	44f B NC VA NC
		Samuel D.	25m B MI VA NC
		Daniel S.	19m B MI VA NC
		Susan B.	13f B MI VA NC
		Ida L.	11f B MI VA NC	married 1892 D-22
		John C.F.	15m B MI VA NC
		Jennie M.	9f B MI VA NC	BC
		Lina T.	5f B MI VA NC
		Oliver C.	3m B MI VA NC
		(Wm.A.)		1878 BC
		Alfonse	1m B MI VA NC	BC (Alonzo)
126-127	Radford,	John	81m B VA VA VA	cripple (Parents ??)
		Cynthia	68f •B VA VA VA	"
		William	22m B MI VA VA
		Frederick	20m B MI VA VA
		Rosetta	16f B MI VA VA
144-146	Sanders,	Calvin	26m B VA VA VA	s/Levi
		Gerturde	24f M VA VA VA	(Brown)
		Mary J.	5f M MI VA VA	married 1893 D-77
		Oscar	4m M MI VA VA	married 1905 D-251
		Carrie	2f M MI VA VA	*Cass Vigilant* d 1887
146-148	Sanders,	Woodford	44m B VA VA VA
		Arbella	38f B NC NC NC
147-149	Sanders,	Jason J.	38m B VA VA VA	*Cass Vigilant* b 25 dec 1840 Cabell co. Va
					d 6 sep 1897 Porter Twp. bur Ch LK
		Caroline	29f B IN NC NC
172-175	Sanders,	Elijah	42m B VA VA VA	s/Daniel (Williamsville)
		Laura	33f M IN KY KY
		Cora T.	16f M MI VA IN	(or 10 ?)
		George A.	4m M MI VA IN	BC
		Rosa L.	1f M MI VA IN
	Cousins,	Ary	76f B VA VA VA	mother

NOTE: Cora, daughter of Elijah, passed for white and left community.

Cass Vigilant 1897 Harvey Radford and wife formerly of Cassopolis moved from Kalamzoo to Battle Creek

* Solomon Jr. married 3 times 1 Phymuda McCullon 1859 (dead by 1860)
                2 Mary died 13 apr 1876
                   3 died 2 nov 1876 only married 2 weeks *Cass Vigilant*
must have been a fourth because none of above produced children

Appendix 9A

Cass County - Census - 1900 Cenus Cass County, MI

Calvin Township

301	Sanders,	Elihu	m Aug 1858	41	MI	VA	VA	s/Levi/Solomon
		Ellen	f Mar 1858	42	MI	NY	OH	
		Ralph	m May 1897	3	MI	MI	MI	
5858	Sanders,	Solomon	Aug 1831	68	VA	VA	VA	s/Solomon
		Edgar	Mar 1882	18	MI	VA	VA	

Porter Township not Available

1910 Census Cass County, MI

Cass Township

61-61	Sanders,	Oscar	m33	MI	NC	OH	s/Calvin/Levi/Solomon	
		Edna	f24	MI	MI	MI	2ch - 2 living	
		Lester	m 4	MI	MI	MI		
		Srella	f 1/2	MI	MI	MI		

Porter Township

53-55	Sanders,	Calvin	m61	VA	VA	VA	s/Levi/solomon	
		Anna G.	f56	OH	VA	VA	4ch - 2 living	
85-87	Sanders,	Samuel D.	m55	MI	VA	OH	s/Monteque/Daniel	
		Rosa	fm45	MI	VA	VA	4ch - 3 living	
93-96	Sanders,	Laura F.	f63	IN	KY	KY	10ch - 4 living	w/Elijah/Daniel
	East,	Clyde K.	m21	MI	MI	MI	grandson	
	Lucas,	Myrtle F.	f 8	MI	MI	MI	grandson	

Military Census

Michigan Soldiers and Sailors Individual Records. Michigan Historical Records, Lansing, Michigan, 1915.

Sanders,	Albert	Co	H	1st	MI	Col	Inf	(102 USCT)	s/Moses
Sanders,	Elijah	Co	H	1st	MI	Col	Inf	(102 USCT)	s/Daniel
Sanders,	Hamilton	Co	B	1st	MI	Col	Inf	(102 USCT)	s/Daniel
Sanders,	Jason J.	Co	H	1st	MI	Col	Inf	(102 USCT)	s/Solomon
Sanders,	John	Co	B	1st	MI	Col	Inf	(102 USCT)	s/Moses
Sanders,	John J.	Co	E	1st	MI	Col	Inf	(102 USCT)	s/Moses-bro/Albert
Sanders,	Peter	Co	H	1st	MI	Col	Inf	(102 USCT)	--

APPENDICES

Appendix 9B

Cass County Cemetery Records
Chain Lake Baptist Churchyard Burials

Located on Chain Lake Road, Calvin Township
(unpublished materials on file at Cassopolis Library "DAR Cemeteries of Cass County - 1943"
(USCT= United States Colored Troops originally 1st Michigan)

Sanders, Adre	1850	age	87	(Ader-Ada) 1850 census(Halestock) 1801 Wm. sale
Sanders, Zebedec	1850	age	87	
Sanders, DANIEL	1853	age	44	(are these Daniel's parents? - he names son Zebedee)
Sanders, Malinda --------				
Sanders, Martha	1878	age	20	d/Montique - s/Daniel DC
Sanders, Joseph F.	1878	age	15	d/Montique Josephine DC?
Sanders, Hamilton --				(1871 death cer) (s/Daniel ? age 27)
Halestock, Eli	Co B	102nd	USCT	s/Peggy/Mergaret - Gr son Ada ?
Halestock, Elisha	1875		30	(Eliza ? d/Margart)
Halestock, Elizabeth	1877	(?)	26	dau/Margaret
Sanders, Jacob B.		age	38	s/Solomon d 1855
Sanders, Jane	1870	age	45	d/Charlotte w/Levi
Sanders, Levi	1879	age	53	s/Solomon mar Jane/Charlotte
Sanders, Solomon	1863	age	77	
Sanders, Phillis	1863 (?)	age	55	(maybe 1861) 1st wife Solomon Sr.
Sanders, Jeremiah	1859	age	5	
Sanders, Hezekiah	1871	age	11	s/Moses
Sanders, Eliza	1870	age	14	dau/Moses
Sanders, Woodford	1887	age	52y	s/Solomon
Sanders, J.J.	Co H	102	USCT	s/Solomon (Jason)
Sanders, Peter	Co H	102	USCT	
Sanders, Elijah	Co H	102	USCT	s/Daniel 1838-
Sanders, Laura	1847-1921			w/Elijah ?
Steward, Elisha	1866	age	5	
Steward, Minerva Jane				
Sanders, Calvin	1848-1926			s/Levi & Jane by 1860 census
Sanders, Gerturde	1852-1921			w/Calvin- a Brown
Sanders, Arthur	1882-1909			
Sanders, Carrie	1878-1905			d/Calvin & Gerturde
Radford, John	1798-1889			m Cynthia before arriving Michigan
Radford, Cynthia	1902-1920			
Radford, Fred	1862-1908			s/John & Cynthia
Sanders, Elihu	1855-1931			(s/Levi & Jane ?)
Sanders, Ralph	1891-1935			
Radford, Jacob	1854 6yr			s/John & Cynthia 0n 1850 census
Radford, James M.	1853 7m			s/John & Cynthia
Smith, Harriet	5 sep 1896			(died Toledo) (d/Mary)
Sanders, Rolley B.	1885-1938			s/Jason/Solomon
Sanders, Helen M.	1885-1978			
Sanders, Oscar	1876-1965			(s/Calvin/Levi/Solomon & Jane/Charlotte)
Sanders,Edna B.	1885-1980			w/Oscar
Sanders, Lester H.	1904-1940			s/Oscar & Edna

Sanders, Rosa Henderson   1864-1936 (beside brother George his stone illegible
    & d/Elijah) others records give Henderson as surname

NOTE: These graves are not side by side, but are scattered over the whole graveyard. Stones were read as grouped. Most of the stones are down and unreadable today. It is difficult to tell just how many unmarked Sanders graves there may be.

Appendix 9B

Chain Lake burials from other sources:
deaths listed in the *"Cassopolis Viligant"* newspaper abstracted by local DAR chapter.

2	nov	1876	------Sanders 3rd wife of Solomon Sanders, they had been married 2 wk (Sol Jr.)
15	may	1878	Josephine Sanders 16 dau/Monatcue & Jane- 4 daughter in 2 yrs to consumption
21	jun	1888	Woodford Sanders 12 aug 1832-25 jul 1887 one of counties first settlers b Cabell Co. VA m Arbella Lowe
12	oct	1889	Charoltte Sanders aged 103 sermon was preached at Chain Lake Church
5	sep	1896	Harriet Smith of Toledo (dau/Mary Sanders)
6	sep	1897	Jason J. Sanders b Cabell Co. VA 1840 served in Civil War

Maurice Sanders, a direct descendant, has kept a personal list of family burials. Some of the above listed burials are from his list and in addition:
BETHEL CEMETERY west of Calvin Center -Calvin Twp - Methodist
Sanders, Mary E.   1878 age   38y   2nd   w/Solomon Jr.
Sanders, Matilda   1877

Rough outline of burials at Chain Lake Cemetery

Chain Lake Road

```
==================================================================================
CHURCH         ! ! ! S  S ! !   S  !  !  "  ! ! ! ! ! ! ! ! ! !
                       s  s           s        "
               !      s  s                     "
                      s     s     s  s         "
               !     s s s       s             "
west                   SS           s          "                           east
               !       s                       "
                     s                         "
               !    s   s                      "
                                               "                  s
               !                               "
                                               "
               !                               "
               -------------------------------  -----------------------------------
               ! !                             "
                                               "
               ! !                             "
                                               "
               ! !                             "
                                               "                                s
               !                               "
                                               "
               !       s                       "       s  s
                                               "
               !      s  s                     "          s
                                               "
               !        s                      "       s  s  s
                                               "
               !       s s s                   "                    s
                                               "                    s
                         s
                         s
```

Most of the markers are damaged or down, some covered with dirt & grass.

APPENDICES

Appendix 9C

KNOWN FACTS of the MANUMITTED SANDERS who lived in both Cabell County, Virginia and Cass County, Michigan
All listed Sanders have one or more recorded document connecting them to Sanders families.

1. Ada (Ader-Adre)
   Ada/Ada
   1. adult listed in 1802 William Sanders' bill of sale (Ader and her children see appendix 2)
   2. 1850 Cass census age 80 home of Alex. Halistock with James & Peggy Sanders
   3. (August)1850 Buried Chain Lake Cemetery beside Zebedee age 87 (b 1773)

2. Alicia (Lethia, Lucy, Lelia, Leicia, Alissia)
   /Daniel
   1. 1849 deed part of Daniel's family
   2. 1850 adult 23 - daughter of Daniel by deed & will
   3. 1850 Cass census living in Solomon's home
   4. 1850 marries Peter Sanders
   5. 1853/4 named in father Daniel's will
   6. mother of 9 to 11 children including twins
      L.A.m 1851   Mary 1855   Jesse 1863   ?Amanda 1852   neice?
      Gerturde 1852-1921   Jasper twin 1859   Arbillion 1868   ?America V. 1854   "
      Mary 1855   Newton twin 1859   Philis f 1861   Alice 1871   (Janetta (Eli's dau) 1856)
   6. 1850,60,70,80 Cass census, and deed, marriage, birth & death records of Cass Co.
   7. still living 1880 (Probably buried beside Peter at Chain Lake.)   (b 1827)

3. Albert
   /Moses
   1. child 7 - son of Moses 1849 deed
   2. son/Moses 1850 Cass census
   3. 1860 Cass census age 17 years
   4. Civil War part of Co H 102 USCT (1st MI)
   5. moved of dead by 1870   b 1843

4. Calvin
   /Jane&Levi
   1. child 2 - son of Jane & Levi born 1848 in VA but not listed on 1850 Cass census nor any deeds
   2. 1860 Cass census age 11   1848-1926
   3. 1870 Cass census age 22
   4. 1880 Cass census married to Gerturde Brown with 3 children (from ch DC)
      Mary Jane 1874   Carrie 1878-1905
      Oscar 1876-1965   Arthur 1882-1909
   5. buried Chain Lake 1848-1926

5. Calvin
   /Calvin
   1. adult - 1849 Cabell sale
   2. 1849 witness in Cass County(Gregg Docket Book)
   3. Sampson Simmons "Cal came back and worked at iron furances in Lawrence County, OH"
   4. possible marriage 1856 to Margaret McMillon of Lawrence Co. OH (Ironton Register)
   5. obit in Ironton Register 1894 : Calvin Sanders, colored man and long time collier at the Etna and
      Vesuvius Furances, died 20 Mar 1894 after having a leg amputated
   6. long a resident of Vesuvius Furnace with pay vouchers from furnance, never listed census

6. Caroline
   /Moses
   1. adult 28 - wife of Moses by census
   2. Cass census 1850,60,70
   3. 4 children
      Albert 1843 -102 USCT   J(m) 1853 -102 USCT   Eliza F.1860-70   Hezekiah 1860-1870
   4. death prior to 1875 when Moses remarried   b1822-(1870/75)

7. Charley
   /Charles
   1. adult - 1849 Cabell estate sale
   2. 1850 Cass County will - everything to sister Mary Ann & her children,
      he has "neither mother or father or children"

8. Charles
   /Mary
   1. child 8 - 1849 deed son of Mary
   2. 1850 Cass census s/ Mary
   3. 1860 Cass census with stepfather John
   4. moved or dead 1870   b1842

9. Charlotte

   /Charlotte
   1. 1813 Cabell deed by Daniel Witcher transfers "Charlotte & Jenny
      slaves of son Sanders Witcher,decd"
   2. 1850 adult 50 - (born before turn of century no aggrement on age)
   3. 1849 Cabell sale but no deed
   4. 1850 Cass census head of house age 50 with daughter Jane
   5. 1860 Cass census age 70 with daugther Jane & husband Levi(Eli) #624
   6. 1870 Cass census with Jane & Levi #85
   7. 1870 - on daughter Jane's death certificate with "father" Sanders Witcher
   8. 1880 Cass census age 93 with grandson Elihu #183
   9. 1889 dies age 107 sermon is preached at Chain Lake - obit in Cass Vigilant 12 Oct 1889
   10. age 50 on 1850 census, 70 in 1860, 70 in 1870, 93 in 1880 and 107 at death- maybe b 1800-1889

10. Columbus
    /Luke
    1. child 4 -1850 census son of Luke
    2. moved or dead 1860   b1846

11. Cynthia
    Radford
    1. adult 38 - 1849 Cabell sale
    2. 1849 Cass deed as Cynthia Radford with son (no husband listed on deed)
    3. 1850 Cass census with husband John and son Jacob
    4. 1860,70,80 Cass census 6 children

Appendix 9C

        Jason 1848-54 John 1853   Fredrick 1862-1908 mD85
        James 1853 William 1858 mD85 Rosetta 1864-1936 m C2-283
5. still living 1880 Porter Twp. she and daughter purchased at Dorcas sale as Radd
6. sometimes used name Radd / son William Radd - teamster at Williamsville b1812 d after 1880

12. Daniel
    /Daniel
    1. adult 46 - 1849 Cabell sale   1804-1853
    2. 1849 Cass deed - head of house
    3. 1850 Cass census
    4. 1853 will
    5. buried at Chain Lake with Ader & Zebedee   (see Dorcas for ch) 1804-1853

13. Dorcas
    /Daniel
    1. adult 50 -1849 Cass deed wife of Daniel   1800-1877
    2. 1850 Cass census (also listed as Darkey)
    3. 1860 Cass census home of son William
    4. 1870 Cass census age 76 head of house
       Alicia   1827   Eliza   1832   Robin(Robert)   1834
       Montesque 1831 Zebedee 1830   William   1836   (raises Halistock daughters)
                           Elijah   1838   Hamilton   1844
    5. 1877 death & will (no burial location   1800-1877

14. Eli
    /Peggy
    /Halistock
    1. child 2 - 1849 Cass deed- son of Peggy Sanders who marries Alex Halistock and takes his name
    2. 1850 Cass census Halistock mother Margaret (grandmother Ada ?)
    3. 1860 Cass census Halistock living with Solomon family
    4. 1860 owns property (mother's share)
    5. 1870 married to Elmore M. -- 1 dau. (plus 3 Brown ch)
    6. served in Civil War CoB 102nd USCT
    7. buried Chain Lake no dates   b 1848

15. Eli
    /Eli
    1. adult ? - probably on 1849 Cabell sale (possibly same as 16)
    2. 1849 Cass deed single   (is he son of Solomon)(1860 census says Eli means Levi ?)
    3. Does he have 2 shares? If not 2 adult Eli's

16. Eli
    /Solomon
    1. adult 25 - 1849 Cabell sale (son of Solomon by will)
    2. 1849 Cass deeds with 2 lots in Williamsville
    3. 1850 Cass census single
    4. 1860 Cass will probate, death prior to 26 jan 1860
    5. 1860 minor child Jeanett receives Eli's 1/8 share of Solomon's deed -
    6. daughter Janette with Peter & Alicia 1870   Eli b 1825-1860

17. Elijah
    /Daniel
    1. child 12 -1849 Cass deed as son of Daniel & Dorcas   1838 - (prior 1921)
    2. 1850 Cass census son of Daniel & Dorcas
    3. 1860 Cass census Brother Wm. & mother
    4. 1870 Cass census with mother
    5. 1874 married Cass D-37 (no name) (Laura Cousins)
    6. 1880 Cass census with Laura 3 children
       Cora T. 1870   George 1876   Rosa L. 1877
       George noted quitar player & singer in Williamsville in 1900 (operated a show)
    7. Civil War Co H 102nd USG (from tomb stone)
    8. buried Chain Lake beside Laura (Laura 1847-1921)   Elijah b 1838 d prior to 1921

18. Eliza
    /Daniel
    1. child 18 - 1849 deed daughter of Daniel & Dorcas
    2. 1850 Cass census ch/Daniel & Dorcas
    3. 1855 Cass married to Jacob Sanders s/ Solomon
    4. 1860 Cass census 1ch plus Joseph Ward orphan child of Susan Sanders & Isaac Warrd
    5. 1870 Cass census   Elihu   1860   Fannie A. 1864
                           Mary J. 1862   Martha E. 1869
    6. 1880 not listed Jacob died 1871   b1832 d between 1870-80

19. Hamilton
    /Daniel
    1. child 6 - 1849 deed son of Daniel & Dorcas   1842-1871
    2. 1850 Cass census son of Daniel & Dorcas
    3. 1860 Cass census with mother
    4. Co B 102 USCT
    5. 1870 Cass census with mother- unmarried
    6. Cass death Book 19 Feb 1871 s/Daniel & Dorcas
    7. buried Chain Lake no dates   1842-1871

20. Hamilton
    /Hamilton
    1. adult ? listed with wife Sarah on 1851 Cass deed for 20a with Daniel & Dorcas & Peter & Letia
       possible son of Daniel as Alicia is daughter of Daniel ??
    2. no other reference Cass County

APPENDICES

Appendix 9C

21. Harriet /Mary
    1. child -14 - 1849 Cass deed daughter of Mary 1836-
    2. 1850 Cass census daughter Mary
    3. 1856 Cass marries Peter Smith b-363 (Robert) in home Mary Sanders - Wit: Solomon
    4. 1860 Cass Census (husband Robert) 2ch plus her brother Sampson (twin to Theodore) and possible 2nd brother M. 6 (Mother Mary's youngest son Mordica)
    5. 1870 Cass census - Harriet head , 5ch plus sister's son Nathan Ward (also Beth Morgan & twins)
        Mordica 1852 brother   Mary J. 1860   Elizabeth 1866
                                  (J.E.) James W. 1855   John W. 1863
    6. 1880 not listed - moved
    7. 1896 died in Toledo
    8. buried at Chain Lake obit Cass Vigilant   1836-1896

22. Isom /Isom
    1. adult 52 -1849 Cabell sale
    2. 1850 remains in Cabell County(petition to court)
    3. 1860 Cabell census wife Sarah & daughter Diana b 1845
    4. not in Cabell 1870   b1798 d after 1860

23. Jacob /Cynthia /Radford
    1. child 2- 1849 Cass deed as son of Cynthia Radford
    2. 1850 Cass census as son of John & Cynthia Radford
    3. buried Chain Lake 1854   1848-1854

24. Jacob /Solomon
    1. child 17 - 1849 Cass deed as son of Solomon
    2. 1850 census as son of Solomon & Phillis
    3. 1855 Cass marriage to Eliza dau/ Daniel
    4. 1860 Cass census 1 ch plus Joseph Ward (son of Susan/Mary and isaac Ward)
    5. 1870 Cass census with 4 ch
         Elihu 1860-1912 m Martha Ash 1881   Fannie A. 1864
         Mary J. 1862   Martha E. 1869
    6. m 2nd Ellen Stephenson who d1932 in Jefferson Twp. obit
    7. 1871 dies at 38 buried by Chain Lake no dates   1833-1871

25. James /James
    1. adult 40 - 1849 Cabell sale   1810-(prior 1860 ? moved ?)
    2. 1849 Cass deed single
    3. 1850 Cass census in Halistock household Peggy Sanders Halistock & Ada Sanders 80 (mother ?)
    4. lot in Williamsville
    5. no other reference

26. Jane /Charlotte
    1. adult 30 - daughter of Charlotte   (b1820 put Cabell deed proves 1813)
    2. 1850 Cass Co. census (no deed)
    3. ch Calvin b 1848 in Cabell County, VA
    4. 1852 Cass marriage to Levi s/ Solomon (house Alex Halistock wit: Luke Sanders)
    5. 1860 Cass census - wife 3 ch and her mother Charlotte
    6. 1870 Cass census same Calvin (b/VA but not on 1850) 1848
                        Mary Francis   1853-1870
                        Elihu   1856- (prior 1895)m S.J.Mitchell
    7. 28jul 1870 Cass death certificate mother Charlotte Sanders(VA), father Sanders Witcher(PA)
    8. Cabell deed 1813 transfer mother Charlotte from estate of Sanders Witcher
    9. Probably at Chain Lake with rest of family 1813-1870

27. Jane /Luke
    1. adult 23- wife of Luke 1850 census 2 ch Columbus - Mary
    2. no other reference   b1827-

28. Jason /Solomon
    1. child 11 - 1849 Cass deed s/ Solomon 1839-1897 DC
    2. 1850 Cass census s/ Solomon & Phillis
    3. m Rebecca Sanders Cordia
    4. served 102 USCT under J.J.
    5. not listed on any census after 1860 when single
    6. Cass death certificate 1897
    7. d 1897 buried Chain Lake obit in Cass Vigilant   1839-1897

29. John /John
    1. adult 58 - 1849 Cabell sale
    2. not on 1850 census
    3. 1851 marries Mary (sister of Charles) they have ch 1854 Mordaci
    4. 1860 (no Mary) John head of house with Mary's children
    5. not listed 1870   1792/4-prior to 1870

30. Joseph /Mary
    1. child 19 - 1849 Cass Co. deed son/Mary   1831-
    2. 1850 Cass Co. census s/Mary
    3. moved or dead 1860

31. Levi /Solomon
    1. adult 23 - 1849 Cabell Co. sale   1827-1880 heart attact at dentist obit CV
    2. 1849 Cass. deed s/Solomon
    3. 1850 Cass census s/Solomon & Phillis
    4. 1852 Cass marriage to Jane dau/Charlotte B-218 Halistock home, wit: Luke Sanders
    5. 1860, 1870 Cass census wife Jane 3 ch, mother-in-law Charlotte (listed Eli)
         Calvin 1848   Mary Francis 1853-1870   Elihu 1856-(1895)
    6. 1879 died age 53 buried Chain Lake   1827-1879/80

Appendix 9C

32. Luke /Luke
    1. adult 39 - 1849 Cabell sale (He purchased the most equipment.)
    2. no deed 1850 Cass census wife Jane 2 ch Columbus, Mary
    3. 1852 witness to marriage of Levi and Jane Sanders Cass County
    4. no other reference   b 1821

33. Mahala /Mary
    1. child 15 - 1849 Cass Co. deed daughter /Mary
    2. 1850 Cass Co. census dau/Mary
    3. 1854 Cass Co. marriage to Thomas Jefferson Carter B-323 Wit: Woodford & Montique Sanders
    4. no other reference (both dead ??) moved??   b1853

34. Margaret (Peggy) /Halistock
    1. adult 29 - 1849 Cabell sale as Peggy
    2. 1849 Cass deed with son Eli
    3. 1850 Cass marriage to Alex Halistock (unrecorded but on census)
    4. 1850 Cass census wife/ Alex Halistock (LaGrange Twp)
       with James Sanders 40 & Ada Sanders 80   plus son Eli 2
       daughters Elizabeth 1850-1877 Ch Lk & Eliza 1854 (1870 with Dorcas)
    5. son Eli living with Solomon in 1860
    6. daughters living with Dorcas 1870
    7. Peggy & husband Alex both dead prior to 1860 (Eli receives deed share) 1821-after 1854 prior 1860

35. Mary /Luke
    1. child 2 - 1850 Cass census as daughter of Luke
    2. moved or dead by 1860   b1848

36. Mary /Mary
    1. adult 41 - 1849 Cabell sale   1809-(prior 1860)
    2. 1849 Cass deed as head of house
    3. 1850 Cass census Susan 1829 Harriet 1834 Mahala 1835 Theodore 1849
       7 ch including twins Joseph 1831   Charles 1841 Sampson 1849
                M. (Mordica- youngest b 1854 - 1860 living with sister Harriet Smith listed
                    separate from her children and with his brother Sampson Sanders
    4. 1851 Cass marriage to John Sanders Porter Twp. Wit: John Radford & Thos. Christopher
    5. 1860 Cass census John with children
    6. dies prior 1860 census

37. Montesque /Daniel
    1. child 19- 1849 deed s/Daniel
    2. not listed 1850 Cass census
    3. 1851 Cass Marriages B-206 to (Martha) Jane Byrd home of Moses Sanders
    4. 1860 Cass census 5ch (twins) plus one ch with grandfather Byrd
    5. 1870 Cass 9 ch - wife missing
    6. 1880 4 more ch wife Sarah -

M.J.(Martha Jane)	1852	Daniel W.	1860- 1937	Ida Leona	1869
Samuel	1854- 1932	Josephine	1862- 1878	Jennie M.	1871
C.A.(with Byrd grpd)	1855	Charlotte E.	1864- 1884	Lina T.	1875
Charity	1856- 1873	Charles		Oliver C.	1877
Mary - twin	1857	or (John C.F.)	1865	Alfonse	1879
Martha -twin	1857- 1878	Susan E.	1867		

    7. two wives -Montique still living 1880 16ch
       Montesque lost 4 daughters to consumption in 2 years *Cass Vigilant*) b1831 d after 1880

38. Moses /Moses
    1. adult 37 - 1849 Cabell sale
    2. no deed
    3. 1850 Cass census wife 2 ch
    4. 1860 wife Caroline & 4 children also William Ward ch of Susan/Mary & Isaac Ward
       Albert   1843 102USCT   Eliza F.   1857-1870
       J.   1853 102USCT   Hezekiah   1860-1870 ch buried with Solomon (grandfather ?)
    5. 1870 2ch (Eliza & Hezekiah) wife dies by 1875
    6. 1875 Cass remarries to Martha Keith
    7. 1880 Cass census still living with Martha her 3 ch & gr dau.
    8. Cass Vigilant 20 Feb 1890 very ill and dying   1813-1890

39. Peter /Peter
    1. adult 28 - 1849 Cabell sale 1821-(after 1880)
    2. 1849 Cass deed single
    3. not on 1850 Cass Census
    4. 1850 Cass marriage to Alicia(Melita) Sanders daughter of Daniel wit: Moses Sanders
    5. 1860 5ch (see Alicia)
    6. 1870 8ch plus daughter of decd Eli/Solmon
       L.A.m   1851   Newton twin 1859   Jesse   1863   ? Amanda 1852
       Gerturde   1852-1921 Jasper twin 1859   Arbillion 1868 ?America V. 1854
       Mary   1855   Philis f   1861   Alice   1871   (Janetta (Eli's dau) 1856
    8. Served Civil War marker 102 USCT at Chain Lake

40. Phillis /Solomon
    1. adult - 55 wife of Solomon - 1849 Cabell sale
    2. 1849 Cass deed wife of Solomon
    3. 1850 Cass Census 6 ch on census & deed (possibly 4 others - older)
       Eli   1825   Woodford 1831   others possible   Peggy 1819
       Levi   1826   Jacob   1833   Peter 1821
       Solomon Jr. 1829   Jason   1839
    4. not listed 1860 Cass census
    5. 1863 burial listed (can not be right because Solomon already remarried)
    6. buried Chain Lake age 55 (death must be 1853 ?becuse Sol remarries in 61)   1795-death or d prior to 1860

APPENDICES

Appendix 9C

41. Robert /Daniel
    1. child -16 - 1849 Cass deed s/Daniel (Robin)
    2. 1850 Cass census s/Daniel & Dorcas
    3. 1860 & 1870 Cass census with mother unmarried
    4. Cass death certificate 13 nov 1877 b VA s/ Daniel & Dorcas 1834-1877

42. Robert / Moses
    1. child 1 - 1850 Cass census son/Moses
    2. no deed, no other reference   b1849

43. Sampson /Mary
    1. child twin 1 - 1849 Cass deed son/Mary
    2. 1850 Cass census son/Mary twin to Theodore
    3. 1860 Cass census living with sister Harriet Smith
    4. 1870 not listed - moved or dead   b1849

44. Solomon Jr. /Solomon
    1. adult 21 - 1849 Cass deed s/Solomon
    2. 1850 Cass census as s/Solomon & Phillis
    3. 1859 Cass marriage to Phymuda E. McCullon C-8 (she is not on 1860 census)
    4. 1860 Cass. with father Solomon (no wife)
    5. 1870 Cass census living alone
    6. 1871 Cass marriages C2-86 to Mary Meathews she d 1871
    7. wife Mary died April 1871 married 6mo later, 3rd Susanah Nov 1871 she died two weeks later obit CV
    8. must be 4th wife who dies before 1880 then maybe 5th (or wife just not listed)
    9. 1880 Cass census no wife 3 ch   Fred   1869 (hers?)   Edgar   1882-1971
                                         William O. 1872   Blanch
                                         Melvin   1874
    10. 1906 will named 5 children and reserved property to family for 25 years   1829-1906 DC

45. Solomon Sr. /Solomon
    1. adult 62 - 1849 Cabell sale & other records   1788-1863
    2. 1849 Cass deed (primary head of family)
    3. 1850 Cass Co. census wife Phillis & 6 sons (plus Daniel's daughter Alicia)
        Eli   1825-1859   Solomon Jr. 1829-1906   Jacob J. 1833-1871
        Levi   1827-1880   Woodford   1831-1887   Jason J. 1839-1897
    4. 1860 Cass Co. census with son Solomon & gr/son ? Eli Halistock
    5. 1860 Cass Co. probate for son Eli and his daughter Janetta
    6. 1861 Cass Co. marriage to widow Francis Oglesby C-103
    7. 1863 will and burial at Chain Lake   1788-1863

46. Susan /Mary
    1. adult 21 - 1849 Cass co. deed daughter/Mary   1829 -(1855-1860)
    2. 1850 Cass Co. census dau/Mary
    3. 1850 Cass marriage to Isaac Ward (from Solomon's will)
    4. 1860 both dead leaving 3 sons
       William Ward 1852) twin ? living with Moses
       Nathan Ward 1852) twin ? living with Woodford
       Joseph Ward 1855   living with Jacob & Eliza
    5. no other mention of children (Nathan 1870 with Harriet Smith)

47. Theodore /Mary
    1. child 1 - 1849 Cass deed s/Mary
    2. 1850 Cass census s/Mary twin to Sampson
    3. 1860 Cass census living with Mary's husband John Sanders
    4. no other mention b1849

48. William
    1. child 14 - 1849 Cass deed s/Daniel
    2. 1850 Cass census s/Daniel & Dorcas
    3. 1860 Cass census head of house with mother
    4. 1870 Cass death certificate 20 sep 1870   1836-1870

49. Woodford /Solomon
    1. child 19 - 1849 Cass deed son/Solomon
    2. 1850 Cass census s/Solomon & Phillis
    3. 1860 Cass census married to Arabella Lowe (Cass Vigilant) with Nathan Ward in home
    4. 1870 & 1880 Cass census no children
    5. 1886 Cass will probated (put paper says died 1887)
    6. b 12 Aug 1832 Cabell Co. VA, died 25 Jul 1887 Cass Vigilant   1832-1886/7

50. Zebedee /Daniel
    1. child 20 - 1849 Cabell sale   1830- ( )
    2. 1849 Cass deed s/Daniel
    3. 1850 Cass census s/Daniel & Dorcas
    4. no other information

51. Zebedee
    1. adult -87 -
    2. buried at Chain Lake 1850 aged 87

Appendix 9C

    unk Martha J.   1. adult 23 - marries W.M.Stuart 1855 Porter Twp.
    unk Sarah   1. adult   wife of Hamilton - deed
    unk Susan   1. adult 19 - in Gray house 1850 363-370 possible Susan m Isaac Ward different age
unk Elijah Sanders 1860 census age 20 bVA in home of William Jones possible s/Daniel counted twice Penn Twp
unk William Sanders 1860 census age 27 bVA in home of Nathan Jones possible s/Daniel counted twice Penn Twp
unk George 34 & Margaret 36 Sanders b VA in Howard Twp 1860

not on 1850 census	not on deeds	
Hamilton & wife Sarah	Ada	Moses & Caroline & children
John who marries Mary	Zebeedee	Luke & Jane & children
Eli with lot in Williamsville	Calvin Sr.	
Calvin s/Jane	Calvin Jr.	
Calvin adult witness 1849	Charlotte	
Montique s/Daniel	Jane/Charlotte	
Charles who dies 1850	John	
Peter who marries Alicia	Hamilton	
Zebedee who dies 1850	Isom (remains Cabell)	

DISAPPEAR

Luke, Jane & children after 1850 & no deed
Albert/Moses after war service b1843 (age25)
Charles/Mary after 1860 census b1849 (age 11)
Hamilton no deed or census,
  but listed with Sarah on deed with Daniel
James with lot in Williamsville

Joseph/Mary after 1850 census b 1831 (age 19)
Mahala/Mary after marriage in 1854 to Carter
Sampson s/Mary after 1860 census twin b1849 (11)
Theodore s/Mary after 1860 census twin b1849 (11)
Zebedee s/Daniel after 1850 census b1830 (age 20)
Eli if there are 2

Appendix 9C

Sanders family members --
(dates based on sale, deed, census and other information) (DEED HOLDERS in BOLD type)

name	Cabell 1849 sale	Cass 1849d	census 1850	1860	1870	1880	marriage	death	will	burial	
1 Ada			x							Ch LK age 87 (Halistock)	1763-1850
2 Albert/Moses	x	x									1843-
3 Alicia (LethaMelitaElessa)	x		x(Sol)	x	x	x	mPeter Sanders 1850 (Daniel's daughter-deed)				1827-
4 Calvin(Calvary	x						(witness a deed 1849- returned to OH) d Ironton,				OH 1894
5 Calvin/Levi				x	x	x	mGerturde/Peter/Sol Sanders				1848-
6 Caroline w/Moses			x	x							1822--
7 Charley (adult)							----------------------------1850 will -sister Mary				-1850
8 Charles/Mary	x	x									1842-
9 CHARLOTTE	x	x	x	x	x	x	(Witcher Sanders) 1889 age 107				1782-1889
10 Columbus/Luke-			-x								1846-
11 CYNTHIA Radford	x	x	x	x	x	x	John Radford				1809-1853
12 DANIEL	x	x	x				-- 1853 1854 Ch LK				1804-1853
13 Dorcas w/Daniel	x	x	x	x	x		--- 1877 1877 Ch LK				1800-1877
14 ELI	x	x					(maybe s/Sol who buys own property)				
15 Eli/Margaret ((Halistock)	x	x	x	x	x		mElmore			Ch LK Civ.War	1848-
16 Eli/Solomon		x-					----------------------------------- 1860 dau/Janetta				1825-
17 Elijah/Daniel	x	x	x	x	x		mLaura			Ch LK civil war	1838-
18 Eliza/Daniel	x	x	x	x	x		mLevi/Daniel Sanders 1855				1832-
19 Hamilton/Daniel	x	x	x				-- d 1871				1842-1871
20 Hamilton(adult)							--with wife Sarah on a Daniel Deed				
21 Harriet/Mary	x	x	x	x			mPeter Smith 1856/ Peter dead '70, Harriet'80				1836-1896
22 Isom							--remained in Cabell Co.				1798-
23 Jacob/Radford		x	x	x							1848-
24 Jacob/Solomon		x	x	x			mEliza/Daniel1855 @1871 Ch Lk				1833-1871
25 JAMES	x	x	x-				('50 Halistock with ADA '60 dead ch Janetta(Sol)				1810-
26 Jane/Charlotte			x	x	x		mLevi/Sol ch Calvin b in Cabell d1870 Ch Lk				1813-1870
27 Jane w Luke			x								1827-
28 Jason/Solomon		x	x							DC	1839-1897
29 John	x			x			m Mary Sanders 1851				1792-
30 Joseph/Mary		x	x								1831-
31 Levi/Solomon	x	x	x	x	x		mJane/Charlotte				1827-1879
32 Luke			x								1811-
33 Mahala/Mary		x	x				mThos.Jeff.Carter 1854				1835-
34 Margaret/PEGGY	x	x	x				m Alex Halistock				1821-
35 Mary/Luke			x								1848-
36 MARY	x		x	x	x		mJohn Sanders 1851				1809-
37 Montesque/Daniel		x	x	x	x		mJane Byrd 1851				1831-
38 Moses	x	x	x	x	x		w/Caroline 2nd w Martha Keith 1875				1813-1890
39 Peter		x	x	x	x	x	m Alicia Sanders/Daniel 1854				1822-
40 Phillis w Solomon	x	x	x					d p1860		Ch Lk	1795-
41 Robert/Daniel	x	x	x	x				dc 1877			1834-1877
42 Robert/Moses			x								1849-
43 Sampson/Mary	x	x	x	x						twin	1849-
44 Solomon/Solomon	x	x	x	x	x	x	3ch in 1880 at least 4 wives (all die)				1829-1906
45 SOLOMON Sr.	x	x	x				w/Phillis 2nd w 1861 d1863 will Ch LK				1788-1863
46 Susan/Mary		x	x				m Issac Ward 1850 d p1860				1829-
47 Theodore /Mary	x	x	x	x						twin	1849-
48 William/Daniel	x	x	x	x				dc 1870			1836-1870
49 Woodford/Solomon	x	x	x	x	x		m Arabella		will 1886		1832-1886
50 Zebedee/Daniel	x	x									1830-
51 Zebedee							-- Ch LK d 1850 age 87				1763-1850

NOTE: ALL THESE SANDERS HAVE ONE OR MORE DIRCET CONNECTIONS TO THE REST OF THE FAMILIES.
*capitalized --head of household
reported anywhere from 41 to 50 slaves freed---- Calvin/Levi 2 not listed on deeds or census   (all listed b VA)
Ada, Zebedee, Daniel buried together at Chain Lake
2 other possible : 1850 Cass Census Susan Sanders (19) in Gary house (Is this Susanna who marries Ward?)
          1850   Martha Jane Sanders(23) m Wm. M. Stuart 1855 (Stewart ch with Byrd grparent 1860)

Appendix 10A

Solomon Sanders Sr. inventory   Cass Co. MI   22 sep 1863

Parcel of land N20'E   SE corner of the E 1/ of SE 1/4 of Sec 12 Twp 7 S of
Range 14 N88 20'   etc. containing 36 1/4a (?) $547.20 (?)

personal property	
3 quilts	$5.50
1 feather bed	4.50
1 counterpane	3.50
1 coverlid - 3 glass dishes	2.00
1 pillow slip, 1 chest, 1 trunk, 1 bedstead	1.50
1 brass kettle & 1 12 gal kettle	3.00
	$20.00
one 20 gal kettle 3.50 one (ten) 3.50	7.00
one old harness & one fanning mill 5.00	5.50
one lot wheat,18.00, apples on trees	25.00
corn on the ground 30.00	73.00
one barel flour 8, a lot of tobacco 20	
11 head hogs & 9 pigs 22.00	48.00
one bay mare	100.00
cash on hand at death	30.00
4 certificates of deposit on A.Kingsbay	156.60
3 promissary notes on Woodford Sanders	
amounting to $111.14 appraised	55.57
xxx one note xxx	
	$1037.87
widow selects 1 20 gal kettle	$3.50
half of wheat 9.00, cash 30.00	
4 certificates at Kingsberries 156.60	199.10
household furniture	20.00
I assign the above selections to the widow of same	
deceased also the house hold furniture	818.77
I also grant her an order for provisions	52.00
Deduct real estate	-547.20
Amount of assesment	$271.57

Judge of Probate

Will of Solomon Sanders Jr. 3rd March 1906
Solomon Sanders of Calvin Township Cass County Michigan being of Sound mind and memory, do declare this to be my last will and testament.
After all my Lawful debts are paid I give and bequeath to my sons: Fred Sanders, William Sanders, Melvin Sanders, Edgar Sanders and my daughter Blanch Sanders all the land I own in Calvin Township which is to be divided equally with my heirs described as follows: South 1/2 of the North East 1/4 of the South East 1/4 of section 12 town 7 Range 14 West.
It is further understood that none of my heirs can sell or mortage the above described land to anyone except it be to one of the heirs at law for the period of twenty five years after my death. After my death sell all my chattels and pay funeral and other expenses that may occur. All moneys that is left after my expenses are paid to be divided equally among my heirs.
I appoint Green Allen executor of my will.
In witness whereof I Solomon Sanders have hereunto set my hand and seal this third day of March in the year of our Lord 1906   Solomon Sanders (seal)

Appendix 10B

Dorcas Sanders estate sale 1877 & Appraisal
(wife of Daniel)

Item	Price	Purchaser	Item	Price
old iron	.25	W.C. Rinehart	feather bed & bedding	7.00
Barn Door Hinges	.30	"	1 feather bed	3.50
Iron Kettle	1.15	"	1 bed tick	1.00
Cow Bell	.55	Norris Richardson	1 white blanket	.30
Iron Kettle	.05	"	1 checked blanket	.25
Tea Pot & contents	.05		1 " " " "	.50
Fan Mill & cradle	.10		1 quilt 4 blankets old	1.00
Hay knife & bedstead	.10		2 sheat	.20
Sheep Shears	.10		1 table cloth linen	.50
Clock	1.10		1 bureau	3.00
Bedstead	1.00		1 clock	2.00
Cord Bedstead	.25		1 stand table	1.00
Wagon	30.25		5 chairs	1.00
Cow & calf	40.00		1 bedstead	1.00
1 Bay Horse	50.00		1 bedstead	.50
1 Bay Mare	85.00	"	1 table full leaf	.50
Chairs	1.00	Moses Sanders	1 brass kettle	2.50
Side Saddle	.25	"	jars & crocks	1.50
2 Fruit Jars	.10	Laura Sanders	cook stove & furniture	3.00
Brass Kettle	3.00	"	milch safe	2.00
1 Butter Dish	.15		Sundries-Sadle ?	.75
1/2 doz Plates	.10		apple parer	.25
1 check blanket	.20		dishes	.75
1 bureau	4.30		Box of irons	.25
Flat Iron	.20	"	Bell	.75
Milk Crock	.10	Allen Hunt	Fanning mill	1.00
1 Crock	.05	"	Hay Rake	14.00
Milk Crock	.05	"	3 sugar kittles	5.00
4 gal Jar	.45	Calvin Sanders	1 wash kittle	1.75
Lot Tin Ware	.50	"	3 turkeys	2.50
Lard Can	.30		1 hoe	.25
Pail & Dipper	.35		17 chickens	4.25
3 Tumblers	.25		1 cow 6 yr old	25.00
1 Sauce Dish	.13		1 spinning wheel	.50
Cream Pitcher	.14		1 churn	.75
Biscuit Cutter	.01		wash board & flat iron	.25
Stove & Furniture	2.45		Bay Mare mortaged	40.00
1 quilt	.40		R & W cow 4yr old	20.00
2 Stand Covers	.05	"	waggon	30.00
Six Gallon Churn	.70	Eliza Sanders	pr horses 40.00 each	80.00
Check Blanket	.50	"	interest in 120a of land	
Feather Bed	4.75	"	clk of Cass	
4 gal Jar	.45	Silas Copley		
3 gal Jar	.10	Henry Hunt		
1 Stand & Roll Pin	1.35	"		
Iron Kettle	1.55			
Six Chickens	1.50			
Pork Barrell	.21	"		
Oil Can	.10	Solomon Sanders		

Appendix 10B

Item	Price	Buyer
Auger	.10	"
Tea Pot	.40	
Glass Dish	.50	
4 Sauce Dishes	.35	Solomon Sanders
3 Widow Curtains	.45	"
Spinning Wheel	.35	Cynthia Radd
Platter & Pepper Box	.05	"
2 Wool Blankets	.25	
2 Pillows	.50	
Pillow & Sheet	.15	
Feather Bed	5.75	
3 Turkeys $.70	2.10	"
1 Bottle	.10	Otis Moor
Lamp Chimney & can fruit	.10	Mrs. T. Cannady
Wool Blanket	.35	"
Wool Blanket	.10	"
Milk Safe	1.55	Elias Rinehart
1 table	.05	"
Iron Kettle	1.00	"
1 Stove Shelf	1.30	Thomas Stover
1 Barrell	.05	"
Hay Rake	20.00	Lot B. James
Table Cloth	.30	Rosa Radd
Bed Quilt	.50	"
Wool Blanket	.30	"
1 Brown Horse	26.00	Orlow Williams
	$290.19	

I hereby certify the above to be the true account of the sale of the estate of Dorcas Sanders May 26, 1877 Otis Moor clk

Dorcas Sanders account with W.C. Rinehart

1871
May 12 Repair on plow wheel .50
Jun 18 Repair on plow wheel .15
1872
May 10 Repair on hoes .40
Jun 27 Sharpen 2 shovels .25
Jul 13 Repair 2 heel wedges .10
Sep 11 Repair on 2 forks .25
Nov 25 4 new shoes 4 set 2.30
Dec 12 2 new shoes 2 set 1.25

1873
Mar 27 Singletree hook/wedge sharp .30
Jul 30 Repair on Wagon .25
Aug 5 Lenying cutter sharp spear 1.00
Aug 30 Sharp 4 shovles/singletree .75
Sep 2 Shoe set per Elijah .20
Nov 8 Sow & pigs 10.00
Dec 31 3 chain links .15
   12.65

Mar 5 1 1/2 day work   1.50

APPENDICES

Appendix 10B

			Nov 8	2 bushel wheat	3.00	
	interest for 5 yr 1.82	5.20	Nov 8	34 cabbage heads	2.04	
		7.02	Nov 8	1/2 bu potatoes	.36	
					6.90	3.75
			interest to 4 yr		1.61	7.36

```
1874
Jan   2   2 chain links              .10
Feb   6   1 shoe on Bob Sleigh       .75
Mar  24   Elijah Sanders acct       9.05
Apr  15   2 shoe set                 .40
Aug   5   1 set door hinges         1.25
                                   11.55
Apr  10   Cr 1 cord wood            1.00
                                   10.55      interest 3 yr  2.22   12.77
                                              Amount Total  $27.15  against estate
```

Appendix 10C

Cass County Marriage Books

B-162	1850	Susanna Sanders (22) d/Mary Porter Twp.
		to Isaac Ward (43) wit: E.W.Artis & Beth Brim
B2-170	26 dec 1850	Peter S.Sanders (28) home Solomon Jones -
		Melita Sanders (24) d/Daniel Porter Twp.
		wit:Stephen Trane & Moses Sanders
		Peter- Porter Twp.- Alicia- Calvin Twp
B-20	22 oct 1851	John Sanders (59) home John Sanders (Calvin twp)
		Mary Sanders (45) Wit:John Radford, Thomas Christopher
B-206	2 oct 1851	Montique Sanders (22) s/Solomon - home Moses Saunders
		to Jane Byrd (17-Porter Twp)
B-218	12 feb 1852	Levi Sanders (34) s/Solomon - home Alex Hailstock)
		Jane Sanders (32) d/Charlotte wit: Luke Sanders
B-323	14 dec 1854	Mahala A. Sanders (18) Calvin twp) wit: Wood Sanders &
		to Thos. Jefferson Carter(24) Monticue Sanders
B-333	5 apr 1855	Jacob Sanders (21) s/Sol Brownsville, Calvin Twp.
		Eliza Sanders (22) d/Dan wit:Levi Newton,Thos.J.Carter
B-	1855	Mary Jane Sanders (23)
		to William M. Stuart
B-363	1856	Harriet Sanders (21) Calvin Twp. home Mary Sanders Mother
		to Peter Smith (21)
C-8	17 mar 1859	Solomon Sanders Jr.(24) s/Sol Calvin Twp.)
		to Phymunda E. McCullon
C-103	21 nov 1861	Solomon Sanders Sr. (70) wit:John Rolson-Penn Twp
		to Francis Oglesby (50)wit: Mary Haley-Calvin Twp
C2-86	12 jun 1871	Solomon A. Sanders (28)Calvin Twp Jr. s/Sol
		to Mary Meathews
C2-160	15 sep 1875	Moses Sanders (63) Calvin Twp
		to Martha J. Keith
C2-175	1877	Elihu Sanders (22) wit: Jason J. & Charlotte Sanders
		to Sarah J. Mitchell (16) (s/Levi/Sol
C2-231	1881	Elihu Sanders (21) of Williamsville s/Jacob/Sol
		to Martha Sanders(28) d/Mont ???

Appendix 10C

C2-261	1878	Levi Sanders (49) of Cabell Co. VA Calvin Twp. to Martha Ash wit: Moses & Martha Sanders
D-37	1874	Elijah Sanders --

Cass Death Records

20 sep 1870	William Sanders	37	Porter Twp	
	b VA s/Daniel & Dorcas Sanders (both b VA)			
24 jun 1870	Eliza Sanders	13	Calvin Twp	
	b MI dau/Moses & Martha Sanders (both VA)			
9 mar 1870	Hezekiah Sanders	11	Calvin Twp	
	b MI s/Moses & Martha Sanders (both VA)			
28 jul 1870	Jane Sanders	50	Calvin Twp wife of Levi/Solomon	
	b VA dau/Sanders Witcher (PA) & Charlotte (VA) Sanders			
20 aug 1870	Mary J. Sanders	17	Calvin Twp b MI dau/Levi & Jane Sanders	
19 feb 1871	Hamilton Sanders	27	b VA s/Daniel & Dorcas Sanders	
13 nov 1877	Robert Sanders	43	b VA s/Daniel & Dorcas Sanders both dead	
28 may 1878	Martha Sanders	19	Porter Twp b MI d/Monticue & Sarah	
15 may 1878	Josephine Sanders	15	Porter Twp b MI d/Monticue & Sarah	
12 par 1879	Jesse Sanders	14	Porter Twp b MI s/Peter & Elissa Sanders	
12 oct 1889	Charlotte Sanders	107	Jefferson Twp---	

Appendix 11 CALVIN TOWNSHIP
Adapted from "Map of the Counties, Van Burn and Berrien, Michigan" Geil Harley & Siverd - Philladelphia 1860.

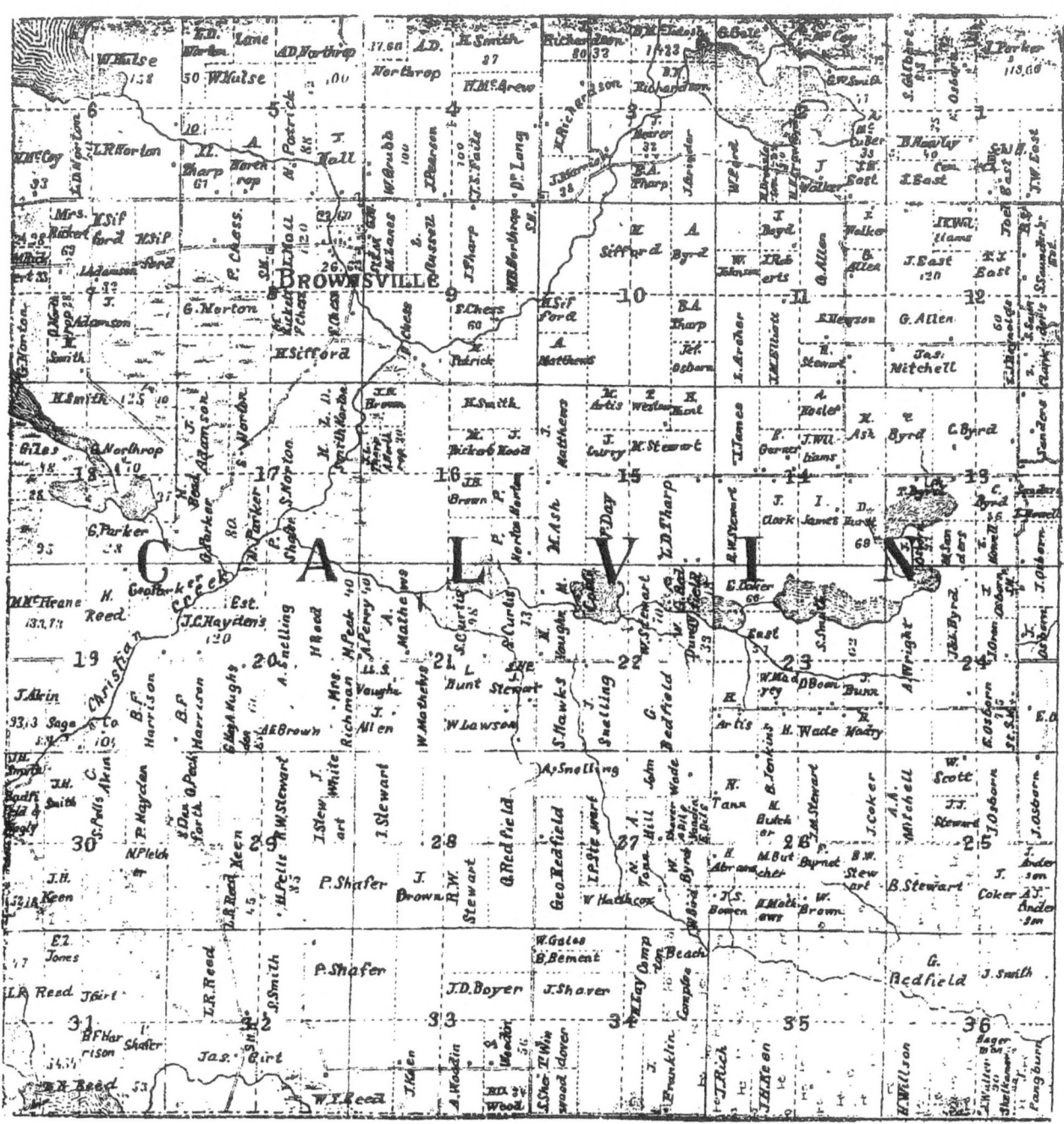

Sanders settled in northeastern quadrant along township line.

Appendix 11 PORTER TOWNSHIP
Adapted from "Map of the Counties of Cass, Van Buren and Berriem, Michigan" Geil Harley and Siverd - Philadelphia 1860.

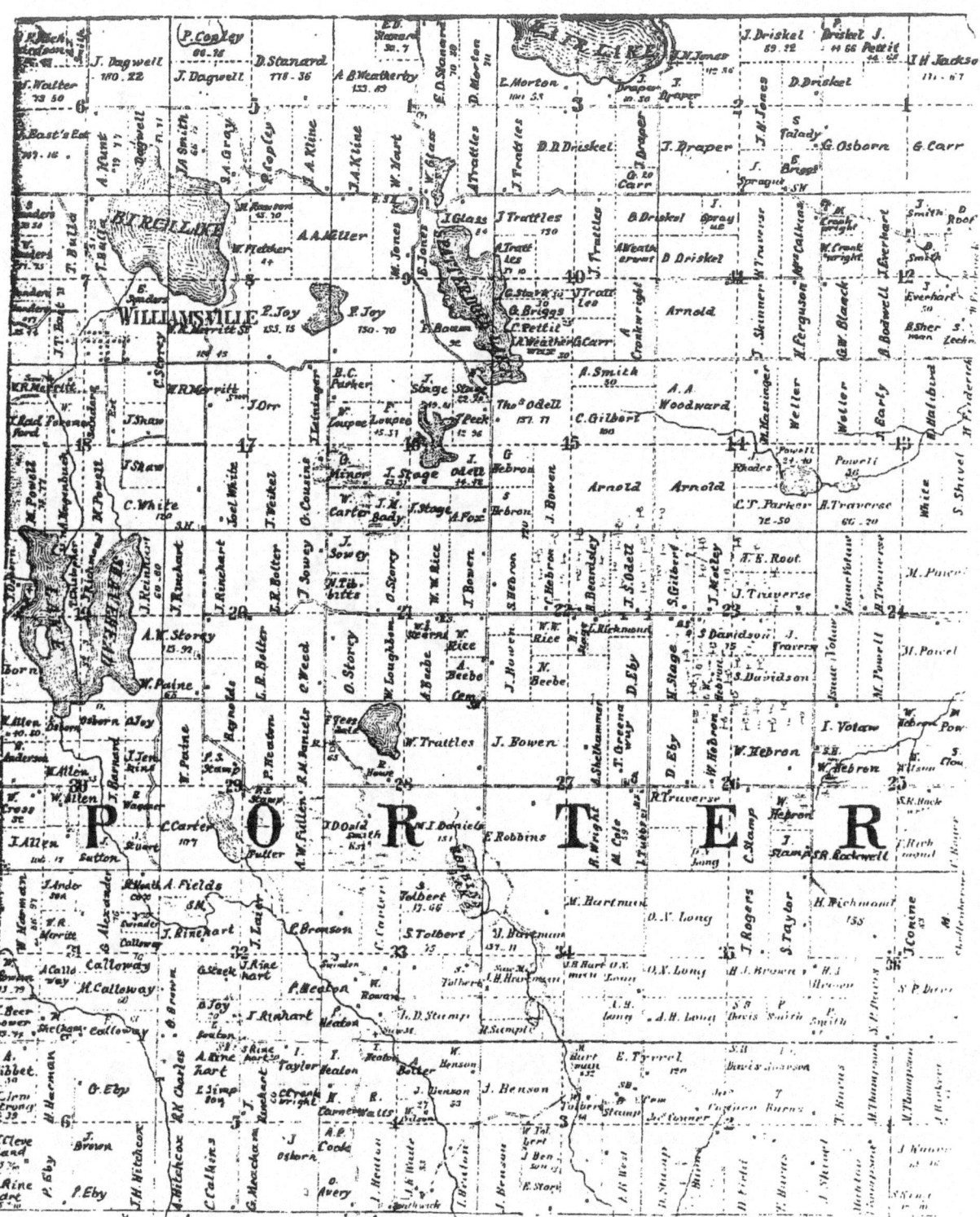

Sanders settled in northeastern quadrant west of Williamson

Appendix 11 CALVIN TOWNSHIP
Adapted from "Atlas of Cass County Michigan" D.J. Lake Philadelphia, 1872.

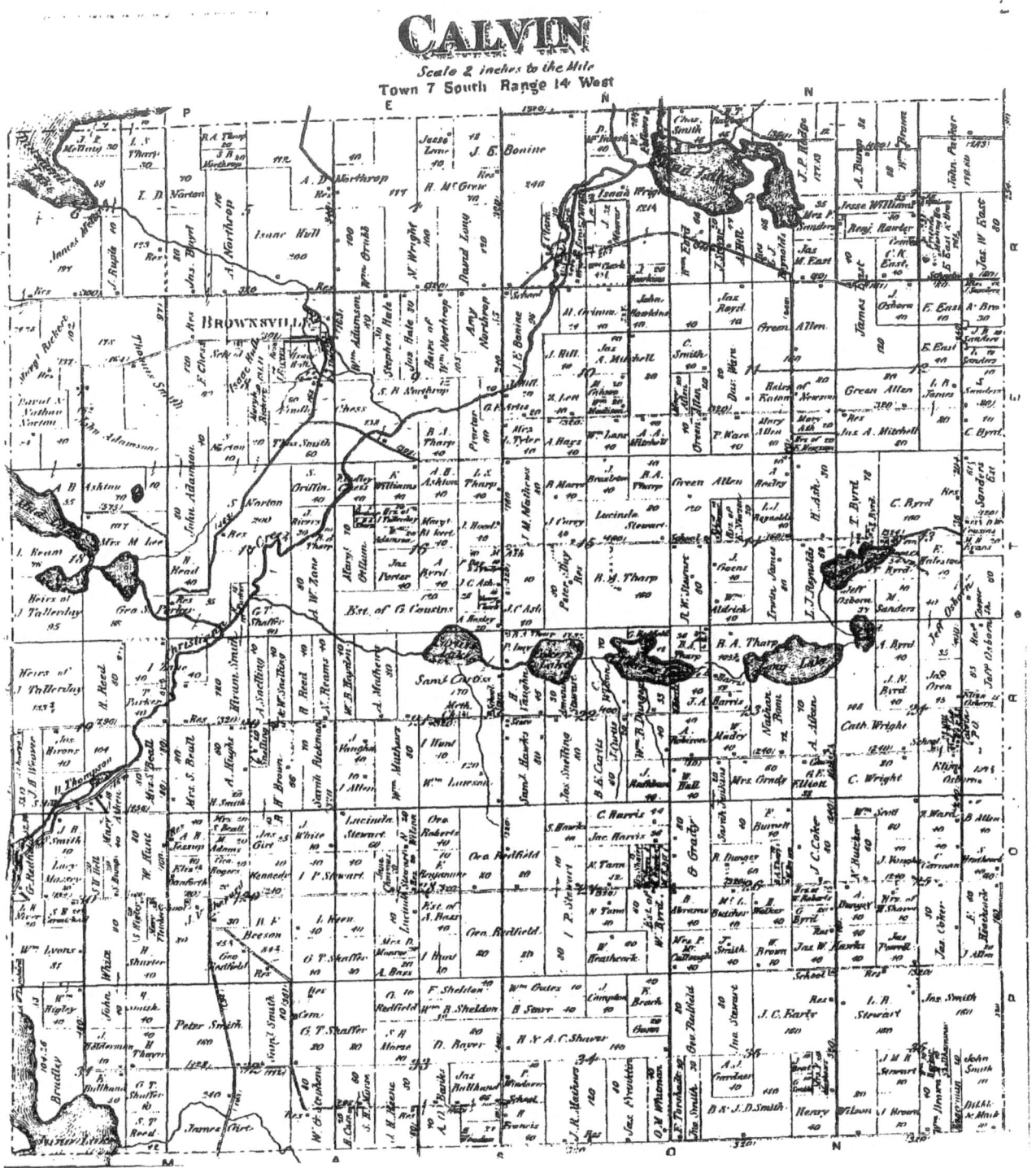

Sanders settled in northeastern quadrant along township line.

Appendix 11 PORTER TOWNSHIP
Adapted from "Atlas of Cass County Michigan" D.J. Lake Philadelphia, 1872.

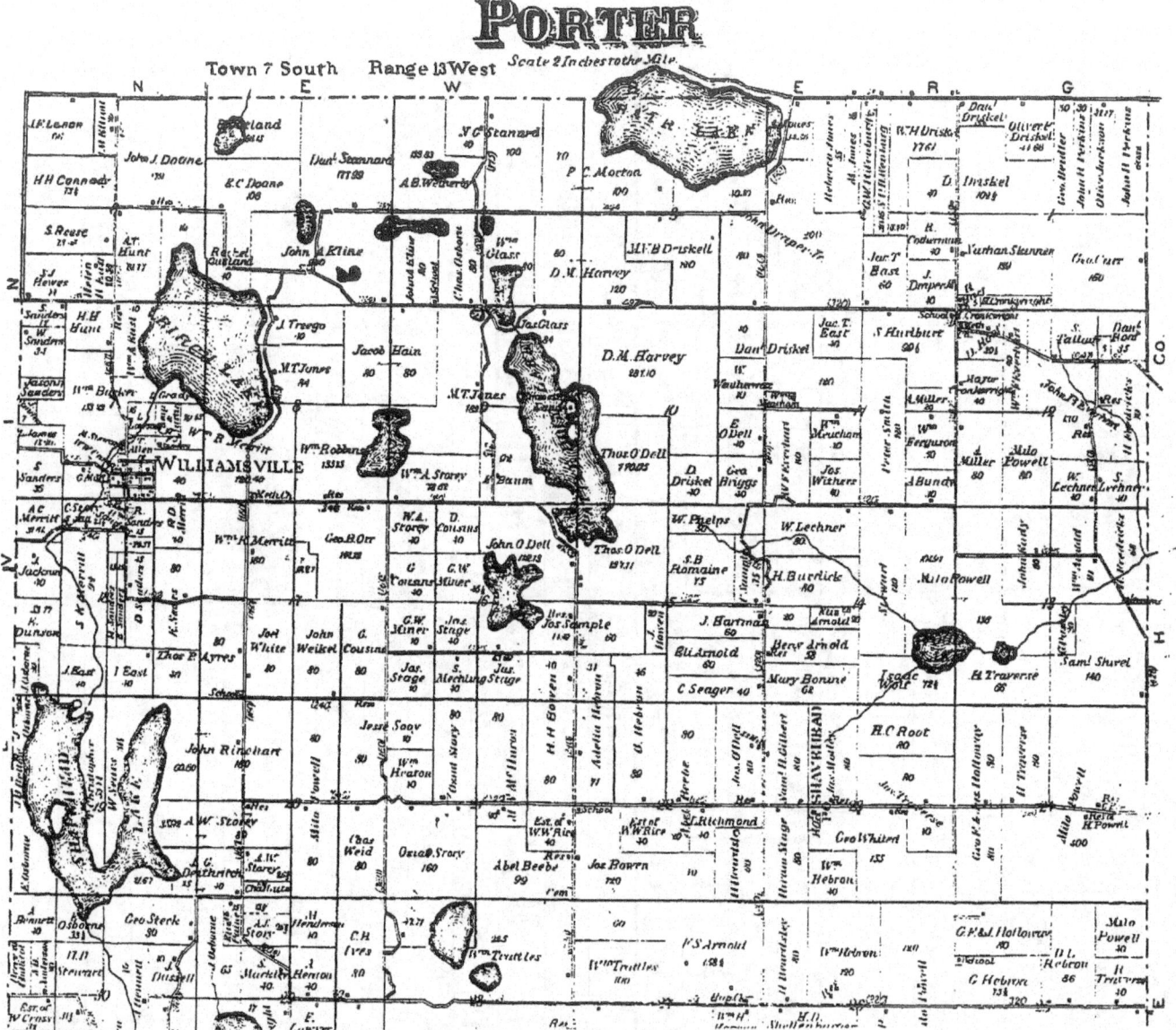

Sanders settled in northeastern quadrant west of Williamsville.

Appendix 12A

Descendants of Hetty Sanders Kilgore
    William Sanders (17--)-1801   Kanawha will
        m Martha Green(Gwinn) 1761-1831   Cabell will
            (possibly Loudoun Co. VA @1782)
    1 Hetty   1782-1852   Cabell will
    2 Sampson m 1821 Ann Gwinn (Cabell) one girl both died young @1836-40
        1786-1849   Cabell will

Thomas Kilgore m Hetty Sanders probably Kanawha, VA 1801/2
    1 Hetty b 1782 VA (lived Anson Co. NC ? and Smith Co. TN)
        d 8 apr 1852 (aged 70) buried Kilgore Cem. Milton
children

11 <u>Emaline (Linie-)</u> @1802-(1849) m <u>Henry Ball</u> Cabell Co.
    111. Telitha 1827(died young not on deeds)
    112. Marietta 1831   m Washington Gwinn(FBL deed)
        1121 Elizabeth 1852
        1122 Sampson 1855
        1123 Conwesley 1857 m Louisa Billups 2)Mary Erwin CCM
        1124 Charles
        1125 Thomas 1860
    113. Lafayette 1834 m 1856 Mary Gwinn   CCM
        1131 Josephus 1858
        1132 William 1860
        1133 Martha E. 1863
        1134 Jennie 1864
        1135 Fannie 1865
        1136 Emily 1867
    114. Jeremiah 1836   m 1864 Jennie Keyser (2nd)
        1141 Albert 1865
        1142 Louisa 1867
        1143 Mary 1869 m Tom Perry
        1144 Thomas
            11441 Lee (living 1997)
        1145 Jefferson
        1146 Benj. Franklin 1870 m Estella Heck
            11461 sister
                4 infs
            11462 Benj. Frederick (living 1997)
        1147 Susy m Curry
            11471 Mary Curry Davis (living 1997)
        1148 Hettie
        1149 Julius (killed RR)
    115. Hetty Ann 1838 (21 in 1860 in Washington Gwinn house)
    116. Martha Ann 1841   m 1866 James Rece   CCM
        1161 Charles 1868
        1162 Walter 1869
    117. John D.S. 1849(not listed deeds or 1850 census)

Appendix 12A

12 <u>George 1803-af1880</u>　　m 1st <u>Elizabeth Margaret Newman</u> Cabell Co.
   121. Matthew inf　　(Geo d Boyd Co. KY)
   122. Eliza 1827-1847(?)　m 1847 James Jordan
   123. Malinda 1828-1856　m 1856 John T. Hatfield
      1231　Effie Aton 1856
      1232　Millard F. 1857
      1233 Margaret 1858
   124. James 1830-1912　m 1850　　(1)Malinda Riggs
                            m　　　　(2) Lucretia Alexander
   125. William 1831-　m 1854 Rachael McCune　　CCM
   126. Martha 1834-　m 1878 James Jordan (sister Eliza's widower)
   127. Mary Ann 1836-1896 m 1854 Isaac Blake 1834-1902
      1271　Anne 1857-1879 m Frank J. Lesage
         12711　Ethel A.
         12712　Sidney
      1272　Emma 1859　m Levi Jones
         12721　Anna
         12722　Sallie
         12723　Mary
      1273　Ceres 1861 m William Shipe
         12731　Nettie May
         12732　James A.
         12733　William
      1274　Virginia 1865 m Cassius Merritt
         12734　Angie
         12735　Robert
      1275　Margaret 1868 m William Hendrick
      1276　Martha 1871　m Dr. Thomas Hallanan
         12761　Walter S.
         12762　John P.
      1277　Nellie Blake 1874　m Arthur McClean
         12771　Norman 1887-1887
         12772　Birdie
         12773　Mary
         12774　Virginia McClean 1904-1970 m Charles M. Payne
            127741　Charlene Payne m Jack Leist
            127741　Carla Sue Leist m Paul A. Templeton
               1277411　Sara Dare Templeton
               1277412　Wesley Cole Templeton
            127742　Jennie Lou m Thomas W. Hughes
   128. Sarah 1838-　m 1854 John Heath
   129. Elizabeth Margaret 1841- m 1856 Geo. W. D. Williams
        (source Charlene Leist CC Hertiage)

13 <u>Jeremiah (?)1803-@1847</u>　　m 1821 <u>Nancy Fullerton</u> Law.Co.OH
   131. Mary Ellen　　　m James Duncan to Illinois
   132. Eliza Jane　d 1913 m Samuel Woodrow Johnson 1812-1883 (FBL 14ch)
      1321　Mary　　　　1837 m (James)Gallaher
      1322　Ann　　　　　1839
      1323　Napeleon　　1841 m Sarah Dundas
      1324　Fannie C.　　1844 m Pollard

Appendix 12A

      1325 Martha   1846/8
      1326 Emily   1840/2
      1327 Abner T.   1852
      1328 Benjamin F.   1856 m Patty Taylor
      1329 Samuel W.   1858
      132+0 Albert M.   1859
      132+1 Daniel W.   1860
      132+2 Robert M.   1864
      132+3 Thomas K.   1866
      132+4 N.Bell(son)   1868 Source: FBL interview Mrs. Johnson
  133. Hetty Frances 1829   m 1849 John Gwinn (FBL-census)
      1331 Emma 1853
      1332 Albert 1855
      1833 Randolph 1860
  134. Julia Ann 1821-1865 m James T.McKeand m 1845 CC
      1341 Sampson Sanders   1846-1935 m Harriet E. Symns
      1342 Martha Pricilla   1848-1886 m Guy F. Plymale
      1343 Columbietta   1850-1868
      1344 Aroanna   1852-1853
      1345 Henry Bascom   1853-1937 m Eliza Ann Garrett
      1346 Thomas Ceon   1856-1857
      1347 Mary Summerville   1858-1933 m Martin Keyser
      1348 James Kilgore   1861-1891 m Minnie Price
      1349 Horatio Seymore   1864-1943 m Minnie Plymale
      James remarried 2nd had 5 more children, 3rd wife
  135. Thomas W. Gwinn 1822 m Mary Jane Rogers or Mary McCormick
      (1860 CCcen) ch on deed
      (source Phillip Hatfield CC Heritage)

14 <u>Mary (Polly) 1806-1845   m 1823 William Simmons(1797-1845)</u> Cabell Co.
    Simmons from Baltimore cabinet & bridge builder-legislator
    FBL W.S.Vinson had Bible (family lived Guyandotte)
    (Conwelsey b there.) His furniture owned by Mrs. Gus Northcott
    from Geore W. Summers. Dr. Vinson had table & secretary/bureau
        W.S. Vinson also had picture (Mary & Wm. ??)
        Vinson had picture Peter Love & wife and
        George Gallaher & wife Malinda(Benton Co.MO)
        FBL interview card Mrs. Mary Frances)
  141 Conwelsey   1824-1870 m Elizabeth Ann Handley no ch
  142 Martha Green 1826-1847 m Warren P. Rece
  143 Emily   1825-1845
  144 Naomi 1831-1854 m George Gallaher(1822-1900)(Benton Co.MO)
      1441 Georgia
* 145 Ann Amelia 1833-1910 m Peter Everett Love/s-Wm.A. 1833-1912
      CCM   (FBL Amelia McDonald) she had pictures
      (C.A. Love biography in FBL) addional FBL no author
    1451 Charles A. Love 1853-1942 m 1893 Edith Branough
    1452 John W. Love 1856-1940 m MO- Catherine Jackson
    1453 Conwelsey Simmons Love 1858-1941 m Mary J. Dundas (Cabell)
    1454 James Sampson Love 1861-1900 m Agnes Sedinger
    1455 Thomas Lee Love 1865-1897 m Katherine Hereford (no ch)

Appendix 12A

        1456 Leonidus Lewis Love 1866-1918 m Cynthianna Love 1891(Cabell)
        1457 Allen Vinson Love 8-1942 m Lillian Tozer (WA)
        1458 Henry Edward Love 1934 m Minnie McComas 1894 (Cabell)
        1459 Mary Elizabeth Love 1923 m William G. Williams 1894 (Cabell)
        145+1 Anna Eliza Love 1941 m Shelton Reynolds 1897 (Cabell)
  146   Elizabeth 1836-36
  147   Malinda 1837-   m George B. Gallaher (her sister's husband)
  148   Mary Francis 1840 m Dr. Bennett Clay Vinson (d 1888)
        (FBL interview W.S. Vinson) (Vinson from St. Louis)
        1481 Clara Grace 1862- m Sheriff Wm. Walton b MO
        1482 Charles Clinton 1865-1900 m Brenda Lane CC killed RR
        1483 William Sampson 1868- never married
        1484 James Albert 1870-1893 killed RR
        1485 Lulu Maud 1873-1905 single teacher
        1486 Frances V. 1875- m. W.T. Cooley
        1487 Bennett Clay Jr.
  149   Sampson Sanders 1843- m Agnes Goodrich(Goody)Ruffner CCM
        (FBL-Will Rece) dau-Col. Ruffner of Charleston
        1491 William Sanders   1870-1873
        1492 Charles Ruffner   1873-1873
        1493 Naomi Anne 1874-   m Dr. George T. Klipstein
        1494 Elizabeth Wilson   1876 m 1 Isaac N. Lively
                                        m 2 William P. Mahood
        1495 Mary Frances   1878-1925 m John W. Platt
           14951 John Leighton 1900-(Fayetteville) m Virginia Turner
              149511 John Turner 1927- (Los Angeles, CA)
              149512 Richard Leighton 1929-1929
           14952 Albert Simmons 1901- m Georgianna Thornton
           14953 Mary Virginia 1904- m Paul S. Hahn
           14954 Naomi Simmons 1906- m Frank B. Boyd
           14955 Agnes Rose   1909-
        1496 Samuel Watson 1880-1880
        1497 Bennett Erwin 1882- m Myrtle Zoe Maddy
        1498 Grace Josephine 1884-1886
        1499 Goodrich Kilgore 1887- m Ruby Kuns
        1499+1 Conwelsie Ruffner m Ruth Lucas

15 <u>Martha Green 1819-1897</u>   m   Charles K. Morris Cabell Co.
  (given in Dusenberry) Chas./s/John of Berkeley Co. 1819-1900
    151. Mary 1838/9   m 1855 Dr. V. R. Moss   CCM
    152. Ellen 1842   m 1880 Arthur Williams   CCM
    153. John A. 1845   m 1866 Emily Gwinn/dau/And. CCM
        1531 Mary E. 1867
    154. Thomas(James J.) 1847 d Civil War
    155. Edna E. 1849   m 1870 T. Heber Rece/s/Edmund CCM
    156. Allie d before war
    157. Ida K. 1855   m 1880 T.S. Berkely   CCM
    158. Charles R. 1859-1935   m Myrtle Ayers
  FBL interview Wm. Rece card (moved to VA during Civil War)
      interview Mr. & Mrs. Wentz   (Carter Co. VA)
      interview C.A. Love grandson of Ann Amelia Kilgore Simmons

Appendix 12A

(Wintz- Dick Kilgore (black & half bro to Martha- very fond of each other)

16 <u>Malinda   1822-1855</u>   m   Thomas Lee Jordan   Tennessee
    161. Ella
    162. John
    163. Charles
    164. Mary
    165. Martha

*14 Mary Kilgore & Williams Simmons (Line Stilling in Cabell County)
    145   Ann Amelia Simmons   m Peter Everett Love/s-Wm.A. 1833-1912 CCM
        (FBL Amelia McDonald) she had pictures
        (C.A. Love biography in FBL) addional FBL no author
      1451 Charles A. Love 1853-1942 m 1893 Edith Branough
        14511   Edith 1860 inf
        14512   Edwin inf
        14513   Grace inf
      1452 John W. Love 1856-1940 m MO- Catherine Jackson
        14521   Walter Head 1885-1887
        14522   Marie Quida 1887- m Wm. R. Harrington (Htgn)
          145221   Nancy L. 1919- m Samuel S. Shumate (Kanawha)
          145222   Mary Jane 1924-
        14523   Bertie (son) 1889-1889
        14524   Fred Alfred 1889 m Nona C. Alderman
          145241   Wm. Alderman 1916-
          145242   Robert Hiram 1919
          145243   Sarah Francis 1921 m Ray Justice KY
          145241   Bobbie Ray 1922
          145244   Janet Lee 1927-
          145245   Frederick Wesley 1929-
      1453 Conwelsey Simmons Love 1858-1941 m Mary J. Dundas (Cabell)
        14531   Madge Everett 1887- m Clyde R. Salmons   Appendix 12A
          145311   Clyde R. Salmons Jr. 1913 (Buffalo NY)m Ruth
              Konopaska (Tulloma, TN
          145312   Mary Elizabeth 1916(Crestwod,KY) inf
          145313   John Grant 1920(Cincinnati)
        14532   Ruth Dundas 1891-m George W. Raike (Greenup)
          145321   Betty Anne b1919(Logan) m Oscar W. Sellars (KY)
          145322   George W. II 1925(Logan)
        14533   James Donald 1894 m Alice M. Terry
        14534   Lillith L. 1897 m Russell V. Lewis (FL)
      1454 James Sampson Love 1861-1900 m Agnes Sedinger
        14541   Ilma Estelle 1896 (Milton) m 1918 Andrew W. Johnston (ND)
          145411   Virginia Love 1919(ND) m Robert A. Peterson (ND)
          145412   James Wm.1923 (CO)
      1455 Thomas Lee Love 1865-1897 m Katherine Hereford (no ch)
      1456 Leonidus Lewis Love 1866-1918 m Cynthianna Love 1891(Cabell)
        14561   Lewis A. 1892 m 1916 Elizabeth Morrill (WA)
          145611   Lewis M. 1918(WA)-1942
          145612   Robert Fielding 1920(WA)

Appendix 12A

```
1457  Allen Vinson Love 8-1942 m Lillian Tozer (WA)
   14571   Dorothy 1904-1989 m George W. Lee (WA)
      145711   George W. II 1932
   14572   Allen Vinson II 1907 m Mae Sievers (WA)
      145712   Peter J. 1933
1458  Henry Edward Love 1934 m Minnie McComas 1894 (Cabell)
   14581   Paul Everett 1896 m Lucille Brooksher 1923(AK)
      145811   Doris Ellis 1924
   14582   Amelia Alene 1900 m Silas E. McDonald 1928 (Cabell)
      145821   Donald Elmer 1929
      145822   Marilyn Love 1931
   14583   Mildred Bess 1904-1925
1459  Mary Elizabeth Love 1923 m William G. Williams 1894 (Cabell)
   14591   Allen Graves 1895 (Portsmouth) m Virginia Denver
      145911   Allen G. Jr. 1933(Portsmouth)
      145912   Brook Anthony 1935
   14592   Forrest Love 1897 m Evelyn Billiam (OH)
      145921   Karen 1937
      145922   Forrest Love Jr.1899
   14593 Paul Grant 1899 m Mabel M. Phillips (OH)
      145931   Paul Jr. 1920 (Huntington)
      145932   William Grant 1923 (Portsmouth)
      145933   Keith Phillips 1927
145+1 Anna Eliza Love 1941 m Shelton Reynolds 1897 (Cabell)
   145+11  Hunter Love 1903 m Evelyn Dowling (MD)
      145+111  Hunter Love Jr. 1927 (Huntington)
   145+12  Shelton Ellsworth 1907 m Matilda Roane 1936 (VA)
      145+121  Mary Elizabeth 1937
```

Appendix 12B

s=Solomon
d=Daniel
m=Mary
L=Luke
ms=Moses
c=Charlotte
R=Cynthia Radford
H=Peggy Halistock

Sanders descendants
information acquired from census, deed, marriage, will, death records and
cemetery records in Cass County, MI & personal information of family
++
s1 Solomon Sanders 1787-1863 m Phillis 1795-1853
                               m Francis (Ogselby) she died 1899 age 96 CH LK
       other older children possible born between 1817-1825
s11 Eli   1825-1859 m?
    s111 Jannetta A. 1856-   (deed transfer)
s12 Levi   1827-1880 m Jane Sanders/Charlotte 1852 Cass ML
             m Martha Ash 1878
      died Heart attack in dentist's office 26 feb 1880 (obit)
    s121 Calvin 1848-1926 (b Cabell) m Gerturde Brown (ch DC)
        s1211 Mary Jane   1874-1956 m 1893 James Wilson - d (South Bend, IN)
        s1212 Oscar   1876-1965 m Edna B. Vaughan   (b Porter) ML
           s12121 Lester 1905-1940 m Doris Steele (garage Calvin Center)
           s12122 Estella 25 feb 1909 m 1927 Forest Lawson (LIVING CASS)
               garage Calvin Center, Cass Co. MI
              s121221 Imogene 1927 m Preston Brown (Granger,IN)
                  s1212211   Larry W. (Westminster Co. MI)
                  s1212212   Karen L. Holmes (Littleton Co.MI)
              s121222 Sandra 1939 m Joseph White (Kalamazoo)
                  s1212221   Dawn R. McDonald (Grand Rapids, MI)
                  s1212222   Aaron D. (Grand Rapids, MI)
                  s1212223   Kevin A. (Kalamazoo, MI)
              s121223 Audrey 1941   (Calvin Center, Cass Co. MI)
              s121224 Paul Dean 1945 (m 3) (Elkhart, IN))
                  s1212241   Paul Dean Jr. (Elkhart, IN)
                  s1212242   Damon Eugene (Elkhart, IN)
           s12123 Marshall H. 1911-1962 m Ester (b Cass- d Detroit)
              s121231 Marshall H. Jr. 1940 (Flint, MI)
                  s1212311   Valencia (t) 1963
                  s1212312   Elizabeth (t) 1963 m Williams
                        s12123121   Taylor Elizabeth 1996
                  s1212313   Marshall Howe III 1964
                  s1212314   Jennifer 1981
              s121232 Maurice W. 1942 (Detroit, MI)
                  s1212321   Telecia Renee 1969
                  s1212322   Sharon (t) 1973
                  s1212323   Shirley (t) 1973

Appendix 12B

```
                    s12124  Myrl(son) 1918 m 2 ch (LIVING-Dowagiac,CASS Co. MI)
                       s121241  Donna Lee (Citrus Heights, CA)
                       s121242  Donald E. (Diamond Bar, CA)
                s1213 Carrie   1878-1905   (Cass Co. MI)
                s1214 Arthur   1882-1909 DC (Cass Co. MI)
        s122 Mary Frances 1853-1870 (Cass Co. MI)
        s123 Elihu  1856-(1895-) m Sarah Jane Mitchell 1877(she remarried 1896)
                witness Jason J. & Caroline Sanders
            s1231 Jacob 1878
            s1232 Robert Sr. m Jessie Scott
                s12321  Esther m Fisher
                s12322  Ethel
                s12323  Harriet
                s12324  Helen
                s12325  James    (info from Stella Lawson & Maurice Sanders)
                            (additional info available)
    s13 Solomon Jr.1829-1906(77) DC m 1 Phymuda McCullon 2 Mary Meathews 1871
                    Cass m 3rd Susannah  Ch Lk (obit says 2w in 6mo)
        s131  William O. 1872- BC
        s132  Melvin 1874-
        s133  Fredrick 1869  -m 1889 Louise Brown (s/Sol & Mary)
            s1331 Alpha  (ch lk ?)
        s134  Edgar 1882-1971 (Ch Lk)
        s135  Blanch
            (ch listed Sol.Jr. will 1906)    (MS)
    s14 Woodford   1831-1887 DC S&P  m Arabella   (Ara at Ch LK)(no children ?)
    s15 Jacob J.  1833-1871 m Eliza Sanders/Daniel 1855 Cass
        s151  Elihu  1860-1912 DC J&E  m Martha Ash 1881
            s1511 Rollie 1885-1938 Ch Lk
            s1512 Rosemary
                2nd 1894 Ellen Stephenson (Ch Lk 1932)(CV in Jefferson Twp)
        s152  Mary J.1862
        s153  Fannie A.     1864
        s154  Martha E.     1869                         (MS)
    s16 Jason J.           1839-1897 DC obit married Rebecca Sanders Cordia (spelling?)
        CoH 102 USCT obit - CH LK
```

UNKNOWN RELATIONSHIP
(Ada is possibly Mother to many of the Sanders- see separate chart.)

---

*1 Ada(Ader) 1773-1850 (87)(listed William Sanders' will 1801)
       may be mother to most of group, buried Chain Lake1850 aged 87
    11 Daniel 1804 buried beside her
    12 James 1810 living with her 1850
    13 Margaret(Peggy) 1821 living with her in 1850

---

*1 Zebedee 1773-1850 (87) buried with Ada & Daniel

Appendix 12B

```
d1   Daniel Sanders 1804-1853    m Dorcas 1800-1877
     other older children possible (Margaret m Halistock dau/sister)
     d11   Alicia 1827-            m Peter Sanders 1850 Cass   102 USCT CoH
           d111  L.Amanda          1851
           d112  Gerturde          1852-1921
           d113  America     V.    1854
           d113  Mary              1855
           d114  Newton            1859t  m 1899 Maggie Fowler Witcher (South Bend)(CV)
           d115  Jasper            1859t
           d116  Phillis 1861
           d117  Jesse             1863-1879 DC P&A
           d118  Arbillion         1868
           d119  Alice             1871
     d12   Zebedee                 1830
     d13   Montesque 1831-1891 DC  m Jane Byrd 1851 Cass  2nd Sarah (16ch)
           d131  Martha Jane 1852
           d132  Samuel D.         1854 m1907 (53) Rose Henderson 1855-1932 DC
           d133  C.A.              1855 (with grandparent Byrd 1860census)
           d134  Charity           1856-1873 Ch Lk
           d135  Mary              1857t
           d136  Martha            1857t-1878 DC M&S age 19
           d137  Daniel W.         1860-1937 Ch Lk
                 d1371  Bertha (26) m Fred Gault 1908
           d138  Josephine         1862-1878 DC M&S age 15
           d139  Charlotte E.      1864-1884 DC M&S age 21(CV article said 4th dau in 2yr)
           d13+  Charles(John C.F.)1865
           d13+1 Susan E.          1867
           d13+2 Ida Leona         1869        m 1892 Joseph Ramsey Jr. of Vadalia
           d13+3 Jennie M.         1871
           d13+4 Lina T.           1875
           d13+5 Oliver C.         1877
           d13+6 Alfonse           1879 (Alonzo)
     d14   Eliza                   1832-(1880)       m Jacob Sanders/Solomon 1855 Cass
           d141  Elihu             1860
           d142  Mary Jane         1862
           d143  Fannie A.         1864
           d144  Martha E.         1869
     d15   Robert(Robin) 1834-1877 DC (no children)
     d16   William  1836-1870 DC age 65(no children ?)
     d17   Elijah  1838-1905 (age 65)DC ChLk m Laura Cousins 1874 Cass  102USCT
           d171  George A.         1876  m 1901 Mrs. Anna Koser
                       noted singer & guitar player in Williamsville (had own show)
           d172  Rosa Lee 1877 m John Thomas 1903 2nd Jackson
                 d1721  (Elsie m 1908 Blaine Stewart 2nd Mathews
           d173  inf son           1885 BC E&L
           d174  Clara m G.W.Franklin 1904
           d175  Cora
           d176  Margaret m Lucas/Norris
                 d1761  Fern Lucas
                 d1762  (George)
     d18   Hamilton                1844-1871 DC age 27  102 USCT  ChLk
```

Appendix 12B

c1 Charlotte Sanders 1782-1889 (father of Jane was Sanders Witcher ?)
    (There is a Witcher deed in Cabell Co. from Daniel Sr. to Daniel Jr transferring
    Charlote & Jenny from property of deceased son Sanders Witcher)
    obit (Jefferson Twp in County Home)
    c11 Jane 1820-1870 DC m Levi Sanders/Solomon 1852 Cass
        c111 Calvin 1848-1926 (b Cabell) m Gerturde Brown
            c1111   Mary Jane 1874
            c1112   Oscar   1876 m Edna B. Vaughan   (b Porter)
                c11121   Lester 1905
                c11122   Marshall H. 1911 m Ester
                      c111221   Marshall H. Jr. 1940
                            c1112211   Valencia (t) 1963
                            c1112212   Elizabeth (t) 1963   m Williams
                                    c11122121   Taylor Elizabeth
                            c1112213   Marshall Jr. 1964
                            c1112214   Jennifer 1981
                      c111222   Maurice W. 1942
                            c1112221   Telecia Renee 1969
                            c1112222   Sharon (t) 1973
                            c1112223   Shirley (t) 1973
                c12123   Myrl(s) 1918 m 2 ch (living-CASS)
                c12124   Estella 25 feb 1909 m 1927 Forest Lawson (LIVING CASS)
                      garage Calvin Center
                      c121241   Imogene 1927 m Brown (Dowagiac)
                      c121242   Sandra 1939 m White (Kalamazoo)
                      c121243   Audrey 1941   (Calvin Center)
                      c121244   Paul Dean 1945   (Elkhart)
        c1213   Carrie   1878-1905
        c1214   Arthur   1882-1909 DC

Mary had brother Charles (by Cass Co.will) no other kin
m1 Mary Sanders 1809-(1860) m John Sanders 1851 Cass
    other children possible
    m11 Susan   1829-(1860) m Isaac Ward (both d by 1860)
        m111   William 1852t(?)
        m112   Nathan 1852t(?)
        m113   Joseph 1855
    m12 Joseph 1831-
    m13 Harriet 1834-1896 Toledo Ch LK   m Peter Smith 1856 Cass
        m131   James W. 1856
        m132   Mary J. 1860
        m133   John W. 1863
        m134   Elizabeth 1866
    m14 Mahala   1835-   m Thomas Jefferson Carter 1854 Cass
    m15 Charles 1841-
    m16 Theodore 1849t
    m17 Sampson 1849t
    m18 Mordica 1854 living with sister Harriet 1860

Appendix 12B

```
ms1   Moses Sanders 1813-1890 (lib) m Caroline 2nd Martha Keith 1875 (her 3ch)
ms11  Albert       1843      102 USCT
ms12  J.           1853      ?102 USCT
ms13  Eliza F.     1857-1870 DC
ms14  Hezekiah     1860-1870 DC
```

```
L1  Luke Sanders        1811       m Jane
    L11   Columbus      1846
    L12   Mary          1848                    no other references
```

R1 Cynthia Sanders Radford 1812- m John Radford (1798-1889 Ch Lk)
    estate sale Cynthia & Rosa Radd - Frederick is married as a Radd

```
R11  Jacob Radford      1848-1854 6yr Ch Lk
R12  John               1853 (m Susan Loomis) ?
     R121   Harry R. m 1895 Nellie Adams ?
            R1211   Cynthia 1902-1920 DC ?
R13  James              1853-1853 7m Ch Lk
R13  William    (R.)    1858- (1915 DC age 56) teamster in Williamsville
R14  Fredrick           1860 (1862-1908 Ch Lk)
        m 1893 Jennis Churchina Nlyene (s/ John & Cynthia)
        Fred Radd South Bend  s/ John & Cynthia m Millie Artis 1892
R15  Rosetta            1864-1936 obit m 1884 Geo. A. Henderson
        obit is Rosa Radford Sanders
        (1870 Fredrick Sanders in home age 1 ?)
```

```
h1  Margaret (Peggy) Sanders Halistock  m Alexander Halistock 1850 Cass
    h11    Eli          1848-          ChLk m Elmore M.         (Civil War)
           h111  Coravida
    h12    Elizabeth    1850-1877
    h13    Eliza        1854                     (living with Dorcas
```

One cora left home and passes as white

Missing

1 Hamilton m Sarah adult on deed with Daniel
2 Calvin witness 1849 -returned to Cabell
3 Charles of will
4 John who m Mary
5 Peter who m Alicia

CV=obits from *Cassopolis Viligant*

Appendix 13

"Henning's Statues at Large of all the Laws of Virginia"
Volume 11 Chapter 21 - 1782 - printed 1823

An act to authorize the manumission of Slaves.

I. WHEREAS application hath been made to this present general assembly, that those persons who are disposed to emancipate their slaves may be empowered so to do, and the same hath been judged expedient under certain restriction: Be it therefore enacted, That is shall hereafter be lawful for any person, by his or her last will and testament, or by any other instrument in writing, under his of her hand and seal, attested and proved in the county court by two witnesses, or acknowledged by the party in the court of the county where he or she resides, to emancipate and set free, his or her slaves, or any of them, who shall thereupon be entirely and fully discharged from the performance of any contract entered into during servitude, and enjoy as full freedom as if they had been particularly named and freed by this act.

II. Provided always, and be it further enacted, That all slaves so set free, not being in the judgement of the court, of sound mind and body, or being above the age of forty-five years, or being males under the age of twenty-one, or females under the age of eighteen years, shall respectively be supported and maintained by the person so liberating them, or by his or her estate: and upon neglect or refusal so to do, the court of the county where such neglect or refusal may be, is hereby empowered and required, upon application to them made, to order the sheriff to distrain and sell so much of the person's estate as shall be sufficient for that purpose. Provided also, That every person by written instrument in his life time, or if by last will and testament, the executors of every person freeing any slave, shall cause to be delivered to him or her, a copy of the instrument of emancipation, attested by the clerk of the court of the county, who shall be therefor, by the person emancipating, five shillings, to be collected in the manner of other clerk's fees. Every person neglecting or refusing to deliver to any slave by him or her set free, such copy, shall forfeit and pay ten pounds, to be recovered with costs in any court of record, one half therof to the person suing for the same; and the other to the person to whom such copy ought to have been delivered. It shall be lawful for any justice of the peace to commit to the gaol of his county, any emancipated slave traveling out of the county of his or her residence without a copy of his or her emancipation, there to remain till such copy is produced and the gaoler's fees paid.

III. And be it further enacted, That in case any slave so liberated shall neglect in any year to pay all taxes and levies imposed or to be imposed by law, the court of the county shall order the sheriff to hire out him or her for so long time as will raise the said taxes and levies. Provided sufficient distress cannot be made upon his or her estate. Saving nevertheless to all and every person and persons, bodies politic or corporate, and theirs heirs and successors, other than the person or persons claiming under those so emancipated their slaves, all such right and title as they or any of them could or might claim if this act had never been made.

Although the laws were ammended in 1849, Sampson Sanders' will that year would probably have been executed under the older statues.

Selected Bibliography

Public Documents

Cabell County, Huntington, West Virginia, County Clerk, [Deeds] Books 1-10, 1809-1850.
----------,[Marriages] Book 1, 1809-1850.
----------, [Wills] Book 1, 1820-1850.
----------,[Minutes] Book 1 and Book 3, 1809-1815, 1826-1835.
Caswell County, North Carolina, County Clerk, [Bonds] 1790-1810. (Court House, Carthage, Tennessee.)
----------,[Tax List] 1784 and 1787. (Carthage, Tennessee.)
Cass County, Cassopolis, Michigan, County Clerk, [Deeds] Book 1848-1852.
----------, [Marriages] Books 1,2, 1840-1920.
----------, [Wills] Books 1-5, 1840-1920.
----------, [Deaths] Books 1-3, 1854-1920.
"Documents of the Guyandotte Navigation Company 1849-54." Richmond, Virginia: Virginia Department of Public Works and the Virginia Assembly. (Lambert Collection, 76-8-21.)
Kanawha County, Charleston, West Virginia, County Clerk, [Deeds] Book B-F, 1800-1810.
Loudoun County, Leesburg, Virginia, County Clerk, [Wills] Books 1760-1800.
Pittsylvania County, Chatham, Virginia, County Clerk, [Tax List] 1784. (Microfilm)
Smith County, Carthage, Tennessee, County Clerk,
    Deeds of North Carolina Grants 1790-1800.
United States Bureau of the Census, Population. Washington:National Archives Microfilm Publications, *Second Census 1800 Virginia*, Kanawha County(printed).
----------, *Third Census 1810, Virginia*, Cabell County(printed).
----------, *Fourth Census 1820, Virginia*, Cabell County, Microcopy M33, Roll 130.
----------, *Fifth Census 1830, Virginia*, Cabell County, Microcopy M19, Roll 190.
----------, *Sixth Census 1840, Virginia*, Cabell County, Microcopy M704, Roll 555.
----------, *Seventh Census 1850, Virginia*, Cabell County, Microcopy M432, Roll 938
----------, *Seventh Census 1850, Virginia*, Slave Schedules, Microcopy M432, Roll 984.
----------, *Eighth Census 1860, Virginia*. Cabell County, Microcopy M653, Roll 1338.
----------, *Eight Census 1860, Virginia*, Slave Schedules, Microcopy M653, Roll 1387.
----------, *Seventh Census 1850, Michigan*, Cass County, Microcopy M432, Roll 349.
----------, *Eighth Census 1860, Michigan*, Cass County, Microcopy M653, Roll 541
----------, *Ninth Census 1870, Michigan*, Cass County, Microcopy M593, Roll 668.
----------, *Tenth Census 1880, Michigan*, Cass County, Microcopy T9, Roll 575.
----------, *Twelveth Census 1900, Michigan*, Cass County, Microcopy T623, Roll 706.
----------, *Thirteenth Census 1910, Michigan*, Cass County, Microcopy T624, Roll 640.
Virginia Personal Property Tax Lists, Virginia State Archives, Richmond, Virginia.
    Cabell County 1809-1850
----------. Kanawha County 1790-1810
West Virginia Property Tax Lists, West Virginia Archives and History Library, Charleston, West Virginia.

Books

Billington, Ray Allen. *Western Expansion-A History of the American Frontier*. New York: Macmillan Publishing Co., 1974.
Chiarito, Marian Dodson. *Old Survey Book I, 1746-1782 Pittsylvania County, Virginia*. Nathalie, Virginia: Clarkson Press, 1988.

----------, *Old Survey Book II, 1797-1829 Pittsylvania County, Virginia*. Nathalie, Virginia: Clarkson Press, 1988.

Comstock, Jim. *Encyclopedia of West Virginia*. Richwood, West Virginia, 1976.

"1860 Plat Maps for Calvin and Porter Townships." Cassopolis, Michigan: Cass County Historical Commission. 1983.

Eldridge, Carrie. *Cabell County Cemeteries, Volume 1*. Chesapeake, Ohio. Privately printed, 1990.

----------. *Cabell County Locator 1810-1850*. Chesapeake, Ohio. Privately printed, 1992.

Fulcher, Richard Carlton. *1770-1790 Census of the Cumberland Settlements*. Baltimore: Genealogical Publishing Co., 1987.

Goodspeed's History of Tennessee. Nashville, Tennessee: The Goodspeed Publishing Co., 1887.

Glover, L.H. *A 20th Century History of Cass County*. Chicago: Lewis Publishing Co., 1906.

Harlan, Louis R. and Raymond E. Smock. *The Booker T. Washington Papers Vol. 7*. University of Illinois Press, 1984.

Henning, William Waller. *Statutes at Large Being a Collection of the Laws of Virginia*. Richmond, 1823.

Hiatt, Marty & Craig Roberts Scott. *Index to Loudoun County Virginia Chancery Suits 1759-1915*. Athens, Georgia: Iberian Press, 1995.

----------, *Implied Marriages of Fairfax County, Virginia*. Athens, Georgia: Iberian Press, 1994.

----------, *Loudoun County Virginia Tithables 1758-1774, 1775-1785 & 1786-1790*. Athens, Georgia: Iberian Press, 1995.

Historical Atlas of the United States. New York: Rand McNally, 1984.

Historical U.S. County Outline Map collection 1840-1980, Sr. Editor, Thomas. D. Rabanhorst. Baltimore: Department of Geography, University of Maryland & Baltimore County, 1984.

Hopkins, Margaret Lail. *Index to the Tithables of Loudoun County Virginia and to the Slaveholders and Slaves*. Baltimore: Genealogical Publishing Co., 1991.

Jackson, N. Wayne. *Our Ward Family*. Salt Lake City: Artistic Printing Company, 1995.

Joyner, Peggy Shomo. *Abstracts of Virginia's Northern Neck, Warrants and Surveys 1697-1784 Volume 4*. Portsmouth, Virginia: Private Publication, 1987.

Kendall, Katherine Kerr. *Caswell County North Carolina Deed Books 1777-1817*. Easley, South Carolina: Southern Historical Press, 1994.

Mathews, S.S. *History of Cass County, Michigan*. Chicago: Waterman, Watkins & Co., 1882.

McKernon, Mary L. *The Church at the Blue Sulphur Springs, Mud River Baptist 1807*. Huntington, West Virginia: OIC, 1987.

Michigan Soldiers and Sailors Individual Records. Lansing, Michigan: Wynkoop Hallenbeck Crawford Co. State Printers, 1915.

Paullin, C.O. *The Atlas of Historical Geography of the United States*. Washington, 1932.

Pratt, J. Earl. *The Promised Land*. New York: Vantage Press, 1964.

Ray, Worth S. *Tennessee Cousins*. Baltimore: Genealogical Publishing Co., 1968.

Register, Mrs. Alvaretta Kenan. *State Census of North Carolina 1784-1787*. Baltimore: Genealogical Publishing Co., 1983.

Rogers, Howard S. *History of Cass County 1825-1875*. Cassopolis, Michigan: Vigilant Books & Job Print, 1875.

Schoetzow, Mae. *A Brief History of Cass County, Michigan*. Casssopolis, Michigan: Marcelus News, 1935.

Wallace, George S. *Cabell County Annals and Families*. Richmond: Garrett & Massie, 1935.

Wardell, Patrick. *Timesaving Aid to Virginia-West Virginia Ancestors*. Athens, Georgia:

SELECTED BIBLIOGRAPHY

Iberian Press, 1985.

Wells, Carol. *Sumner County Tennessee Court Minutes 1787-1805 and 1808-1810*. Bowie, Maryland: Heritage Books, 1995.

Interviews

Ball, Fred (descended from Hetty Sanders Kilgore through son Jeremiah)
    interview with Carrie Eldridge, Cabell County, West Virginia. 22 Sep 1997.
Ball, Lee (descended from Hetty Sanders Kilgore through son Jeremiah)
    interview with Carrie Eldridge, Cabell County, West Virginia. 22 Sep 1997.
Sanders, Estella (descended from both Solomon & Charlotte Sanders)
    interview with Carrie Eldridge, Cass County, Michigan. 21 May 1997.
Sanders, Maurice (nephew of Stella Sanders)
    interview with Carrie Eldridge, Detroit, Michigan. 23 May 1997.

Magazines

Dancy, John C. "The Negro People in Michigan." *Michigan History*, 1940.

Fields, Harold B. "Free Negroes in Cass County Before the Civil War." *Michigan History*. 1960.

Huntley, Fred J. "Colored Farmers settle the Race Problem." *The Gleaner* (Caro, Michigan,)1911. Ann Arbor, Michigan: From Gregg Papers, Bentley Historical Library, University of Michigan. (Used by permission.)

Leete, Edmund N. and Ann J. Sheedy. "The Ohio Trail," Marietta, Ohio: *The Tallow Light*, Summer and Fall 1995.

Stewart, Roma Jones. "The Migration of a Free People, Cass County's Black Settlers from North Carolina." *Michigan History*, Jan/Feb 1987.

Newspapers

Ball, Frank. "The Kilgore Saga." *The Bullentin*, Barboursville, West Virginia, 1971.

"Calvin Township Home of Early Black Community." Ann Arbor, Michigan. Publication and date unknown.

Cassopolis Vigilant. Cassopolis, Michigan, 1872-1890.

Gawne, Peg. "Birch Lake Ruins Offer History Lesson". *Stateline News Review*, Cassopolis, Michigan: 28 May 1969..

Ironton Register. Ironton, Ohio "Marriages," 17 Apr 1856

------- "Obituaries," 22 Mar 1894.

Perkins, Eunice Proctor. "Early Cabell Settlers." Huntington, West Virginia: *Herald Advertiser*, 1939.

------- "Family Trees Out of History's Forest." (article series) Huntington, West Virginia: Herald Advertiser, 1935.

"Sumner County"*Rural Sun*, Nashville, Tennessee: June 19, 1873.

Unpublished Materials

Allen, Green. (Original)"A History of the Chain Lake Baptist Church."
 Chain Lake Church, Cass County, Michigan. (undated, 2 versions.)
"Cemetery Records of Cass County." Daughters of the American Revolution. Cass County,
 Michigan, 1933. Cassopolis Library.
Cemetery Tombstones, Chain Lake Cemetery, Cass County, Michigan.
Douthat, R.S. "Extracts of the Records of the County Court of Cabell County, West Virginia
 from 2 Jan 1809 to 6 Jul 1863," Huntington, West Virginia, 1932. Special Collections
 Department, James E. Morrow Library, Marshall University.
William F. Dusenberry Diaries. Private collection, Huntington, West Virginia.
 (Used by permission.)
East, Harry & Lavon Breece. "Short Story of Williamsville."
 Private collection of Tom & Betty Griffith, Williamsville, Michigan.
Gregg, Phineas & William C. Records from Cass County, Michigan. Donated by Mrs.
 Marshall Sanders and son Maurice. Ann Arbor, Michigan: Bentley Historical
 Library, University of Michigan. (Used by permission.)
Kanawha County Records 1780-1803. (printed text of original), West Virginia Archives
 and History Library, Charleston, West Virginia.
Fred B. Lambert Collection. Huntington, West Virginia: Special Collections Department,
 James E. Morrow Library, Marshall University. (Used by permission.)
"Records of the Dixon Creek Baptist Church 1799-1853."
 Microfilm, Latter Day Saints Library.
Henry & William Ruffner Papers. Privately held. Montreat, North Carolina: Collection at
 the Historical Foundation of Presbyterian and Reformed Churches.
 (Used by permission.)
Sanders, Maurice. Personal list of Chain Lake Burials. Detroit, Michigan.

Maps

Boye, Herman. *Map of the State of Virginia*. Richmond, 1825. Reproduction by Virginia
 State Historical Society. (James E. Morrow Library, Huntington, West Virginia.)
Geil, Harley & Siverd. *Map of the Counties Cass, Van Buren and Berrien, Michigan*. Philadel-
 phia, 1860. (Cassopolis Public Library.)
United States Geological Survey. "7.5 Topgraphical Maps" of Cabell County, West Virginia,
 and Cass County, Michigan. Washington, D.C., 1982.
University of Maryland, Department of Geography. "1840 Counties of the United States."
 Baltimore, 1952. (James E. Morrow Library, Huntington, West Virginia.)

INDEX 1
PEOPLE

Alexander, "Rowan Bill"; 10
Allen, George; 63
Allen, Green; 57, 63
Allen, T.; 57
Anderson Family; 63
Artis Family; 63
Ash; 54
Ash Family; 63
Ash, Harrison; 54, 55
Ball (nephew); 27
Ball, Emaline Kilgore; 38
Ballow, Capt.; 11
Banks, Thomas; 10
Barker, William; 57
Bet (wife of Spencer); 42
Bristoe, 42
Brown, Benjamin; 43
Brown, Imogene (daughter of Estella); 71
Brown, John; 43
Brown, William; 57
Bump, A.; 57
Byrd, C.; 57
Byrd, Irena; 63
Byrd, Turner; 57, 63
Calloway Family; 63
Calvary; 42
Cannady, H. H.; 57
Carter, Mahala Sanders (daughter of Mary, wife of Thomas); 36, 56, 69, 74
Carter, Thomas Jefferson (husband of Mahala); 69, 74
Chapman, James; 21
Charley (kin to Hannah); 43
Childers, Sam; 26
Cooper; 57
Cousins, D.; 57
Cox, James; 20
Crump, W. W.; 57
Dail, Ransom; 20
Dingess, Peter; 25
Dixon, Tilman; 7, 9, 10, 15
Doane, John J.; 57
Dundass, Thomas; 20
Dunson, E.; 57
Dusenberry, Thorn; 43
Dusenberry, William C.; 25, 26, 29, 30
Dusenberry, William F.; 25, 26, 42, 43
Dusenbury, Charles O.; 45
Dusenbury, William C.; 45
Duvall, John P.; 19
East, C. K.; 57
East, E.; 57
East Family; 73
East, Helen H.; 57
East, J.; 57
East, James; 57
East, Jas. W.; 57
East, William A.; 57
Elliott, C. M.; 57
Ellison, W. L.; 61
Estis, Joel; 7
Evans Family; 63
Evans, M. H.; 57
Everett; 43
Gallaher, George; 45, 46, 47, 48, 52, 53, 54, 55, 56
Galleher, George; 67
Grady, L.; 57
Green, Frances; 5
Green, Garret; 6
Green, Gerrard; 5, 6, 8
Green, James; 5, 6, 8
Green, Jarrett; 6
Green, Martha; see Sanders, Martha Green
Green, Mary; 5
Green, Thomas; 6
Gwinn, Andrew; 45
Halestock, E.; 57
Halistock, Alex; 60, 61, 65
Halistock, Eli Sanders (son of Margaret); 36, 56, 57, 60, 61, 65
Halistock, Margaret (Peggy) Sanders (mother of Eli); 36, 56, 60, 61, 65, 74
Hannah; 5, 6, 9, 17, 33, 41, 42, 43
Hatfield, Andrew; 20
Hawks Family; 63
Hawley, Benjamin; 57
Henderson, Jno; 13
Henderson, (laidy); 13
Henson; 37
Hewes, S. J.; 57
Hite, John W.; 25
Hunt, A. T.; 57
Hunt, H. H.; 57
Huntley, Fred J.; 60
Ike; 43
Jackson, J.; 57
James; 42
James; 57
James, L. B.; 57
Jenny; 42, 74, 75
Jordan, James; 20
Jordan, Malinda Kilgore; 22, 38
Kilgore, George; 5, 6, 38
Kilgore, Hetty Frances Sanders; 5, 6, 16, 22, 23, 24, 31, 33, 34, 37, 38, 41, 42, 43, 75
Kilgore, Jeremiah; 38
Kilgore, Thomas; 6, 16, 19, 20, 23, 24, 37, 38, 41
Laidley, John; 45, 46
Lambert, Fred B.; 73

Lawson, Audrey (daughter of Estella); 71
Lawson, Estella Sanders (daughter of Oscar and Edna, wife of Forest); 71, 76
Lawson, Forest (husband of Estella); 76
Lawson, L.; 57
Lenon, J. F.; 57
Lewis, Thomas; 6
Lorry; 42
Love, Charles; 20
Love, Peter; 26, 42
Love, Samuel; 5, 20
Lunsford, Lewis; 21
Manuel; 37
McComas, William; 20
McConnel; 11
Merritt, A. C.; 57
Merritt, R. D.; 57
Mill, G.; 57
Mill, S.; 57
Mitchell, Joseph A.; 57
Moore, Martin; 20, 42
Moore, Wilson; 43
Morris, Charles; 26, 43
Morris, Martha Kilgore; 22, 31, 38, 42
Neal, Jack; 14, 15, 16, 33, 34
Osborn, A.; 57
Osborn, Jeff; 57
Osborne, J.; 57
Osbourn, Jefferson; 60
Paine, William; 45
Parker, Edmund; 43
Parker, John; 57
Parker, Lillie; 43
Patience; 37
Pegalis Marget; 42
Pettengill, Moses; 67
Peyton, Henry; 5, 20, 26
Plott, George W.; 45
Radford (Radd), Cynthia Sanders; 36, 46, 56, 62
Radford (Radd), Jacob; 36, 46, 56
Radford (Radd), John; 46
Radd, William (son of Cynthia); 62
Reese, S.; 57
Reynolds, John; 12
Rinehart, W. C.; 68
Robin; 42
Roffe, C. L.; 26, 42, 43
Rogers, Bennett; 9, 10, 11, 12, 13, 14, 15, 16, 19, 34
Rogers, William; 26
Ruffner, William; 34
Russell, John; 37
Samuels, John; 45, 46
Sanders, A.; 57
Sanders, Albert (son of Moses and Caroline); 36
Sanders, Ada (Ader); 17, 33, 36, 41, 42, 59, 60, 61, 67, 74, 78

Sanders, Alicia (daughter of Daniel and Dorcas); 36, 56, 62, 66, 67, 68
Sanders, Ann Guin; 27, 28, 31, 73
Sanders, Arabella Lowe (wife of Woodford); 66
Sanders, Arthur (son of Calvin and Gertrude); 71
Sanders, Benjamin; 6
Sanders, Calvin (adult); 36, 46, 61
Sanders, Calvin (son of Levi and Jane, husband of Gertrude); 36, 54, 61, 65, 70, 71
Sanders, Caroline (wife of Moses); 36
Sanders, Carrie (daughter of Calvin and Gertrude); 71
Sanders, Charles (brother of Mary); 36, 42, 59, 60, 61, 69, 73
Sanders, Charles (son of Mary); 36, 56, 69
Sanders, Charlotte (mother of Jane); 33, 36, 42, 46, 52, 61, 65, 66, 70, 71, 74, 75, 76
Sanders, Columbus (son of Luke and Jane); 36
Sanders, Daniel (husband of Dorcas); 36, 42, 53, 54, 55, 56, 57, 61, 62, 66, 67, 68, 78
Sanders, Dorcas (Darky) (wife of Daniel); 36, 53, 56, 67, 68
Sanders, Edna B. Vaughn (wife of Oscar); 71
Sanders, Eli; 36, 56, 62
Sanders, Eli, see Halistock, Eli Sanders
Sanders, Eli (son of Solomon and Phyllis); 36, 66
Sanders, Elijah (son of Daniel and Dorcas); 36, 56, 62, 67, 68
Sanders, Eliza (daughter of Daniel and Dorcas); 36, 56, 66, 67
Sanders, Estella, see Estella Lawson
Sanders, Esther Rosanna Wilson (wife of Marshall H.); 71
Sanders Families; 59, 60, 61, 62, 63, 66, 68, 69, 71, 74-75, 77, 78
Sanders, George (son of Elijah); 62
Sanders, Gertrude Brown (wife of Calvin); 71
Sanders, Hamilton; 36
Sanders, Hamilton (son of Daniel and Dorcas); 36, 56, 57, 67
Sanders, Harriet, see Harriet Smith
Sanders, Isom; 36, 43, 46
Sanders, J. (Miss); 57
Sanders, J. B.; 57
Sanders, Jacob (son of Solomon and Phyllis); 36, 56, 65, 67
Sanders, James; 9, 36, 56, 60, 61, 62, 74
Sanders, Jane (daughter of Charlotte, wife of Levi); 33, 36, 42, 61, 65, 66, 71, 74, 76
Sanders, Jane (wife of Luke); 36
Sanders, Jane Byrd (wife of Montesque); 67
Sanders, Jason (son of Solomon and Phyllis); 36, 56, 57, 62, 65
Sanders, John (husband of Mary); 36, 65, 69
Sanders, Joseph (son of Mary); 36, 56, 69

Sanders, Laura Cousins (wife of Elijah); 67
Sanders, Lester (son of Oscar and Edna); 71
Sanders, Levi (son of Solomon and Phyllis, husband of Jane); 36, 56, 61, 65, 66, 71, 74, 76, 78
Sanders, Luke; 36, 46, 57
Sanders, M.; 57
Sanders, Mahala, see Mahala Carter
Sanders, Margaret (Peggy), see Halistock, Margaret (Peggy) Sanders
Sanders, Marshall H. (son of Oscar and Edna, husband of Esther); 71
Sanders, Marshall H., Jr. (son of Marshall H. and Esther); 71
Sanders, Martha Green; 5, 6, 8, 9, 11, 12, 16-17, 19, 20, 21, 22, 23, 24, 25, 27, 28, 30, 31, 33, 37, 41-42, 46, 62, 73, 77
Sanders, Mary (daughter of Luke and Jane); 36
Sanders, Mary Ann (sister of Charles, wife of John); 36, 42, 56, 60, 61, 65, 69, 73, 74
Sanders, Mary Jane (daughter of Calvin and Gertrude); 71
Sanders, Maurice W. (son of Marshall H. and Esther); 71
Sanders, Montesque (son of Daniel and Dorcas); 36, 56, 67, 68
Sanders, Mordica (son of John and Mary); 69, 74
Sanders, Moses (husband of Caroline); 36, 62
Sanders, Myrl (son of Oscar and Edna); 71
Sanders, Oscar, (son of Calvin and Gertrude, husband of Edna); 71, 76
Sanders, Paul Dean (son of Estella); 71
Sanders, Peter; 36, 46, 56, 62, 66, 67, 78
Sanders, Phyllis (wife of Solomon); 36, 46, 56, 65, 66, 71, 76
Sanders, Polly; 5
Sanders, Rebecca; 27, 31, 46, 73
Sanders, Rebecca Sanders Cordia (wife of Jason); 66
Sanders, Robert (son of Daniel and Dorcas); 36, 53, 56, 57, 67
Sanders, Robert (son of Moses and Caroline); 36
Sanders, Sampson; 5, 6, 7, 9, 10, 16, 17, 19, 20, 21, 22, 23, 24, 25-26, 27-28, 29-30, 31, 33, 34, 35, 36, 37, 38, 39, 41, 42, 43, 45, 46, 48, 52, 54, 61, 65, 69, 73, 74, 75, 77
Sanders, Sampson (son of Mary); 36, 56, 65, 69, 74
Sanders, Solomon (husband of Phyllis); 36, 46, 51, 53-54, 55, 56, 57, 61, 62, 65, 66, 67, 70, 71, 76, 78
Sanders, Solomon Jr.; 36, 46, 56, 65, 66
Sanders, Susan, see Susan Ward
Sanders, Theodore (son of Mary); 36, 56, 65, 69

Sanders, Colonel William; 5, 6, 7, 8, 9, 10, 11, 12, 13, 14, 15, 16, 17, 19, 20, 25, 33, 34, 41, 42, 61, 73
Sanders, William (son of Daniel and Dorcas); 36, 56, 57, 67
Sanders, Witcher see Sanders Witcher
Sanders, Woodford (son of Solomon and Phyllis); 36, 56, 65, 78
Sanders, Zebeedee; 36, 53, 59, 61, 67, 73, 78
Sanders, Zebedee (son of Daniel and Dorcas); 36, 56, 61, 67
Sears, E.; 57
Shed (kin to Hannah); 43
Simmons, Conwelsie; 26, 43, 45, 46, 47, 48, 52, 53, 54, 55
Simmons, Lizzie; 46
Simmons, Mary Polly Kilgore; 31, 38
Simmons, Sampson; 31, 41, 42, 43, 46, 73
Simmons, William; 31
Smith, Harriet Sanders (daughter of Mary, wife of Peter); 36, 56, 69, 74
Smith, Harvey; 26
Smith, Percival; 25
Smith, Peter (husband of Harriet); 69, 74
Spencer (husband of Bet); 42
Spurlock, Stephen; 45
Stewart Family; 63
Stewart, M.; 57
Storey, Jeff; 62
Strupe, Melcher; 20
Summers, Francis George; 5, 6, 46, 47, 48, 52, 53, 54
Terrell, Mr.; 11, 12
Thayer, Congressman Eli; 43
Thompson, Pat; 43
Thompson, Widow; 26, 27
Thornburg, Solomon; 20, 25
Turley, James; 5
Turley, Sampson; 6
Turner; 26
Twyman, James; 36
Uncle Tom; 42, 43
Vincent, John; 6
Vinson, W. S.; 46
Ward, Evermont; 25
Ward Family; 75
Ward, Isaac (husband of Susan); 69, 74
Ward, Jeremiah; 7, 16, 20, 42, 75
Ward, Jeremiah (wife); 16
Ward, Susan Sanders (daughter of Mary, wife of Isaac); 36, 56, 69, 74
Washington, Booker T.; 69, 73
White, Sandra (daughter of Estella); 71
Williams, Jesse; 57
Wilson Family; 63
Witcher, Daniel, Jr.; 42
Witcher, Daniel, Sr.; 42, 74

Witcher Family; 75
Witcher, Sanders; 33, 42, 65, 71, 74

INDEX 2
PLACES

Appalachian Mountains, 41
Blue Ridge; 8
California; 71
Canada; 49, 63, 73, 74
Carolina Road; 8, 9
Crick Creek; 13
Cumberland; 12
Cumberland Gap; 12
Cumberland River; 9, 10
Dan River; 8
Dixon Creek; 13
Fort Pitt; 11, 13
Gallipolis; 14
Illinois
    Chicago; 70
Indiana; 47, 48
    Elkhart; 48, 55, 70, 71
    Granger; 71
    South Bend; 69, 70
James River and Ohio Turnpike; 20
Kanawha River; 14, 15, 17, 20, 41
Kentucky; 43, 48, 73
    Greenup; 43
    Harrison County; 8
Louisiana; 15
Maryland; 7, 10, 14, 15
    Baltimore; 10, 11, 12, 13, 14, 34
Massachusetts; 43
Menton; 13
Michigan; 5, 34, 43, 46, 47, 48, 51, 53, 59, 61, 62, 63, 73, 74
    Angle Creek; 62
    Ann Arbor; 70
    Battle Creek; 70
    Bethel Methodist Church; 62
    Birch Lake; 62
    Calvin Center; 62
    Cass County; 5, 17, 35, 41, 42, 47, 48, 49, 55, 56, 57, 59, 60, 61, 62, 63, 65, 66, 68, 69, 70, 71, 73, 74, 75, 78
        Calvin Township; 49, 56, 57, 60, 61, 62, 63, 66, 69, 71, 74
        Howard Township; 49
        Jefferson Township; 49
        LaGrange Township; 49, 61
        Marcellus Township; 49
        Mason Township; 49
        Milton Township; 49
        Newberg Township; 49
        Ontwa Township; 49
        Penn Township; 49
        Pokagon Township; 49
        Porter Township; 49, 56, 57, 61, 62, 67, 71
            Williamsville; 57, 62
            Williamsville Academy; 62
        Silver Creek Township; 49
        Volinia Township; 49
        Wayne Township; 49
    Cassopolis; 63
    Chain Lake; 54, 65
    Chain Lake Baptist Church; 48, 54, 55, 61, 62, 63, 67, 69, 74, 75, 78
    Chain Lake Baptist Cemetery; 59, 61, 66, 68, 73, 74, 78
    Detroit; 70, 71
    Flint; 70, 71
    Kalamazoo; 71
    Union Road; 56
Mississippi Territory; 11, 12
Missouri; 23, 74
Natchez; 10, 11, 12, 13, 15
Natchez Trail; 10, 12, 14
National Road; 14
New Orleans; 10, 12, 15
New York; 10, 11, 12, 13
North Carolina; 5, 7, 25, 41, 48
    Caswell County; 7, 8, 9
Ohio; 43, 47, 48, 52, 56, 67, 74
    Burlington; 43
    Cincinnati; 28, 47, 48, 52, 53
    Ironton; 36
    Lawrence County; 46, 61
        Etna Furnace; 61
        Vesuvius Furnace; 61
    Porkopolis; 28
    Toledo; 70
Ohio River; 14, 20, 27, 30, 34, 41, 43, 47, 52, 59, 61, 74
Ohio Valley; 61
Pennsylvania; 6, 7
    Pittsburgh; 14
Piedmont Trail; 8
Potomac; 12
Rogues Road; 8
Tennessee; 5, 7, 10, 16, 25, 41, 51
    Caswell County; 15
    Dixon Springs; 9, 10, 15
    Gallantin; 9
    Nashville; 10, 12
    Nashville Road; 9
    Sandersville; 9
    Smith County; 9, 10, 14, 15, 16, 34
    Sumner County; 9, 10
US 60; 19, 20, 30
Virginia; 14, 15, 19, 24, 25, 34, 35, 36, 37, 39, 41,

42, 44, 45, 48, 51, 65, 69, 73, 75
    Ashland PO; 26
    Barboursville; 20, 25, 26, 43, 51
    Bloomingdale PO; 26
    Booten Road; 26
    Cabell County; 5-6, 7, 16, 17, 20, 21, 23, 24, 25, 26, 27, 29, 33, 35, 36, 37, 41, 42, 43, 44, 45, 46, 47, 48, 51, 53, 56, 59, 60, 61, 62, 65, 69, 70, 74, 75
    Campbell County; 43
    Ceredo; 43
    Charleston; 14, 16
    Cyrus Creek; 20
    Dolittle's Mill; 20
    Dusenberry Mill; 26, 29
    Estis Mill; 26
    Fudge Creek; 20
    Guyandotte; 20, 26, 43, 48, 51
    Guyandotte Navigation Company; 25, 26
    Guyandotte River; 7, 20, 23, 25, 26, 27, 29-30, 46, 51
    Heath Creek; 26
    Hinchman Bend; 26
    James River Turnpike; 19, 20, 21, 42
    John Everett, Sr. Tavern (Ona); 19, 20, 42
    Jordan/Morris Cemetery; 20
    Kanawha County; 6, 7, 12, 14, 15, 16, 17, 19, 23, 24, 25, 27, 33, 34, 41, 42
    Kilgore Cemetery; 20
    Lock Number 4; 26
    Loudoun County; 5, 6, 7, 8, 9, 16, 41
        Cameron Parrish; 6
        Shelburn Parrish; 6
    Love PO; 26
    Love's Store; 42
    Martha; 25, 26
    Martha Bridge; 25
    McComas Road; 20
    Morris Tavern & Ferry; 20
    Mud Bridge (Milton); 19, 20, 27, 62
    Mud River; 19, 20, 23, 24, 30, 46
    Mud River Baptist Church & Cemetery; 20, 62
    Pittsylvania County; 7, 8, 9
    Point Pleasant; 14
    Poore's Hill; 20
    Richmond; 15
    Sanders Cemetery; 20
    Sanders Creek; 19
    Sanders Graveyard; 27, 46
    Sanders Mill; 25, 26, 28, 29, 42, 46, 51
    Teay's Creek; 20
    Teays Valley; 16, 19, 41
        Diamond Tract; 19, 23
    Thomas Maupin Tavern; 20
    Trouts Hill; 23
    Twelve Pole Creek; 23, 24
    Union Baptist Church; 20, 62
    Virginia Valley; 12
    Wayne County; 23
    Wheeling; 13
    William Merritt's Mill; 20
    William Yates Crossing; 20
    West Virginia; 17, 30
    Ashland; 30
    Balls Gap; 30
    Barboursville; 30
    Brownsville; 30
    Cabell County; 17, 30, 38, 73, 74-75, 77
    Cabell Creek; 30
    Clover; 30
    Crown City Ferry; 30
    Cox's Landing; 30
    Cross Roads; 30
    Culloden; 30
    Dudley Gap; 30
    Fudges; 30
    Gallaher Village; 30
    Greenbottom; 30
    Guyandotte; 30
    Guyandotte River; 30
    Gwinn; 30
    Harvey Town; 30
    Hodges; 30
    Holderby's Landing; 30
    Howell; 30
    Howells Mill; 30
    Inez; 30
    Isabell; 30
    James E. Morrow Library; 73
    James River Turnpike; 30
    Johnson; 30
    Lacede; 30
    Lom; 30
    Long Level; 30
    Love's Store; 73
    Lower Creek; 30
    Marshall University; 73
    Martha; 30
    McComas/Logan Road; 30
    McCurdy; 30
    Melissa; 30
    Millersport Ferry; 30
    Milton; 27, 30, 46, 73
    Mt. Union; 30
    Mud Bridge; 30
    Mud River; 30, 77
    Ona; 30
    Ousley Gap; 30
    Poors Hill; 30
    Raccoon; 30
    Reid; 30
    Roach; 30
    Salt Rock; 30

Sanders Cemetery; 73
Sanders Creek; 77
Sarah; 30
SR 2; 30
Swann; 30
Toson; 30
Tylers Creek; 30
Union Ridge; 30
US 60; 30
Wilson Switch; 30
Yates Crossing; 30

ABOUT THE AUTHOR

CARRIE ELDRIDGE is a product of Appalachia with deep roots in Ohio, West Virginia, Kentucky, and Tennessee. Her life-long interest in history and family has lead her to a bachelor's degree in secondary education, emphasizing Social Studies and Music, followed by a master's degree in historical geography emphasizing maps and remote sensing. These degrees were earned from Marshall University in Huntington, West Virginia where she volunteers in the Special Collection Department of Morrow Library and teaches Geography classes as an adjunct professor after many years as a classroom teacher. For the last twenty-five years, she has abstracted and compiled local documents in West Virginia, Kentucky and Ohio, acted to preserve county records, and created maps to display geographical and genealogical information. Mrs. Eldridge has published thirty compiled court records and ten volumes of local history, including ten original maps. A series of pioneer migration atlases and a regional study on slave manumissions have brought nationwide recognition of her work.

The President of ELDERKIN, Mrs. Eldridge, acts as a local history consultant for numerous groups and university classes. She has created a brochure of historical cemetery sites for the Cabell County Landmark Society and speaks at local, regional and national genealogical events. Currently, an adjunct teacher of Geography at Marshall University and Shawnee State University, she is also involved in West Virginia records preservation and is assisting in the creation of an underground railroad society for West Virginia. Carrie Eldridge has been honored by Who's Who of the Midwest, by Who's Who of American Women, and by the Special Collections Department of Marshall University's Morrow Library.

www.ingramcontent.com/pod-product-compliance
Lightning Source LLC
Chambersburg PA
CBHW080551230426
43663CB00015B/2791